Eating the Black Body

AFRICAN AMERICAN LITERATURE AND CULTURE

Expanding and Exploding the Boundaries

Carlyle V. Thompson
General Editor

Vol. 10

PETER LANG
New York • Washington, D.C./Baltimore • Bern
Frankfurt am Main • Berlin • Brussels • Vienna • Oxford

CARLYLE VAN THOMPSON

Eating the Black Body

MISCEGENATION *as* SEXUAL CONSUMPTION
in AFRICAN AMERICAN LITERATURE *and* CULTURE

PETER LANG
New York • Washington, D.C./Baltimore • Bern
Frankfurt am Main • Berlin • Brussels • Vienna • Oxford

Library of Congress Cataloging-in-Publication Data

Thompson, Carlyle Van.
Eating the Black body: miscegenation as sexual consumption
in African American literature and culture / Carlyle Van Thompson.
p. cm. — (African American literature and culture; v. 10)
Includes bibliographical references.
1. American literature—African American authors—History and criticism.
2. African Americans—Intellectual life. 3. Sexual abuse victims—United States. 4. African
Americans—Crimes against. 5. African Americans in literature. 6. Miscegenation in literature.
7. Body, Human in literature. 8. Violence in literature. 9. Race in literature.
10. Sex in literature. I. Title. II. Series.
PS153.N5T48 2006   810.9'3552—dc22   2005013511
ISBN 0-8204-7931-4
ISSN 1528-3887

Bibliographic information published by **Die Deutsche Bibliothek.**
Die Deutsche Bibliothek lists this publication in the "Deutsche
Nationalbibliografie"; detailed bibliographic data is available
on the Internet at http://dnb.ddb.de/.

Cover design by Sophie Boorsch Appel

The paper in this book meets the guidelines for permanence and durability
of the Committee on Production Guidelines for Book Longevity
of the Council of Library Resources.

© 2006 Peter Lang Publishing, Inc., New York
29 Broadway, New York, NY 10006
www.peterlang.com

Printed in the United States of America

This book is proudly dedicated to
Cynthia Pullen-Thompson and Jabari James Joseph Jawara Thompson,
along with the intellectually tenacious students at Medgar Evers College of the
City University of New York, and especially those thoroughly engaged
students in my African American Literature from the
Harlem Renaissance to the Present classes.

contents

acknowledgments

As with my first book, *The Tragic Black Buck: Racial Masquerading in the American Literary Imagination*, where I examine the issue of racial passing in the fiction of Charles Waddell Chesnutt, James Weldon Johnson, F. Scott Fitzgerald, and William Faulkner, my scholarly work and research here is directly related to my teaching of African American literature at Medgar Evers College, City University of New York. Here, the enduring mission is to educate and give academic access to those individuals who have been most disadvantaged, most denied, most discriminated, and most educationally deceived. Intellectual, spiritual, psychological, and moral empowerment remains the agenda for many of us at Medgar Evers College as our students reach scholarly heights that amaze the world. Since I began teaching at Medgar Evers College, Edison O. Jackson, the president, has been a staunch and unwavering supporter of my scholarship.

Indeed, this scholarly work comes out of some unresolved questions in my first book. It was in the classrooms at Medgar Evers College that I first began to explore the theme of miscegenation as sexual consumption in African American literature. As with many other scholars, the classroom becomes fertile ground to explore new ideas, especially around African American texts and African American writers who have not been given the scholarly attention they deserve. In my classes, I have had the chance to ask questions such as: How does miscegenation manifest as sexual consumption? What African American novels best explicate the issue of miscegenation as sexual consumption? How does race intersect with sexuality? How does the classroom provide one an opportunity to test out, pedagogically, one's theories about how white supremacy continues to operate in American society? What are the complex forces that construct racial and sexual identities? How does the transgenerational transgression of trauma affect the sexuality of Black males and Black females? What effect does trauma have on participants and witnesses to violence?

Many of the students in my African American Literature from the Harlem Renaissance to the Present classes deserve special thanks for the intellectual rigor that infuses this work. Medgar Evers College students including Oladapu Yeku, Tyeast Fullerton, and Christopher Walker are among the stellar students who will be movers and shakers in their future academic careers. They will pursue their academic and professional goals in manners that do not reinforce and reinscribe white supremacy, gender oppression, class prejudice, and color hegemony. Indeed, Medgar Evers College gives its students intellectual and professional opportunities that few other institutions can provide.

For this project I would like to express special thanks to James de Jognh and the Institute for Research on African Diaspora in the Americas and the Caribbean for their continuous support of my work. For me and other CUNY scholars working in the areas of African American and African Studies, IRADAC has been a critical intellectual space in which to flesh out our ideas and present our work to other CUNY scholars. The annual Works in Progress at CUNY on the African Diaspora, an Interdisciplinary Conference has been tremendous in advancing my work by obtaining feedback from other CUNY professors working on critical issues in African American literature, in particular George P. Cunningham, my longtime Brooklyn College, CUNY colleague, confidant, and comrade. I would also like to warmly thank the distinguished professor Haki R. Madhubuti, and the journal editors at *WarpLand: A Journal of Black Literature and Ideas*, at Chicago State University, for allowing me to include in this project my revised essay on white-male police brutality and Abner Louima. Phyllis Korper and Lisa Dillon at Peter Lang, here in New York City, have been extremely helpful to me in making my ideas reach people all over the world; the quality and attention to detail to my scholarship have been truly outstanding.

And to Cynthia Pullen-Thompson, I am extraordinary grateful for all of your assistance, love, nurture, and support. You were always available for me to test out my ideas and theories concerning these novels. Without your providing the intellectual space for me to work, this book would not exist.

introduction

This project examines the explosive issue of miscegenation as an act of sexual consumption in African American literature and culture. The four literary texts that are examined here are Richard Wright's surreal poem on lynching, "Between the World and Me," John Oliver Killens' *Youngblood*, Gayl Jones' *Corregidora*, and Octavia Butler's *Kindred*. These African American texts represent the most powerful explications of racial subjugation and the enduring effects of the transgenerational transgression of trauma associated with some white people's enduring desire for the Black body. The lynching of Black males and the rape of Black women, as acts of racialized sexual violence, are encompassed in the issue of miscegenation. Miscegenation represents one of the most paradoxical aspects in African American literature and culture because it illustrates the intersectionality of race, gender, and sexuality. Beyond the literature, an ominous and consistent cloud of police brutality in New York City comes under examination in the case of the Haitian immigrant Abner Louima, who was beaten and viciously sodomized with a broomstick by white-male police officer Justin Volpe, who had a long-term relationship with a Black woman, New York City Police Department employee Susan Lawson. Louima's sexual assault represents one of the most disturbing incidents of police brutality in American history because it was done within the bathroom of the Brooklyn police precinct and not one police officer came to his assistance. Hence, equally disturbing is the level of complicity of the other police officers involved and those officers on duty at the police precinct. For me, this is not simply a case of physical violence on the part of the police officer, but also a case of subliminal and repressed sexual desire acted out in a manner that reflects the racialized violence that Black people experienced under slavery.

Slavery's legacy is not only evident in much of African American literature, but it is also especially present in many of the current Hollywood films. Clearly, D.W. Griffith's *Birth of a Nation* (1915) has institutionalized the issue of miscegenation, especially between Black males and white females as a social issue. Equally important, the arrogance of white-male supremacy in the film and in the current society continues to inform the relationships between all races and has a significant economic impact when it comes to corruption in the business sector. Accordingly, my discussion and analysis of miscegenation as sexual consumption are framed around current films where miscegenation represents a critical theme, along with a number of national legal and cultural incidents that place emphasis on interracial sexual relationships. For me, these legal and cultural incidents represent national narratives of miscegenation that influence social policies and personal beliefs concerning education, housing, employment, incarceration, and economic development. Most whites in America have no problem working with Black people, but when it comes to public education and housing, segregation seems to be the law of the land—more so, even, than during the Jim Crow Segregation period. Ironically, the northern cities are more structurally segregated in terms of education and housing than are most southern cities. Housing and public education, by their very natures, produce intimacy, and many whites abhor the idea of their white children having sexual contact with Black children, especially their white daughters having sexual contact with Black males. As quiet as it is kept, for these whites, a good neighborhood consists of few if any African Americans or non-white individuals. These whites never view themselves as white supremacists, but through their careful selection of housing and education for their children they make it clear that miscegenation is not only something that should be avoided, but that it represents social debauchery. With very few African Americans around, white children learn an important lesson: you only date or marry within your race. On the other hand, African American children learn a similar lesson because they see whites working in their neighborhoods as teachers, police officers, social workers, firefighters, and utility workers. However, these same whites who work in African American communities do not live in these communities and by extension do not send their white children to schools in these communities regardless of the socioeconomic level of the residents. Beyond the socioeconomic aspect, there is a long history of racial violence that is based on white people's deception, which makes it difficult for Black people to trust whites; this fundamental mistrust has been handed down through the years. The murder of Emmett Till in 1955, the Scottsboro Case, and the destruction of the Black towns in Wallstreet, Oklahoma, in

1921 and Rosewood, Florida, in 1923 are prime example of master narratives in Black society that have informed many Black individuals' relationships outside of their racial group. Black male individuals like the heavyweight boxer Jack Johnson and the football player O.J. Simpson, who somehow believed that their intimate relationships and marriages with white women were free of any social distain, were crudely reminded in terms of legal actions and social criticism from both the African American and white communities.

By approaching African American literature and this horrifying case of white-male police brutality with a focus on miscegenation as an act of sexual consumption, we begin to understand that in America's white-supremacist culture the Black body becomes an enduring site of sexual desire. From the dungeons on the coast of Africa to the slave ships during the Middle Passage and from the auction blocks, slave coffles, and slave plantations to the detention centers and prisons, Black bodies have come under white people's domination and desire. This desire for the Black body is often expressed in sexually violent and sadistic manners—lynchings and rapes represent the violence against Black men and women. Racial subjugation and its legacy become an enduring focus for many African American writers as they simultaneously reflect on slavery's past and explore the current conditions of interracial and intraracial conflict. Race will always matter in America as long as white supremacy and the privileges associated with whiteness exist.

chapter 1

Consuming Hot Black Bodies

Miscegenation as Sexual Violence in African American Literature and Culture

> While I understand that a waved banner of aggressive miscegenation is one
> kind of logical response to the virulent history of anti-miscegenation in the
> United States, I do worry that life is not that simple.
>
> Patricia Williams, *The Rooster's Egg: On the Persistence of Prejudice*

In perhaps one of the most torrid, raw, and steamy interracial sexual scenes in
the history of American cinematography, *Monster's Ball* (2001) set in post-sixties
Georgia and directed by Marc Forster, graphically depicts the African American
Leticia Musgrove (actress Halle Berry) having butt-naked sexual relations with
the white Hank Grotowski (actor Billy Bob Thornton). The film involves a
white-male prison guard who serves as the lead executioner of a Black man convicted of killing a white police officer. Later, this guard becomes emotionally and
sexually involved with the wife of the man he led to his execution. Halle Berry
was nominated for and received an Academy Award in this challenging role of a
Black single mother struggling with family loss, poverty, loneliness, depression,
and alcoholism.[1] The larger context for this tragic film of racial redemption is
the struggles of a young Black woman dealing with the looming execution of
her African American husband, juxtaposed with three generations of a deeply
troubled family of racist white-male prison guards. Hank Grotowski, as the
racially prejudiced, lonely, and frustrated prison guard, assists in the execution

by electrocution of Leticia's husband, Lawrence Musgrove (played by the African American actor, Sean "P. Diddy" Combs). This film reflects the enduring philosophy of white supremacy that Neely Fuller Jr. describes: "White supremacy is now being practiced just for the sake of white supremacy. Racism/white supremacy is the most effective criminal organization that the world has ever known and the most efficient system the world has ever seen for getting things done, but the cost is too high in terms of misery" (25). As a global system of organized behaviour (thought, speech, and action) white supremacy represents white people's racist domination in economics, entertainment, labor, law, politics, religion, sex, and war. Within the context of America's white supremacy culture, the critical importance of Lawrence Musgrove's character is that most Black males become racially coded symbols for pathology and violent criminal conduct.[2] The American public fueled by racist iconography has been socialized to perceive African American men as actual or potential criminals. This racist iconography has its origins in the economic and racial oppression of chattel slavery. Discussing slavery's legacy and Black male subjectivity, in *Black Sexual Politics* (2004), Patricia Hill Collins states:

> Because Blacks did hard manual labor, justifying the harsh conditions forced upon them required objectifying their bodies as big, strong, and stupid. White elites apparently found men of African descent to be more threatening than women because they believed that Black men were naturally violent. Men allegedly possessed the wildness attributed to Blacks as a race, but they carried the additional characteristic of being prone to violence. This combination of violence and sexuality made Black men inherently unsuitable for work until they were trained by White men and placed under their discipline and control. To explain these relations, White elites created the controlling image of the buck . . . White elites reduced Black men to their bodies, and identified their muscles and their penises as their most important sites. (56)

As argued in the *Tragic Black Buck*, too often Black men become characterized as dangerous individuals who need to be controlled, neutralized, or killed. "Many slave owners did use certain black males as studs; here the black man as a buck was born . . . Linking black male slaves to animals, white society considered slaves literally subhuman beasts. They were dangerous, breeding animals who were never more content than when toiling in the fields; idle, they were shiftless drunkards and potential rapists of white women" (Thompson 2). Along with the myth of the Black male as rapist of white women, turning Black women against Black men represents a fundamental of America's white supremacist culture. Leticia's deep-seated antipathy for her husband, Lawrence foreshadows her psychological and sexual embrace of whiteness. Later in this film, Hank and Leticia develop a tenuous relationship after her very overweight son, Tyrell Musgrove (Coronji Calhoun), dies after being hit by an automobile while walking in the rain. At the tragic moment when Tyrell is hit by the car, Hank drives by and stops and then takes them to the hospital where Tyrell dies from his injuries. Based on shared trauma, a quasi-bond between Hank and Leticia occurs at the hospital. Director Forster foreshadows this sexual scene between Hank and Leticia (Halle Berry is a child from a miscegenous relationship) by having his regular consumption of scoops of chocolate ice cream from a white cup with a white plastic spoon served to him by the white waitress, Lucille (Taylor Simpson). Later, Leticia replaces Lucille at the diner and awkwardly serves Hank his bowl of chocolate ice cream and black coffee (no milk, no sugar). While waiting for his ice cream and coffee, Hank calls a white woman prostitute named Vera and asks: "Is it too late?"[3] Immediately after his consumption of blackness, Hank attempts to have sex with Vera but cannot perform. Like a red-lipped whore at the lynch-burning of a Black man, the white prostitute, Vera (Amber Rules), has sexual relations with Hank and Sonny (but not at the same time). Through the graphic execution (a symbolic ritualistic lynching) of an African American male, the death of an extremely overweight African American child, the death by suicide of Hank Grotowski's soft-hearted son Sonny (Heath Ledger), who is also a prison guard, Hank's care for his surly, racist, and disabled father (a retired prison guard), Buck (Peter Boyle), and the sexual relationship between an African American female and a white male, we understand the multifaceted layers of consumption in this film, especially the aspect of miscegenation as sexual consumption.

With the shocking death of Hank's son by a self-inflicted gunshot (he shot himself in front of Hank and Buck), and the sudden death of Leticia Musgrove's son, along with the trauma of Lawrence Musgrove's graphic execution by electric chair after eleven years on death row, the lead characters experience significant psychological pain, loneliness, and frustration. Accordingly, in the film's most explosive sexual scene, these two emotionally desperate characters are looking for some cathartic sexual release. "I want you to make me feel good; I want you to make me feel good," desperately pleads an intoxicated Leticia. Here the perfunctory miscegenous sex between Hank and Leticia is quick and raw, leaving neither of them feeling good, but perhaps feeling better. Since she initiates the embrace by making the call, Leticia's genital space could serve as a trope for a limited emancipatory consciousness, which calls into play an analysis of the role of biological reproduction within a particular form of production that reinforces white-male domination. Despite the courageous behavior of both characters, this film reinforces and reinscribes fundamental aspects of America's white supremacist culture, where the African American female is always available for sexual conquest by white males and the African American male (as some monster or beast) is legally or extra-legally killed by white males. The Black male as monster becomes a metaphor for the cultural body as beasts, demons, freaks, and fiends as symbolic expressions of cultural unease that pervade a society and shape its collective behavior. America's fascination with the monstrous testifies to the continued desire to highlight difference apprehensions. With seemingly little regard for her self-worth (early in the film Hank has regular sexual relations with a white female prostitute), Leticia offers up her Black body for white male consumption. The death of her Black husband by whites, especially this racist prison guard, becomes irrelevant. More disturbing is the fact that, before they have sexual relations, an emotional Leticia shows her husband's pencil drawings to Hank and tells him that her husband was executed at Jackson State Penitentiary. There is no doubt that Hank knows that Leticia was Lawrence's wife. The morning after the sexual scene, we gaze on a reflection of a picture of Leticia's husband in the mirror as Hank washes his face. Hank sees the picture and vomits; he later explains to Leticia that his vomiting has nothing to do with their sexual relations. Later, Hank gives her a pickup truck, and he names his new business venture, a service station, Leticia. Then he puts his racist and infirm father in a convalescent home, and after Leticia is evicted from her home, he moves her into his house.

Despite the statement of emotional desire by Hank and Leticia (after the intimacy), the juxtaposition between the white female prostitute and Leticia is not lost on the audience. Leticia's replacing Lucille at the restaurant has foreshadowed this racial displacement; both serve Hank his chocolate ice cream with a plastic spoon (the white phallus, a signifier of the Father, or better, of the Father's Law), but only Leticia is consumed in a manner that goes beyond the buying of sexual services. Perhaps Leticia, by having sexual relations with this white man, is in some subliminal manner attempting to reverse the birth of her overweight (monstrous) son whom she had with a Black man whom the white male legal authorities characterize as a monster, a characterization that Lawrence validates in his very last conversation with his son, Tyrell. Better still, perhaps Leticia is literally attempting to fuck herself out of the Black race and a Black existence that has brought her so much disappointment, trauma, poverty, and grief. Simply put, hot Black pussy is available for consumption by white males, and white males must destroy the uncontrollable Black penis. Like the authoritative relationship between the white slave master and the Black female slave, the element of power in the film is also critical because Leticia is fired from her waitress job and is evicted from her home; Hank becomes her reluctant white savior, her white knight, and her white foundation symbolized by the white bowl. On this point, bell hooks astutely argues:

> A similar critique can be made of contemporary trends in inter-racial sexual desire and contact initiated by white males. They claim the body of the colored Other instrumentally, as unexplored terrain, a symbolic frontier that will be fertile ground for their reconstruction of the masculine norm, for asserting themselves as transgressive desiring subjects. They call upon the Other to be both witness and participant in this transformation. (*Black Looks* 25)

For many males, especially white males, the watching of this film allowed them the vicarious or subliminal experience of a sexual relationship with the beautiful Black actress Halle Berry.[4] Indeed, Leticia Musgrove's call, "I want you to make me feel good; I want you to make me feel good," as she offers up her breasts, invites an immediate response from Hank Grotowski as well as the male viewers who gaze on her naked flesh, especially white males. Here, white males can openly discuss their desires for African American females and this announces a break with a white-supremacist past that has always articulated such desire as taboo, in secret, and with shame. In the eyes of too many white-male Hollywood filmmakers, white people make sensuous love while Black folks have crude sex. The second love scene is tender, with Hank performing oral sex (cunnilingus) on Leticia, but Hank articulates a desire for his chocolate ice cream immediately after they have sexual relations. All the foreshadowing of the chocolate ice cream culminates with Hank literally consuming Leticia's genitals. Further, it is here that Leticia states that she "needs someone to take care of her." Nonetheless, *Monster's Ball* represents a twisted white-male fantasy about Black women being always available for their desires and perversions. The sensuous sex scene seems to convey Leticia's transformation by having the relationship with Hank. In the film, Hank's father horribly insults Leticia to her face. In an insult involving sexuality and race, he refers to Black women as "juice." Buck tells Leticia, "In my prime I had a thing for nigger juice too" and "you ain't a man till you split dark coal." Here, the issue of the Black female as an object of consumption is brutally racist. Also, like butter on a hot muffin, the word "nigger" rolls off of Buck's tongue. Buck Grotowski is analogous to Bull Connor, the racist police chief, who turned fire hoses and dogs on Civil Rights demonstrators in Birmingham, Alabama, in 1963.[5] However, the naming strategy in the film represents a paradox: that Black men are often characterized as dangerous bucks who are hell bent on the consumption of white female genitalia. In one particular scene, Buck refers to two neighborhood Black boys as "porch monkeys" and articulates his horror of miscegenation (he calls it race mixing) and tells Hank that his mother "hated them niggers too." Buck's discourse has the desire to objectify and render Black people invisible. As bell hooks argues in *Black Looks:* "Reduced to the machinery of bodily physical labor, black people learned to appear before whites as though they were zombies, cultivating the habit of casting the gaze downward so as not to appear uppity. To look directly was an assertion of subjectivity, equality. Safety resided in the pretense of invisibility" (5). Later, Leticia pawns her wedding ring and uses the money to buy Hank a new white cowboy hat (his other hat was damaged by Tyrell's blood); this white hat is symbolic of those white males who cleared the American frontier of all dangerous elements and individuals.[6] Happily, Leticia brings the white hat to Hank but meets Buck who unleashes a vile discourse of racism and sexism. Leticia's subjectivity is constantly under attack. With the death of her husband and her son, Leticia's Musgrove's spiritual and psychological bond with blackness is symbolically dead (there is no evidence of her relationship with any Black family, friends, or community. White supremacy, in its new mutated form, includes a seemingly different sexual desire for the Black female body, but the Black male body continues to be a disposable commodity.

The film's title, *Monster's Ball,* literally refers to the "celebration" that is observed the last night before a person on death row will have their execution carried out but also reinforces the symbolic castration of the Black male characters.[7] Lawrence represents a grotesque monster (he tells his son he is a "bad man") because he has killed a white police officer, and Tyrell represents a monster because he eats too much. White legal authorities essentially inform Lawrence that he cannot kill white police officers, and Leticia forcefully informs her son that he cannot be overweight. More specifically, there is a scene with Tyrell where Leticia discovers that he has been secretly eating chocolate ice cream; she grabs his fleshy belly and begins to beat him. Before beating Tyrell, Leticia states, "What did I tell you about eating this shit? Didn't I tell you about eating shit? Look at this. Look all this fat! This fat ass! Look at all this nasty fat!" Tyrell represents a monstrous ball of flesh. The paradoxes of consumption are plenty. First, before this scene Leticia goes out to obtain a small bottle of alcohol, which she consumes. Second, by referring to what Tyrell eats as "shit," this synthesizes consumption and defecation; essentially, she calls her son shit. Later she tells Hank that Tyrell "used to eat his ass off." Leticia's discourse reverses the normal act of consumption as she suggests that Tyrell engages in a process of self-consumption. Finally, while the film shows the graphic scenes of Lawrence's execution, we also view scenes of Leticia brushing her teeth. Consumption of the Black body becomes evident in both scenes. Both Black male characters must depart this life and they do. Death is their punishment for their transgressions, no redemption here. Better still, the title of the film reinforces and reinscribes the ritual of a lynching as a festival or carnival (ball), and here the phallus and testicles (balls) of the Black male victim would be removed. This aspect of the film recalls Ernest J. Gaines' powerful novel *A Lesson Before Dying* (1993) about a young Black man named Jefferson who is sentenced to die by electrocution for his "involvement" in the death of a white-male owner of a liquor store. With the white-male defense attorney labeling Jefferson a "hog," the godmother, Miss Emma, is compelled to have the schoolteacher, Grant Wiggins, help Jefferson die with dignity.[8] Jefferson's redemption and death bring a life lesson to both whites and Blacks in this community. In *Monster's Ball,* the aspect of redemption for the Black-male characters is insignificant. While at the local bar, the other white-male prison guards relate that the racially sensitive Sonny Grotowski will become a "man" (a white man with balls) after he takes part in the execution (a modern-day lynching and de-balling) of Lawrence Musgrove. Sonny's suicide represents a challenge to the consuming hatred and the religiosity of white supremacy that has been passed down from Buck to Hank. It is interesting to note that Sonny, while in the company of other prison guards, throws up (a reversal of consumption) while he escorts Lawrence to the electric chair; Lawrence's death is particularly graphic. Emphasis on the religious aspect of this modern-day lynching is made when Hank asks another white male guard to lead them in prayer. The critical unresolved moral problem in the film is that Hank never tells Leticia that he was the prison guard who directed the execution of her husband, and when Leticia discovers this information, she never confronts him. *Monster's Ball* concludes with them sitting on the porch and Hank feeding Leticia chocolate ice cream, and with her gaze of quasi-acceptance of their situation. Leticia is psychologically and socioeconomically trapped. There is the possibility that the traumatic memories of pain and death that Leticia is creating will later come to haunt and consume her. Nevertheless, in a real sense, Leticia becomes a decapitated body reduced to a mere sexual being—headless bodies are easier to consume. Black bodies become metonymic figures for an entire repertoire of human and social arrangements. Hence, and much too often in America's hedonistic culture, white-male subjectivity becomes defined by these two paradigms (the symbolic rape of the Black woman and the symbolic castration of the Black man), and this film does little to change the fundamental iconography associated with white-male supremacy. On the other hand, turning the movie's title on its head, perhaps we can view Hank Grotowski and his racist male lineage as the real monsters who destroy the Black male phallus, and who consume Black female genitalia. The killing of Lawrence Musgrove allows Hank to ball (fuck) Leticia Musgrove with little regard for the consequences of discovery. Sonny's self-inflicted death represents a tragic break with the consuming discourse of white-male supremacy embodied by his grandfather and his father. Considering the thousands of Black people who have been lynched, murdered, brutalized, fire-hosed, bitten by dogs, and brutally beaten, white America represents some grotesque monster. After the more loving sexual scene, Hank tells Leticia, "I'm gonna take care of you." Leticia replies, "Good, 'cause I really need to be taken care of." However, after Leticia discovers his involvement in her husband's execution, they sit on the steps and eat chocolate ice cream and Hank states, "I think we gonna be alright." Thus, their relationship is an updated version of the *placage,* a long-term relationship of a wealthy white man and a Black woman where financial support is given for sexual relations.[9] In a broader perspective within the culture and iconography of white supremacy the black body regardless of gender has always represented a site on innate biological and intellectual inferiority as both Leticia and Lawrence Musgrove become tragic commodities of consumption.[10]

With *Monster's Ball* in mind, there is little doubt that race continues to define American culture where the philosophy of white supremacy and racist oppression continue to thrive and mutate into more grotesque forms. Tensions between whites and African Americans too often come down to this national narrative, where African Americans have faced centuries of racialized violence and racial hegemony that was designed to exclude them from all vestiges of socioeconomic subjectivity associated with the American Dream poignantly and tragically symbolized by Jay Gatsby in F. Scott Fitzgerald's *The Great Gatsby.* Clearly, Spike Lee's film *Jungle Fever* (1991) captures many of the complex issues in miscegenous relationships. Here, Wesley Snipes stars as Flipper Purify, a Black architect who becomes attracted to Angie Tucci (Lee's name play suggests Angie's behind). Played by Annabella Sciorra, Angie is an Italian woman from a working-class neighborhood. In one critically important scene, Flipper and Angie are in public and engage in a playful lovers' squabble; a white individual looking down from a window misreads the scene and calls the police. Susan Courtney, in *Hollywood Fantasies of Miscegenation* (2004), reads this scene as a taxonomic comment on the familiarity and spectacularity of popular fantasies of interracial desire:

> In Spike Lee's *Jungle Fever* the camera suddenly aligns itself with an unidentified gaze from an apartment window that (mis)sees a playful lovers' quarrel on the street below as a black man's assault on a white woman; this look of white surveillance quickly results in the black man's harassment and a near beating by police. The combination here of the camera's pronounced alignment with an invisible witness (the only such shot in the film), the instantaneous judgment that presumably leads to the phone call to the police, and the police's arrival with blinding lights (and guns) immediately pointed at the accused emphatically places the scene in a history not only of lynching and police brutality but also of vision and visibility. Indeed, the view from the window Lee momentarily forces us to occupy is in part the product of a history of white vision that cannot be read apart from the history of American cinema. And insofar as this is the moment that makes Flipper Purify (Wesley Snipes) turn away from his white lover (Annabella Sciorra), the overwhelming force of that white gaze and the blinding violence it portends are pivotal to the film's final rendering of what the relationship between the black man and the white woman signifies. (4)

This scene, which examines the possible violence in a miscegenous relationship between a Black man and a white woman, along with previous tensions (both of their families oppose their relationship), leads to Flipper returning to his Black community and Angie returning to her Italian community. While the elements of physical, psychological, and economic violence that African American people have been subjected to during the enslavement period and the neoslavery period have dramatically lessened, the transgenerational effects of these traumas are still present; Black bodies have consistently become objects of commodification and consumption, as Black culture is used to sell American products at home and internationally.

There is perhaps no greater image of American sports and the enduring consumption and commodification of the Black male body than the former National Basketball Association mega-superstar, millionaire, and current businessman Michael Jordon. During his incredibly successful time with the Chicago Bulls organization, Jordan became a national and international superstar who became the image of the NBA, especially for the advertisement and promotions units. Jordan's status as a superstar was sealed when he won the slam-dunk contest at the 1988 NBA All-Star Game. His leap from the free-throw line for a dunk ele-vated his popularity beyond the expectations of the league. With the Nike Com-pany, Jordan became an icon as he brought millions of dollars to this company; Jordan's Nike basketball shoes, jerseys, and t-shirts with his number (23), became extremely popular. Many advertisements focused on Jordan's determination and encouraged children to "be like Mike." Jordan led the Chicago Bulls to six NBA championships (1991–1993 and 1996–1998). Michael Jordan in his prime became the world's most idolized athlete and his marketing prowess became a godsend to U.S. corporations. Through the numerous televised games during the season and especially the playoff games, along with the numerous television com-mercials for Coca-Cola, McDonald's, Hanes, and Nike, Jordan had become an international promoter of some of the largest, wealthiest, and most powerful U.S. corporations and their products. Placing Michael Jordon and other Black-male sports figures within a historical context, Michael Eric Dyson argues:

> Black participation in sports in mainstream society, therefore, is a relatively recent phenomenon. Of course, there have existed venerable traditions of black sports, such as the Negro (baseball) Leagues, which countered the exclusion of black bodies from white sports. The prohibition of athletic activity by black men in mainstream society severely limited publicly acceptable forms of display-ing black physical prowess, an issue that had been politicized during slavery and whose legacy extended into the middle of the twentieth century. Hence, the potentially superior physical prowess of black men, validated for many by the long tradition of slave labor that built American society, helped reinforce racist arguments about the racial regimentation of social space and the denigration of the black body as an inappropriate presence in traditions of American sport. ("Be Like Mike?" in The Jazz Cadence of American Culture, p. 373)

With the prominence of many white coaches and owners of NBA teams dur-ing the time Jordan was playing, some would refer to the NBA as a modern-day slave plantation. And the large sum of money that Jordan received by playing basketball did not compare to the significant sum that the owner of the team received. Jordan augmented his large salary by becoming a figure of consumption. As Dyson states: "Jordan eats Wheaties, drives Chevrolets, wears Hanes, drinks Coca-Cola, consumes McDonald's, guzzles Gatorade, and of course, wears Nike. He and his shrewd handlers have successfully produced, packaged, marketed, and distributed his image and commodified his symbolic worth, transforming cultural capital into cash, influence, prestige, status, and wealth" (376). Of course, the message here is that if you eat, drink, wear, and drive what Michael Jordan does, you can "be like Mike." Perhaps the ultimate example of Jordan as an object of consumption was the McDonald's "McJordan" hamburger; here whites and oth-ers could metaphorically consume Jordan and expel him as waste. One downside to Jordan's activities was his highly publicized troubles with gambling and his insensitivity and defensiveness to documented reports of Nike's exploitation of workers. The pedagogy of desire that Michael Jordan created as a fluid metaphor of mobility, power, elegance, and consumption, now manifests in the current commodification and consumption of NBA mega-superstars LeBron James and Dwyane Wade. Hence, Michael Jordan and all the high-profile Black males who follow his lead will participate in America's capitalistic business where Black culture and Black people will be exploited to ensure rapacious consumerism.

African American writers, among others, continue to focus on the traumatic past of African American people to help us understand the present dynamics of race, class, gender, and sexuality, with literary scholars doing their part to analyze and deconstruct these narratives of racialized desire. In *The Tragic Black Buck: Racial Masquerading in the African American Literary Imagination*, the first volume of a trilogy, I examine the paradoxical theme of light-skinned African American males passing for white in Charles Waddell Chesnutt's *The House Behind the Cedars* (1900), James Weldon Johnson's *The Autobiography of an Ex-Coloured Man* (1912), F. Scott Fitzgerald's *The Great Gatsby* (1925), and William Faulkner's *Light in August* (1932). The bottom-line analysis was that the phenomenon of racial passing represents the most complex issues of American culture because it challenges the notion of racial essentialism. If a Black individual can be a white individual, then blackness and whiteness are fundamentally ludicrous racial classifications. However, race and racial classifications still matter as the debunked theory of racial essentialism endures. From Chesnutt to Faulkner, these four writers cover a truly significant period in U.S. history when thousands of African Americans were migrating from the Jim Crow South to the North in search of socioeconomic opportunities, and it is here that masses of light-skinned African Americans seized the opportunities to assume white identities. At the heart of this phenomenon of African American individuals assuming a white identity is the issue of miscegenation between Blacks and whites. This explosively charged subject continues to provide the foundation for many African American writers' exploration of the enslavement of African Americans, the Reconstruction period, and its aftermath.

The endeavor of this second volume of the trilogy is to take a critical look at the issue of racialized sexuality, miscegenation, by means of four seminal works in the canon of African American literature and an incident of police brutality in New York City. Standing in the murky shadows of race, miscegenation is a long-standing national problem that many African American writers have addressed. The term "miscegenation" represents the sexual relations across racial lines and, as I argue, this issue frames white America's obsession with the discourse of racial hegemony and the hypo-descent theory. Accordingly, this project examines the theme of miscegenation, especially between African American males and white females and African American females and white males as an act of sexual consumption in African American literature. The four African American texts to be examined are a poem and three novels: Richard Wright's surreal poem

"Between the World and Me (1935), John Oliver Killens' *Youngblood* (1954), Gayl Jones' *Corregidora* (1975), and Octavia Butler's *Kindred* (1979). These two African American male and two African American female writers bring tendentious views on miscegenation to their narratives of racialized sexual desire. My investigation will focus on miscegenation in the construction of racial hegemony and racial difference, especially with regard to how it becomes constructed by language. This literature of miscegenation and racial passing denotes how white society uses language to racially define an individual. To speak "proper" or standard English can position one closer to whiteness, whereas the "black dialect" can relegate many African American people to a category of subordination and oppression. As significant as skin color and hair texture, language becomes a critical part of the system of racial categories and hierarchies established by social custom and law.

In American society, too often structured on racial, class, and color hegemony, the possibilities for socioeconomic advancement were too often greater for those who are a production of miscegenation (light-skinned individuals) than for unmixed or dark-skinned African American individuals. The limits, on the other hand, are the scorn from some African Americans and whites and the often-tragic results of those who were discovered to be passing for white. To my knowledge, no other work examines these four African American writers, and no other work does an extensive critical analysis of these writers and their novels with regard to the theme of miscegenation as sexual consumption.

In American literature and life, the question of miscegenation between African Americans and whites has been extremely volatile and controversial but nevertheless supremely important, as shown by the social, cultural, and legal dictates, which laws banning miscegenation have enacted. Yet, since the founding of America, the sexual practice flourished and many African American and white writers drew upon this explosive theme to explore the tragic and comic dynamics of language, race, class, and gender in America. As James McKinney astutely argues in *Amalgamation!: Race, Sex and Rhetoric in the Nineteenth-Century American Novel* (1985), miscegenation was a persistent and prejudicial phenomenon:

> During nearly 250 years of slavery in America, black and white men and women lived together and loved together, shared joys and sorrows and together produced a race of mulatto children. With slavery's end, miscegenation declined until the brutal segregation of the 1890s made such relations practically impossible. By 1915, a generation had come of age—black and white—who knew only that miscegenation was forbidden. As our heritage of this taboo, confusion, guilt, and anger still shroud interracial sex in America (3).

Slave owners, slave traders, slave overseers, and slave hunters were all involved in the rape and sexual abuse of Black females, Black males, and Black children. Accordingly, a central focus in this project is the sexual violence during the horrific enslavement period and its aftermath of continued racism and oppression. On the slave ships, on the auction blocks, and on the slave plantations, Black people were often subjected to the most degrading and humiliating sexual violence that can be imagined. White males, females, and their children penetrated, probed, and played with Black people in often-sadistic ways that created a transgenerational transgression of trauma. From slavery and its aftermath, many Black people have inherited some common pathological and destructive behaviors that shackle them and keep them vulnerable to further sexual violence. Summing up the enslavement period, Robin D. Stone explicates:

> Eight generations of families born in servitude, their very existence at the whim of White masters. Property, bought and sold, bred, beaten, and worked to death. Slaveholders systematically chipped away at our dignity, our humanity, and our knowledge of our histories and languages and cultures. They exploited and violated our women, and demoralized and emasculated our men. They tore our families apart. (26)

What is also truth is that white masters and other whites chipped away at their humanity and dignity in the process of denying Black people their fundamental rights as humans. Also, what is important is Stone's use of the word "whim"; too often the sexual violence that Black people were subjected to was random, with Black people most often never knowing what to expect from their masters. White masters' whims created daily terror. However, despite Stone's rather reductive analysis on what happened to Black families, there was a remarkable ability to create and sustain family life during this period. This resilience was illustrated in the numerous acts of rebellion, escapes, destruction of property, caring for each other, sharing of resources, and the killing of white masters. U.S. president and slave master Thomas Jefferson comes to mind when we consider miscegenation and the paradox of race relationships during slavery. The arch-idealist, philosopher, and humanist, the articulator of the principles of freedom and human equality, Jefferson nevertheless viewed Black people as inferior beings. However, Jefferson's relationship with his young Black mistress, Sally Hemings, and the slave children that he sired in this relationship reveals the fundamental schizoid nature and contradictions of American life. Discussing the slave-owning and slave-making Thomas Jefferson, Annette Gordon-Reed states:

> Contradictions are always on display. . . . It is not good enough to say with regard to this question, "Well, we live in the twentieth century and Thomas Jefferson lived in the eighteenth and nineteenth century." People have internal conflicts during these periods as well as today, probably more regarding the question of race and sex. Whites and blacks in the South often lived and interacted with one another under a system that made them, at once enemies and intimates. How could such a system fail to promote internal conflicts? (234)

The contradictions of American life are brought to life in the slave narratives, as powerful documents of pain and desire. Slavery's violent legacy and the singularity of the slave trade have galvanized the racial discourse in the reductive Black and white dynamic and made miscegenation an issue full of paradoxes and apprehension. The crux of slavery represented what Orlando Patterson has brilliantly termed a "social death":

> Not only was the slave denied all claims on, and obligations to, his [or her] parents and living blood relations but, by extension, all such claims and obligations on his more remote ancestors and on his [or her] descendants. He [or she] was truly a genealogical isolate. Formally isolated in his [or her] social relations with those who lived, he [or she] was also culturally isolated from the social heritage of his [or her] ancestors. He [or she] had a past, to be sure. But a past is not a heritage. . . . [Slaves] were not allowed freely to integrate the experience of their ancestors into their lives, to inform their understanding of social reality with the inherited meanings of their natural forebears, or to anchor the living present in an conscious community of memory. (5)

Thus, the period of enslavement and its aftermath was full of anguish and triumphs and poignantly illustrated in American literature and especially African American literature.

After emancipation, American culture was heavily influenced by significant qualms about miscegenation between Black males and white women and the demonization of sexual relations between white males and Black women. Jean Toomer's *Cane* (1923) represents one of the earliest and perhaps most sophisticated 20th-century literary examinations of miscegenation in American life and culture. Toomer's fascination with miscegenation captures both the tragedy and desire of interracial relationships. As Brian Niro notes: "Toomer's characters, both black and white, demonstrate the gamut of complexions that have been delineated within either extreme of the binary trope"(174). Toomer's poem "Portrait in Georgia" captures the complexity of racial bigotry, violence, and the projection of the white woman as a symbol of the Black man's sexual desire:

> Hair—braided chestnut,
>   coiled like a lyncher's rope,
> Eyes—fagots,
> Lips—old scars, or the first red blister,
> Breath—the last sweet sent of cane,
> And her slim body; white as the ash
>   of black flesh after flame. (*Cane* 27)

Miscegenation between white women and Black men represents the central apprehension during the Jim Crow period, with lynching as the white-male response. Here, Toomer juxtaposes the construction of the white woman with the destruction of the Black man. As George Hutchison maintains: "By superimposing the image of the white woman, the apparatus of lynching, and the burning flesh of the Black man, Toomer graphically embodies both a union of Black male and white female and the terrifying method of exorcising that union to maintain a racial difference the poem linguistically defies" (quoted in Niro 175). Here, the presence of the white woman is being juxtaposed with the absence of the Black man; however, the description of the white woman's body, "white as the ash," as analogous to the Black man's flesh, suggests the very act of miscegenation that results in the lynching. A Black body and white body twisted in the throes of sexual intercourse foreshadow the twisted coils of the lyncher's rope. Other African American writers would make a similar connection, but few capture the beauty and the pathos of Southern life.

If we consider Zora Neale Hurston's *Their Eyes Were Watching God* (1937), a narrative illustrating the aftermath of slavery and Reconstruction, this novel among others lays the groundwork for many African American writers who explore the traumatic history of sexual violence between whites and African Americans. The plot features the reconfiguration of three Black male characters as post-emancipation slave masters who attempt to oppress a Black female character. This novel chronicles the life journey of Janie Crawford in her attempt to achieve a subjectivity that was denied her grandmother and her mother. Here we discover that both Janie Crawford's mother and grandmother have been violently raped by white males. This racialized sexual violence forms the transgenerational transgress of trauma that impacts most African American people and their progeny. After seeing that Janie's mother was "wid gray eyes and yaller hair,"[11] Janie's grandmother relates the reaction of the white master's wife to the birth of her daughter:

> She tuh slap mah jaws ever which a'way. Ah never felt the furst ones 'cause Ah was too busy gettin' de kivver back over mah chile. But dem last lick burnt me lak fire. Ah had too many feelin's tuh tell which one tuh follow so Ah didn't cry and Ah didn't do nothin' else. But then she kept on astin me how come mah baby look white. She asted me dat maybe twenty-five or thirty times, lah she got tah sayin' dat and couldn't help herself. (17)

Here the white woman, rather than challenging her white slave-owning husband, challenges the Black female slave who has been the victim of nonconsensual sexual violence, miscegenation. During the enslavement period, Black women neither owned their bodies nor controlled who would become their sexual partners. Frustrated and enraged with the sexual betrayal by her husband, the white woman resorts to the threat of violence; she tells Nanny:

> Ah wouldn't dirty mah hands on yuh. But first thing in de morning de overseer will take you to de whippin' post and tie you down on yo' knees and cut de hide

offa yo' yaller back. One hundred lashes wid a raw-hide on yo' bare back. Ah'll have you whipped till de blood run down to yo' heels! Ah mean to count de licks mahself. And if it kills you Ah'll stand de loss. Anyhow, as soon as dat brat is a month old Ah'm going to sell it offa dis place.'(17)

There are a number of critical aspects that relate to the pervasive issue of miscegenation as sexual consumption. First, the reference to Nanny's "yaller back" suggests that she is a product of miscegenation, which suggests that her slave mother was a victim of sexual violence. Second, the vicious threat of one hundred lashes is designed to kill this Black slave woman who has been the victim. The unsaid discourse here is that the Black slave woman is a licentious seducer of the white slave master who had no control over his sexuality. Lastly, the threat to sell the "white" baby propels Nanny to escape the slave plantation and save herself and her baby. Another aspect of the issues of racialized sexual violence is the issue of Black males' internalization of gender hegemony, where according to Janie's grandmother, the Black woman is viewed as the "de mule uh the world" (16). In the novel, the pear tree with the bee embracing the blossom comes to represent Janie's concept of sexuality and freedom, because sovereignty in sexual matters marked a significant demarcation between life during enslavement and life after emancipation. All of Janie's three husbands, Logan Killicks, Jody Starks, and Vergible "Tea Cake" Woods, are to some extent reconfigurations of the white slave master in that they represent male hegemony by threatening or assaulting Janie. Janie's grandmother coerced her to marry Logan Killicks. He attempts to work Janie like a mule, but she leaves him. Jody, her second husband, is more psychologically abusive but he does slap her in the face when she challenges him. After Jody's death, Janie marries Tea Cakes, who is more loving and sharing but becomes abusive when he becomes jealous. Black-male hegemony is especially evident in Gayl Jones' *Corregidora*. Beyond the content of the novel, Hurston's narrative strategy of intersubjective communion, the creating of a sensibility that the hearer and narrator share equally in the story to the extent of being as involved in its events, of believing oneself to have lived out what another experiences (Rushdy 273), speaks to all of the novels that are examined here. *Eating the Black Body* is offered as an intervention and an urgent call for sustained discussion of the complexity of racialized sexual violence and Black people's agency within a white supremacist culture. Although lynchings and interracial sexual violence are rare, the violation of Black bodies continues to be a pervasive issue in American society. All of these African Americans narratives reflect the strategy of intersubjectivity as we as readers become not only hearers but also tellers of these narratives as sites of the intersections of race, gender, and sexualities.

Chapter two, "Speaking Desire and Consumption of the Black Body in Richard Wright's 'Between the World and Me'" (1935), examines this haunting lynching poem, which explicates a surreal castration and lynch-burning of a nameless

African American male. Wright's diction and symbolism are replete with images of consumption with regard to the lynched individual and the thousands of white participants in this ritual. Through creative structure and shift in point of view, Wright forces the reader to identify with the thousands of African Americans who were victims of lynchings during the Jim Crow segregation period. Although the main reasons African Americans were lynched was because of murder or assault (of white victims), the issue of sexual violence against white females was central to many of the lynchings. At the heart of the lynching is the issue of miscegenation, where African American males were lynched if there was the slight hint or rumor of any relationship with a white female.

Chapter three examines John Oliver Killens' *Youngblood* (1954). This is a novel about an African American family in Georgia during the Jim Crow segregation period. At every turn, this family of determined individuals faces the enduring plague of white supremacy and its elements of physical, psychological, and economic violence. Miscegenation represents Killens' dominant theme as he explores the racial tensions that seek to tear this family apart. Here, we understand the paradox of African American females being exposed to sexual violence by white males with little or no legal recourse, and the full weight of the law and extra-legal measures when there is any suspicion of an African American male having any sexual contact with a white female.

Gayl Jones, one of the most provocative voices in contemporary African American literature, and her novel *Corregidora* (1975) are the focus of my fourth chapter. With brutal and frank language concerning the sexual violence, sexual desire, and incest during slavery in Brazil, Jones chronicles the transgenerational transgression of trauma in the life of an African American female blues singer, Ursa Corregidora. "Make generations," is the charge that Ursa receives from her maternal ancestors, but this dictate becomes impossible when she loses her ability to reproduce children. Again, miscegenation is the dominant theme during slavery. White females were considered sacred and protected, and African American females were viewed as a thoroughfare, vulnerable to sexual violence from both white males and African American males. Like Richard Wright's poem "Between the World and Me," Gayl Jones' novel *Corregidora* links sexuality to racialized violence. However, a key distinction is the critically important aspect of blues music as a healing force to the sexual violence that has been the legacy of life in the Americas. As Portia K. Maultsby relates, the blues represent a central part of the memories of an African past:

> The blues form shares general features and aesthetic qualities with past music traditions. It combines the musical structure and poetic forms of spirituals, work songs, and field cries with new musical and textual ideas. The improvisatory performance style emphasizes call-response (between the voice and accompanying instruments). Integral to the melody are slides, slurs, bends, and dips, and the timbers vary from moans, groans, and shouts to song-speech utterances. The

accompanying instruments—guitar, fiddle, piano, harmonica, and sometimes tub bases, washboards, jugs, a wire nailed to the side of a house and other ad hoc instruments—are played in an African-derived percussive style. (200–201)

Ursa Corregidora sings the blues in order to come to terms with a past that haunts her present relationships with African American males, Mutt Thomas and Tadpole McCormick.

The fifth chapter, "Moving Past the Present: Racialized Sexual Violence and Miscegenous Consumption in Octavia Butler's *Kindred*," examines Octavia Butler's fascinatingly surreal novel *Kindred* (1979). Like most of her science-fiction novels, this neo-slavery novel illustrates how slavery's past informs the racial present. Butler's novel also adheres to the fabulist tradition; fabulism deals with the fantastic, the unobservable, what may exist outside the normal human understanding. While the realist story attempts to explain the world through cause and effect and human free will, fabulism posits cause-and-effect relationships that can be beyond the grasp of mortals. Here an African American woman, Dana Franklin, is transported back to the antebellum South and her present relationship with a white man frames this novel's exploration of slavery and sexual violence. Dana Franklin's relationship with Rufus Weylin, the white son of a plantation owner, is critical because she must protect Rufus and ensure that he will grow to manhood and father the daughter who will become Dana's ancestor. Like his father, Tom Weylin, Rufus Weylin becomes obsessed with his Black female slaves, especially Alice Greenwood. Like most slave narratives, this innovative novel explores the power relationships that made many African Americans so vulnerable to sexual violence, and how miscegenation can be considered consumption of the Black body.

In my sixth chapter, "White Police Penetrating, Probing, and Playing in the Black Man's Ass: The Sadistic Sodomizing of Abner Louima," I examine one of the most disturbing incidents of police brutality to have occurred in New York City. A Haitian immigrant named Abner Louima was beaten and sexually assaulted by a white-male police officer, Justin Volpe, after a disturbance at a Brooklyn nightclub. The issues of racialized sexual violence and miscegenation are evident in this horrific sexual assault as well as in Justin Volpe's relationship with his fiancée, a Black woman named Susan Lawson, who worked at the police precinct. Paradoxically, the sexual assault occurred in the Brooklyn police precinct during a time that police officers were going about their duties. Louima's physical and psychological traumas from this ass fucking with a wooden stick are difficult to contemplate. Many New Yorkers were horrified by this miscegenous rape and sodomy. This incident reveals the legacy of slavery in the Americas, where Black men, women, and children were subjected to racialized sexual violence on the part of white men and white women.

These chapters illustrate the complex and enduring phenomenon of miscegenation as sexual consumption in African American literature and in American culture. The title of the book, *Eating the Black Body: Miscegenation as Sexual Consumption in African American Literature*, articulates my understanding that the sexualized racial violence that Black people experienced during the enslavement period and beyond constructs the trope of eating, which links the violence to vampirism—a human being becomes the source of another's sustenance. Just as the forced labor and the extra-legal violence consumed Black bodies and provided economic sustenance through intimidation, rape and other forms of sexual violence had a similar physical and psychological effect. Accordingly, my enduring concern here is racialized sexual desire and how that desire manifests in the consumption of Black bodies. As bell hooks aptly explicates in *We Real Cool: Black Men and Masculinity* (2004), "Whites seeking to leave behind a history of their brutal torture, rape, and enslavement of Black bodies projected all their fears onto black bodies" (67). A critical analysis of white supremacy involves an understanding that this racial hegemony comes in all races, genders, classes, and colors; white supremacy is an equal-opportunity philosophy—any and all can butt into the discourse. In terms of African Americans, whites who have sexual relations with Black individuals can be white supremacists. White individuals consuming the Black phallus or consuming Black female genitalia are not automatically excluded from being white supremacists. Indeed, many white supremacists have a profound desire to consume the Black body because slavery represented inhalation through labor and forced reproduction. Indeed, America's enslavement of African Americans and the policies that come out of this experience illustrate that most whites, regardless of their status, rally around the illusion of their superiority. As Derrick Bell argues in *Faces at the Bottom of the Well* (1992), the fraudulent philosophy of white people's superiority ensures Black people being continuously disadvantaged:

> Whites are rallied on the basis of racial pride and patriotism to accept their often lowly lot in life, and encouraged to vent their frustration by opposing any serious advancement by blacks. Crucial to this situation is the unstated understanding by the mass of whites that they will accept large disparities in economic opportunity in respect to other whites as long as they have a priority over blacks and other people of color for access to the few opportunities available. (9)

Accordingly, these four African American narratives of racialized sexual consumption, and the horrific incident of white male police brutality and torture in New York City, interrogate white America's ongoing sexual fixation with Black bodies and how the iconography associated with Black bodies reinforces and reinscribes a white-supremacist discourse of hegemony supported by legal and extra-legal violence.

Speaking Desire and Consumption of the Black Body in Richard Wright's "Between the World and Me"

> The ghost is not simply a dead or a missing person, but a social figure, and investigating it can lead to that dense site where history and subjectivity make social life. . . . The way of the ghost is haunting, and haunting is a very particular way of knowing what has happened or is happening. Being haunted draws us affectively, sometimes against our will and always a bit magically, into the structure of feeling of a reality we come to experience, not as cold knowledge, but as transformative recognition.
>
> Avery F. Gordon, *Ghostly Matters: Haunting and the Sociological Imagination*

With searing and ghostly images of blood, wretchedness, suffering, and crucifixion, Richard Wright's compelling alliterative poem "Between the World and Me" (1935), published in the *Partisan Review,* captures the absolutely gruesome horrors of white America's national crime and sadistic psychological-sexual ritual of lynching and burning African American people, especially African American males. Wright's extraordinary depiction of a brutal lynching, as a festival of necrotic violence, places the rabidly violent nature of white-supremacist culture, especially in the South, under the literary microscope; he inherently understands that the Black-male body represents the most immediate and perhaps the ultimate testing ground for debates over racial hegemony and racial subjectivity. For the masses of African American people struggling against white supremacy, the mythology of white superiority, and Jim Crow racial violence, lynching represents the shadowy side of the American Dream in that it was often actively sanctioned and supported by state and local authorities. Lynchings were often a communal occurrence with the participants being the common people. Activist and preeminent scholar W.E.B. Du Bois, who lived through the period of lynching, clearly saw that it was "its nucleus of ordinary men that continually [gave] the mob its initial and awful impetus" to mutilate, torture, kill, and burn innocent African Americans (678). According to the NAACP, lynching in America is defined as: "(1) there must be evidence that a person was killed; (2) the person must have met death illegally; (3) a group of three or more persons must have participated in the killing; and (4) the group must have acted under the pretext of service to justice or tradition" (Tolnay and Beck 260). This last aspect of maintaining some "service to justice or tradition" suggests the issue of miscegenation where consensual or non-consensual sexual relations between Black males and white females would often result in the lynching of the Black male whereas the consensual or non-consensual sexual relations between Black females and white males were often acceptable. The lynching which represents physical, psychological, and economic violence against Black people resulted in the rise of white nationalism and the disenfranchisement of Blacks.

Explaining the power and assiduity of Wright's work, David P. Demarest argues: "A look at two of his well-known works . . . a poem "Between the World and Me" and Black Boy . . . suggests both the care that he lavished on the details of violence and the range of generalization he achieved with those details . . . about the human psyche in general, about race relations in America in particular" (238–239). As a sadistic ritual of consumption and desire, the roots of lynching are in the extra-legal white American racial violence that many African American people experienced during the enslavement period. For Wright, lynching comes to represent an atrocity against God, humans, and nature; where racism stands between African American people and their desire for socioeconomic equality.

Wright's surreal poem represents an exemplary text for an examination of racist white people's often-hysterical desire for and consumption of the African American male body, a ritual of consumption that was designed to enhance their socioeconomic subjectivity. Readers watch and listen in horror as the fragments of the lynching come to life before their eyes, and the Black body, in the presence of thousands of whites, is shamelessly tortured, maimed, beaten, and tarred and feathered before the body is tied to a sapling and consumed by fire. Discussing Native Son as a tragedy, Joyce Ann Joyce's analysis suggests the fundamental aspects of Wright's poem: "Because tragedy concerns itself with ambiguity in the personality of the hero and with irony in the events that affect the hero's life, it is important that we transcend the conceptions of Bigger as a naturalistic victim limited by the strictures of his environment" (xvi). The particular type of lynching that Wright describes suggests a sacrificial murder, possessing all the ritual, communal characteristics of classic human sacrifice. Massive attendance, torture, and burning represent the three main indicators of ritual killings that acquired a sacrificial nature.

In its entirety, Richard Wright's poem "Between the World and Me" reads:

> And one morning while in the woods I stumbled suddenly
>   upon this thing,
> Stumbling upon it in a grassy clearing guarded by scaly oaks
>   and elms.
> And the sooty details of the scene rose, thrusting themselves
>   between the world and me. . . .
> There was a design of white bone slumbering forgottenly
>   upon a cushion of ashes.
> There was a charred stump of a sapling pointing a blunt
>   finger accusingly at the sky.
> There were torn tree limbs, tiny veins of burnt leaves, and a
>   scorched coil of greasy hemp;
> A vacant shoe, an empty tie, a ripped shirt, a lonely hat, and
>   a pair of trousers stiff with black blood.
> And upon the trampled grass were buttons, dead matches,
>   butt-ends of cigars and cigarettes, peanut shells, a
>   drained gin-flask, and a whore's lipstick;
> Scattered traces of tar, restless arrays of feathers, and the
>   lingering smell of gasoline.
> And through the morning air the sun poured yellow surprise
>   into the eye sockets of a stony skull. . . .
> And while I stood my mind was frozen with a cold pity for
>   the life that was gone.
> The ground gripped my feet and my heart was circled by
>   icy walls of fear—
> The sun died in the sky; a night wind muttered in the grass
>   and fumbled the leaves in the trees; the woods poured
>   forth the hungry yelping of hounds; the darkness
>   screamed with thirsty voices; and the witnesses
>   rose and lived:
> The dry bones stirred, rattled, lifted, melted themselves into
>   my bones.
> The grey ashes formed flesh firm and black, entered into my
>   flesh.
> The gin-flask passed from mouth to mouth; cigars and
>   cigarettes glowed, the whore smeared the lipstick red
>   upon her lips,

> And a thousand faces swirled around me, clamoring that
>   my life be burned. . . .
> And then they had me, stripped me, battering my teeth into
>   my throat till I swallowed my own blood.
> My voice was drowned in the roar of their voices, and my
>   black wet body slipped and rolled in their hands as
>   they bound me to the sapling.
> And my skin clung to the bubbling hot tar, falling from me in
>   limp patches.
> And the down and quills of the white feathers sank into my
>   raw flesh, and I moaned in my agony.
> Then my blood was cooled mercifully, cooled by a baptism
>   of gasoline.
> And in a blaze of red I leaped to the sky as pain rose like
>   water, boiling my limbs.
> Panting, begging I clutched childlike, clutched to the hot
>   sides of death.
> Now I am dry bones and my face a stony skull staring in my
>   yellow surprise at the sun. . . . [1]

Structurally the poem moves from the enigmatic to the specific, as the speaker, during a walk in the woods, uncovers the charred remains of a lynched man or the possibility that the narrator of the poem, in a morbidly surreal manner, re-experiences his own lynch-burning demise. Equally important, the poem suggests that the dead acknowledge no borders or boundaries, especially in the sense that the past becomes present. As Wright observed about his youth in the South during the 1920s: "The things that influenced my conduct as a Negro did not have to happen to me directly; I needed but to hear of them to feel their full effects in the deepest layers of my consciousness. Indeed, the white-American brutality that I had not seen was a more effective control of my behavior than that which I knew" (*Black Boy* 190). Wright's forthright psychological-historical analysis of his life in the Jim Crow South fuels his writing as he takes his readers into the psychological-sexual violence of America's white-supremacist culture. In light of Wright's psychosocial experiences and Orlando Patterson's definition of "social death" as a mode of physical and psychological oppression through which slaves, and by extension those who grew up under the control of Jim Crow society, are coerced and controlled, his poem can be seen as a brutal exploration of the sublimated sexual desires within white supremacy. Throughout the South, the level of hatred, apprehension, and horror of African Americans reached points of psychological, political, and religious intensity that are difficult to comprehend. Forest G. Wood cites a prominent white Republican writer's "first commandment": "Thou shall hate the Nigger with all thy heart, and with all thy soul, and with all thy mind and with all thy strength" (Quoted in *Rituals of Blood* 192).[2] Drawing on Christian religious symbolism, Wright succinctly captures this racial antipathy. By closely examining this poem's structure, themes, diction, title, significations, and symbolism we understand that Wright forces us to examine the African American male body as a particular site for some white American's nefarious desire for, and palpable consumption of, Black flesh. As an increasingly Southern phenomenon (especially with the growth of the antislavery movement), this consumption of the Black male body is laden with nuances of sexuality. It should be noted that there were a number of Americans, especially in the Northeast, who were horrified at the escalating rate of lynching. An editorial appeared in a Massachusetts weekly in April 1899, condemning an unusually sadistic lynching where the victim was killed piece by piece:

> The nation and the whole civilized world stand aghast at the revelation. A civilized community numbering thousands, at the drop of a hat, throws off the restraints and effects of many centuries of progress and stands forth in the naked savagery of the primitive man. Men and women cheer and express feelings of triumph and joy as the victim is hurried on to the stake *to make a Sunday holiday in one of the most orthodox religious communities in the United States.* They cut off his ears, his fingers and other members of his body, and strip him and pour oil upon him while the spectators crowd desperately for positions of advantage in the great work of torture and death. (Ginzburg 19)

Of critical importance is that this lynching occurred in a devotedly Christian community. Another point is the level of violence conveyed by the cutting off of body parts, parts that were more than likely kept as souvenirs of the triumph. In many human sacrifices, the participants took vestiges, oftentimes after a feral scramble and fighting for them. This consumption of the Black body also registers sexual desire. As the philosopher and critic, Cornel West makes clear: "Whites' fear of black sexuality is an indispensable ingredient of white racism. And for whites to admit this deep fear even as they try to instill and sustain fear in blacks is to acknowledge a weakness—a weakness that goes down to the bone" (Race Matters 86). If we examine the poem in the context of other Black writers[3] and the historical accounts of lynchings, we understand the sheer power of Wright's depiction of the Black body in pain. Therefore, racist white people, especially white men with their castration anxieties, have a displaced desire for the consumption of Black flesh that is very much within a sexualized context; white people's wrath against any form of Black people's independence appears as a frenzied lust for blackness.

Before closely examining "Between the World and Me," it is critically important to note that the lynching of African American people, as a sexualized ritual of racial hatred, represents the unconscious guilt feelings on the part of the race-haters. They displace this animosity towards those who are different and less able to defend themselves; moreover, these white Americans displace their sexual desires and sexual frustrations to their African American victims whom they consume. Indeed many lynchings involved a sadistic form of torture. In *Shamanism, Colonialism, and the Wild Man*, anthropologist Michael Taussig argues that "the space of death is important in the creation of meaning and consciousness, nowhere more so in societies where torture is endemic and where the culture of torture flourishes. We may think of the space of death as a threshold that allows illumination as well as extinction" (4). Some white males, with no remorse for the consequences of their deadly actions, projected their sexual desires onto innocent Black males. For example, as documented in the *New York Herald Tribune* of February 9, 1936, Carl "Cowboy" Fisher, a white leader of a lynch mob, was convicted of attempted rape; the charge ascribed to Lloyd Warner, the African American man who was killed in Missouri, three years earlier (Ginzburg 227). As Orlando Patterson points out, shifting conditions in the South made violence more rampant: "The changing character of the Southern economy in the early twentieth century; the outmigration of both Euro-Americans and Afro-Americans from the Deep South; and the political and legal disenfranchisement of Afro-Americans—these factors obviated the need for ritualized mob violence as a means of controlling Afro-Americans" (*Rituals of Blood* 181). The South has suffered more isolation than any other section, since "the preponderance of Methodists and Baptists to whom such diversions as card-playing, and theater attendance are forbidden," argues Walter White. "In many parts of the South this circumstance has elevated attendance at church, sex, escapades, and lynching into the principal escapes from the grim and sordid reality of work" (56). And because the lynchings of African American individuals were often long, drawn-out rituals, there is the question of sexualized desire. I argue that the lynching of African Americans is not a simple ritual of racial hatred, but that it is also a ritual of intense sexual desire for the Black body. Controlling the body means controlling desire: not only what people desire but also how they desire it. Similarities in the lynchings suggest a performative aspect to a redemptive sadistic ritual:

> Without studying a script they [white Americans] knew their lines and stage movements: crowds of angry citizens shout their outrage and epithets at the beginning of the spectacle; a knotted rope appears; the mob forcefully removes the victim from the jail; some beat and mutilate him [or her]; fire ignites to burn a dead body; the body remains hanging as symbol; souvenir hunters grab pieces of rope and clothing and in some instances even body parts; a photographer captures the scene of victim, mob, and spectators. The play is ended. Civilization is redeemed. (Madison 69)[4]

Within the discourse of white supremacy, the Black body becomes defined as sexually undesirable, but, in a perverse manner, the ritual of lynching allows the white Americans involved as spectators and participants the freedom to express their often-sadistic sexual desires. Often in perversions and inversions, sexual desires may deviate from culturally sanctioned expectations, but sexual desires are always difficult to categorize because they operate on the fragile threshold between mind and body. Many of the grotesque acts in these lynchings require white Americans to become physically close and intimate with their Black victims. Castrating, dismembering, disemboweling, disfiguring, stabbing, and mutilating of Black individuals require close and intimate contact with the victim's body. This signals desire, a desire that was present when Black men, women, and children were forced to stand naked on the auction blocks for white males' inspection (fingering). Both the lynching of Black bodies and the auctioning of Black bodies represent public spectacles where white males openly expressed their sublimated sexual desires. Indeed, there is a strong element of public necrophilia present at these lynchings. The groping, fondling, sodomizing, and raping of Black women before they were lynched blatantly illustrate some white Americans' sadistic sexual desire. For example, in Toni Morrison's *Beloved* (1987), while on the Sweet Home plantation, a Black slave, Sethe is traumatized when assaulted by the two white American males who violently nurse on her lactating breasts, stealing her milk. Paul D, one of the "niggers" from the Sweet Home plantation, relates the effect it has on Halle, the Black father of her children: "'It broke him, Sethe. . . . Last time I saw him he was sitting by the churn. He had butter all over his face'" (69). For these sadistic white American males, Sethe's milk-heavy breasts become erotic instruments for consumption; this assault is symbolic of the more prevalent sexual violence that Black women experienced. As literary scholar Trudier Harris notes, there is a fundamental paradox in how Black females and white females are viewed by white males with regard to Black males:

> [T]he sexual usefulness of the [Black] female and her role as a mammy could only have the effect of increasing the white man's fear of the Negro male, her rightful mate and legitimate possessor. This could not but help lead to the fantastic exaggeration in the white American man's mind of the Negro's sexual prowess. And this, in turn would necessitate more repressive measures against the Negro male—all caused by the white man's guilt and anxiety. The necessity to "protect" the white male against this fancied prowess of the male Negro thus becomes a fixed constellation in the ethos of the South. (18)

A hysterical lust for body parts (fingers, toes, ears, and penis) of the African American victims signals white people's desire to symbolically consume their victims. This sublimated sexual consumption would manifest itself in whites taking home Black body parts and in some cases keeping them on their persons. Taking the Black body parts home symbolizes the private act of necrophilia in which the white home becomes a necropolis for Black bodies. In Wright's poem blackness and death are analogous. Discussing Black subjects, Sharon Patricia Holland states: "Their presence in society is, like the subject of death, almost unspeakable, so black subjects share the space the dead inhabit" (6). In America, white masculinity has often been culturally and psychologically defined as the beating, lynch-burning, castrating, and overall killing of Black men, and by the sexual conquest (rape) of Black women. The lynching of Black men by white men suggests that white men fear Black men; however, the rape of Black women by white men suggests that white men do not fear Black women. Although most lynchings of African American men were not related to sexual relationships between those men and white women, such relationships were posited as the reason for mob actions.

Beyond the issue of sexuality, socioeconomic control of African Americans fueled lynching. The humiliation of Black people was foreplay to the ritual of the lynching. As William H. Chafe points out, the humiliating system of Jim Crow affected every part of African American people's lives:

> Beginning where statutory restrictions ended, Jim Crow customs and racial etiquette seized every opportunity to belittle and humiliate African Americans. A racist code of social conduct and customs reserved the use of the titles "Miss" and "Mister" for white men, women, and children; disparaging epithets were reserved for black Americans, including, but certainly not limited to such words as "boy" or "gal" regardless of the person's age, "auntie," or simply "nigger." Whites expected black household workers to enter white homes through the back doors, black pedestrians to step off sidewalks when whites passed by, and under no circumstance was a black man to glance, let alone stare, at a white woman. (268)

The dehumanizing discourse of racism had a devastating effect on the psyches of most Black individuals; no matter the age, the status, or the profession of the Black individual, a Black person was almost always referred to in a disrespectful and demeaning manner. Hence, although Wright focuses our attention on the Black male body, certain analogies can be made with regard to Black females who were also victims in the extra-legal violence of lynchings.[5]

In "Between the World and Me," Wright addresses the compelling sadistic nature of lynching and opens the question of the Black body under law. With the specific use of the "I" point of view, the author seeks to illuminate both the individual and communal effects of racial violence on the lives of African American people. The poem's elaborate perspective of the speaker's body at the center of the lynching ritual, according to Trudier Harris, reinforces the brutality: "The general human degradation becomes specific degradation of the Black individual [of the "I"]. The 'I' becomes central for the speaker. As it becomes centralized, or specific, the 'I' reverses itself and becomes simultaneously generalized again" (101). The first-person point of view allows the reader to identify with the speaker, the narrative, and allows us to remove the psychological and emotional distance that may exist between those African Americans who were lynched and others who only view the remains of a lynching or read about a lynching. This perspective represents the voice from the oral tradition, oral voicing. Like other African American writers, Wright is raising the dead, allowing this lynching victim to speak, and provides him with the agency of a physical body in order to tell the story of a death-in-life. Denied a sustainable subjectivity, the victim speaks from a place and space that is familiar. Equally significant, Wright makes use of the elements of prosody to construct this poem, and another fact in the development of the poem is the progression of the images created by the adjectives and nouns. And the end-stop/run-on pattern of the lines of "Between the World and Me" generates and reinforces the tension in the poem. This technique forces us to read and evaluate simultaneously. The anaphora, the repetition of "And" and "There," especially in the beginning and conclusion of the poem, creates added emphasis to his gruesome description of the de-realization and dissolution of the Southern Black male body. Equally important, with the poem beginning with the coordinating conjunction "And," this suggests the continuous aspect of some journey or situation that will now take a drastic turn. With the end of the enslavement period, the Jim Crow segregation period began a different form of oppression reinforced by violence. This transition reflects the transgenerational transgression of trauma with the enslavement period that has now extended to the Reconstruction period. A more personal perspective suggests that the narrator has recently experienced something, and this encounter in the woods is another tragic occurrence for Blacks living in a Jim Crow culture of systemic psychological and physical violence.

With the ambiance of a fairy tale or children's story and with a Whitman-esque style, the poem seductively begins with the nameless narrator in a bucolic setting telling us how he stumbles upon "this thing." Here the ambiguous noun "thing" represents a double entendre, as the word reflects either the scene of the lynch-burning or some physical element at the scene that causes the narrator to stumble. Also, the crux of the lynching as a tragedy is the ambiguity in the characterization of the narrator as victim. The juxtaposition of the diction "I" and the "thing" reinforces the humanity of the speaker and the inhumanity of the actions that produced the "thing": life and death are associated with this juxtaposition. As represented by the "torn tree limbs" and "scaly oaks and elms," nature has come under an unnatural attack, yet in their desecrated state, the trees "guarded" the scene so as to speak to the violence of humans. Mankind's relationship with nature should be a simple existence, but there is something unusual and unnatural in this place. Indeed, the narrator stumbles upon something grotesque in nature, created by man. And as we will see, the unusual and grotesque "thing" represents the malevolence that is fundamental to the extralegal violence of white supremacy, nativism, and racialized xenophobia. Trees guard not just the lynching scene but also secure the evidence at the scene so that the narrator could bear witness to the desecration. In fact, it is possible that the "torn tree limbs" were used in assaulting the Black man, thereby creating a synthesis between the man and nature. "Scaly oaks" render a morbid quality to this pastoral scene, a gruesome scene that has the eerie feel of a cemetery at midnight. These trees recall the famous lyrics of the song "Strange Fruit" that Billie Holiday sang in which the victim becomes food for the birds to pluck and the wind to suck.[6] Lynchings and their aftermaths sent a profound message of intimidation to the masses of African American people, especially in the South. As W. Fitzhugh Brundage explicates: "The accumulation of news accounts, oral testimonies, and lived experiences of racist violence were a constant reminder to . . . all African Americans of their oppression. Lynching was a powerful tool of intimidation that gripped Blacks' imagination whether they lived in a mob-prone part of the South or in the relative safety of a border state" (2). Indeed, the scene speaks to the narrator as he relates that the sooty details are "thrusting themselves between the world and me." Toni Morrison contextualizes the experience of being "outdoors" in her analysis in *The Bluest Eye:*

> Outdoors was the end of something, an irrevocable, physical act defining and complementing our metaphysical condition. Being a minority in both caste and class, we moved about anyway on the hem of life, struggling to consolidate our weakness and hang on. . . . Our peripheral existence, however, was something we had learned to deal with—probably because it was abstract. But the concreteness of being outdoors was another matter—like the difference between the concept of death and being, in fact dead. Dead doesn't change and outdoors is here to stay. (18)

This sagacious critique helps us to understand Wright's analogy of nature and dead. Like our Black narrator and victim, nature is constantly in a state of coming back from the dead, a life-in death existence. To be Black within a white supremacist culture means to be "outdoors" or in the margins of society, constantly subjected to dehumanizing racial violence. The "sooty details" are not just the burnt fragments but the epistemology and cosmology of a white-supremacist culture that dehumanized and defined Black bodies, especially Black males, as a dangerously racial grotesque. As Leonard Cassuto makes clear in *The Inhuman Race: The Racial Grotesque in American Literature* (1987), "Human objectification can result from all kinds of perceived differences, but in American culture it happens most readily to people with dark skin. . . . When the differences polarize, as they tended to in American experience, human objectification follows" (3–4). White supremacy represents the major obstacle that hinders many African American people from embracing the world and realizing their full human potential. David Levering Lewis has characterized lynching as "the apotheosizing of white supremacy."[7] Accordingly, the critical issue for Black people is their enduring attempt to gain and sustain subjectivity within the parameters of white-American patriarchal capitalistic hegemony. As Brundage explains: "Lynching in the American South during the late nineteenth and early twentieth century was but one manifestation of the strenuous and bloody campaign by white Americans to elaborate and impose a racial hierarchy upon people of color throughout the globe" (2). Accordingly, the Great Migration represents a critical site of Black people's resistance in that the number of lynchings of African Americans increased almost threefold—from seven in 1929 to twenty in 1930. As Trudier Harris notes: "Blacks who because of their value as slaves, had not been widespread targets—though certainly they could be lynched—quickly became new game for lynchers. With the increase in punishment directed at this group, the term 'lynching' became common parlance after 1830. Blacks began to be lynched more frequently because of the increase in economic competition" (7). Thus, the enigmatic title of the poem represents not just the lynching of Black people but the enduring racial hegemony of Jim Crow segregation, a system of violence maintained by Ku Klux Klan intimidation, social humiliation, economic exploitation (sharecropping, land theft, vagrancy laws, and enticement regulations), and white-American-male physical violence, a violence arising from uncontrolled racial hatred and uncontrolled fear of difference. As Bertram Doyle notes: "The Ku Klux Klan was established as an agency to secure the return of government to the white South and to assist in a re-establishment of customs which had been undermined" (133).[8] It should be noted that because of the economics of racism, legal authorities did little or nothing to intercede between this world of racial hatred and violence and African American people's desires. This extra-legal white violence served the interest of the state, or at least multitudes of its officials, by discouraging African American protest against the legal structures of white supremacy. In Wright's home state of Mississippi, Black Codes with an economic base were enacted literally to criminalize and re-enslave the African American population. As C. Vann Woodward argues in *The Strange Career of Jim Crow* (1966): "The standard devices for accomplishing disenfranchisement on a racial basis and evading the restrictions of the Constitution were invented by Mississippi, a pioneer of this movement and the only state that resorted to it before the Populist revolt took the form of political rebellion" (83). What is critical in Mississippi and other states is that African American people stayed in their "place" and did not challenge a system that ensured certain social and economic privileges only to white Americans. Indeed, as Orlando Patterson notes, Mississippi had the greatest number of lynchings during the period of 1892 and 1968, followed by Georgia, Texas, Louisiana, Alabama, and Arkansas (*Rituals of Blood* 176).

The issue of economics is especially important because, like segregation, the enduring lynching of African American men insured white Americans the protection of profits. With the loss of the African American female body, which had been the slaveholding white American man's economic base, they began to a focus on controlling African American men. There were a number of economically based reasons for an African American person to be lynched, such as attempting to vote, attempting to buy land, refusing to work for white Americans, and acting in a manner that challenged the Jim Crow system. African American individuals who attempted to integrate theaters, restaurants, or hotels were subject to a serious beating or a lynching. As Jon-Christian Suggs makes clear: "In reality many if not most victims of white-on-black lynchings were out-spoken or independent men, and occasionally women who came to the attention of the white community; they died for their autonomy" (181). Lynching became an integral part of the southern economy and class structure that emerged dur-ing the 1870s and 1880s to replace slavery, and that new system remained more or less intact until the early decades of the twentieth century (Tolnay and Beck 244). Without a doubt, white violence created white wealth; however, there is a paradox in that cheap Black labor is generally valuable under white supremacy, but African American life individually becomes a cheap commodity. Perhaps, the primary value that these African American individuals' tortured bodies have is to instill trepidation into African American people as a group. African American people's terror creates whiteness as property and "matters of law are tied not only to race but to property, as race in America itself is always already a narrative of property" (Suggs 12). However, like race, white American-ness is a complex and impure social construction that encompasses identity, ideology, and institutions: three aspects that consistently marginalize and degrade blackness. As Toni Mor-rison maintains in her analysis of the American literary tradition, blackness must be "enslaved," "repulsive," "helpless," "history-less," "damned," "a blind accident of evolution," so that whiteness can figure itself as "free," "desirable," destined, and so forth (*Playing in the Dark* 52).

By juxtaposing the degradation of African American body with the des-ecration of nature, Wright brilliantly underscores the themes of consumption (human and nature), desolation, brutal violence, crucifixion, and castration. White American people's desire for and consumption of the Black male body is first represented by "a design of white bones slumbering forgottenly upon a cush-ion of ashes." Ironically, only through the ritualistic act of lynching do the frag-ments of the Black body find some element of peace. But the "charred stump of a sapling pointing a blunt finger accusingly at the sky" personifies and provides a synthesis between the lynching and the crucifixion of Jesus Christ. While on the cross, Jesus asks God the Father why He has forsaken him. With adept personify-ing signification, Wright has the sapling asking God why this African American man has been tortured and killed; also, the sapling asks why it has been tortured and killed by mankind. Both the African American man and the sapling that the man has been bound to become sacrificial victims of white people's malfeasance, manifested in ritual violence. The sapling voices a double articulation: the lost of human life and the desecration of nature. The fingers of the man become metas-tasized into the accusing gesture of the sapling, yet there resides some tension here. Whereas Jesus Christ has sacrificed himself for all of mankind, the African American male body becomes an ensanguined sacrifice for the furtherance of the socioeconomic subjectivity of white-male supremacy. Nature has been violated and damaged, evidenced by the violence of "torn tree limbs, tiny veins of burnt leaves, and a scorched coil of greasy hemp." The spiritual relationship between the man and the sun is underscored in the line: "And through the morning air the sun poured yellow surprise into the eye sockets of a stony skull." God's sunlight illuminates the stony skull in an attempt to bring the scene alive to allow the readers to view the lynching from the point of view of the narrator. Wright's use of the "sun" further suggests the Black man is Christlike in the sense that He is the son ("sun") of God. At the end of the poem, the line: "Now I am dry bones and my face a stony skull staring in my yellow surprise at the sun . . ." reverses the spiritual perspective with the narrator articulating to nature his own horror at what has happened to him.

Along with the assault upon nature, Wright illustrates the desolation of African American life: "A vacant shoe, an empty tie, a ripped shirt, a lonely hat, and a pair of trousers stiff with black blood." The simple adjectives here give a strong sense of the desolation and the sexual violence that this Black man experienced. If clothing can be considered a part of an individual's subjectivity (clothing makes the man), this man's subjectivity is stripped when his clothes were violently removed. Wright's list of the man's attire suggests that the victim may have been of an elevated class; many of the African American victims were those who were landowners, preachers, or businessmen. His "empty tie" is especially significant because the symbolic lynch rope would symbolically replace the necktie as the African American man was tied to the sapling. A "ripped shirt" denotatively conveys the physical violence whereas connotatively it suggests the possibility that the Black body will soon be ripped open; of course, this African American man's family would experience emotional devastation if they were to stumble upon his remains. However, the African American man's "trousers stiff with black blood" suggests that a sexual assault occurred while his trousers were still on or positioned at his ankles. The absence of the man's underwear speaks to sexual desire and consumption, as the Black phallus remains a site of fear with regard to miscegenation. As Trudier Harris argues, the castration of African American males represents a paradox of apprehension and identification:

> From one perspective, then there is an ironic reversal in that there is a communal rape of the black man by the crowd which executes him. . . . His death also enables white males to act out a fear of castration even as they are in the process of castrating the black man. Perhaps the worst fear any man can have is the fear that someone will cut off his penis; the white man, heir to that fear just as the black is, designs as the peculiar punishment for black men that which all males fear most. His action simultaneously shows his kinship to the black man and denies the connection. He does to the black what, in his worst nightmares, he perhaps imagines other adversaries doing to him; before he becomes victim, he victimizes. (23)

With white males' hysterical consternation around miscegenation (mostly between African American males and white females), castration of the African

American male's phallus becomes especially significant in this ritual of consumption of the Black male body. The victim's trousers suggest the gender of the victim and the "black blood" suggests both the race and the coagulation of the blood. Wright suggests that the African American male is made tumescent ("stiff") before the castration and the bloodletting begin. This homoerotic element would make the lynching a more sadistic spectacle.

True to historical documentation and eyewitness reports, Wright characterizes that a significant number of white people were present at many of the lynchings, as well as the wide range of the consumptive activities (engaged in) at these extra-legal rituals. In one account a reporter following some white farmers going to a lynching reveals: "Their wives and children were along. Many bought lunches—big six-layer cakes and fried chicken" (Street 35). Wright's narrator reveals, "And upon the trampled grass were buttons, dead matches, butt-ends of cigars and cigarettes, peanut shells, a drained gin-flask, and a whore's lipstick." First, the "trampled grass" reveals that perhaps hundreds or even thousands of white individuals: including men, women, and children, were present at this festival of violence. More specifically, the other vapid elements reveal a celebratory or circus-like atmosphere where food and drink, such as peanuts and gin, are bought and consumed. These items reinforce the concept that both children and adults were present at these festivals of blood—there is something for everyone. Without a doubt, Wright illustrates a rather hedonistic scene ripe with sexuality. Secondly, with the "butt-ends of cigars and cigarettes, peanut shells, a drained gin-flask, and a whore's lipstick," Wright's diction directs the reader's gaze to the mouth, thereby reinforcing and reinscribing the pervasive theme of sexual desire and oral consumption. The declarative listing of cigars, cigarettes, gin-flasks, and the whore's lipstick (the white woman marks her mouth as a site for consumption and a site for sexual desire), as phallic symbols, connect the desires of the white audience to the consumption of the African American male victim, especially his phallus.

Even as they mercilessly kill this African American man, whites with their taxonomic gazes are in a state of leisure, even sexual leisure and licentious lust. Similar to Wright's use of the word "thing," in the first line (recalling Baldwin's description, the Black man's phallus comes to mind here to reinforce his objectification) the "whore's lipstick" represents a phallic object. This object conveys the possibility that sexual activity occurred at this lynching and the possibility that the African American male victim was either accused of some sexual assault on a white female or engaged in consensual sexual activity with a white female. Paradoxically, if the African American man's phallus represents the "thing," this would mean that the most prized possession was either destroyed or discarded. Continuing this phallic analysis: considering the hundreds or even thousands of white individuals present, this would be an excellent opportunity for a white "whore" to make some money by satisfying the sublimated sexual desires of white males. Just as the gin-flask goes from "mouth to mouth," the white whore perhaps goes from white man to white man (phallus to phallus). Here, Wright destroys the notion of the white woman's pedestal purity by having the whore in the midst of the lynching, reinforcing the triangle of desire. The white whore will consume and she will be consumed in the exchange of bodily fluids. By identifying a whore at the lynching, Wright reveals that the white woman's class, status, and consensual sexual conduct are irrelevant when it comes to the lynching of an African American male. However, while Wright suggests specificity with regard to the race of the victim, he is rather ambiguous with regard to the race of the whore. Hence, if the whore is African American and not white, this would reinforce the notion of white male subjectivity being defined by white men killing African American men and having sex with African American women. Indeed, both African American men and women become victims of consumption.[9]

Like the whore, the prize will be the Black phallus, which will be taken home after the lynching, and the white individual may use the dead Black phallus to displace or project his or her sexual desires, sexual anxieties, and sexual inhibitions. Taking the Black phallus home represents a form of necrophilia. As a sadistic sexual ritual, the lynching represents a massive white orgy with short-term psychological gratification and long-term economic benefits to the dominant white-supremacist society.

The protection of the white woman is critical to the dogma and discourse of white supremacy. For an African American man, any relationship with a white woman could be tragic. If the white woman invites the African American man to love, he is doomed. Once the African American man accepts and it is found out, the white woman will scream rape and the man is lynched. On the other hand, if the African American man refuses, the white woman may in humiliation and revenge scream rape and the African American man will be lynched. In his poem "Silhouette," Langston Hughes addresses a "Southern gentle lady" and makes this paradoxical point clear: "They've hung a black man/ To a roadside tree / In the dark of the moon/ For the world to see/ How Dixie protects/ Its white womanhood/ Southern gentle lady,/ Be good!/ Be good!" (171).

Lastly, with the "whore's lipstick" being framed by the "buttons" and the other phallic symbols, there is the implication that perhaps the buttons were lost as white males in their sexual frenzy satisfied themselves with the whore and the African American victim. Cigars, cigarettes, the drained gin-flask, peanut shells, and the whore's lipstick become disposable elements of consumption, just as this African American's Black body becomes a disposable commodity.

In Richard Wright's novel *The Long Dream* (1958), Wright's extremely unequivocal description of the aftermath of a lynching reinforces and reinscribes the theme of miscegenation as a performance of sexual consumption. As he does in "Between the World and Me," Wright juxtaposes elements of nature with this lynching. Here, a Black father, Tyree Tucker—a director of a funeral business in the South (Clintonville, Mississippi)—attempts to teach his son Rex "Fishbelly" Tucker about the grim and deadly realities of any Black male having a relationship with any white female, when the castrated and mutilated body of Chris Sims, Fishbelly's twenty-four-year-old Black male friend, is delivered to Tucker's establishment. At the age of twelve, Fishbelly is initiated into manhood when his father and Dr. Bruce, the town's Black physician, keep Fishbelly with them as they examine Chris' body. However, before this examination, Chris' mother in an extremely emotional plea seeks an answer to her son's brutal demise:

> "Chris baby this ain't you! Naw, naw, Gawd! This can't be! It ain't true! It ain't right!" Mrs. Sims cried clinging hysterically to the dead body. Then she keened with shut eyes: "Gawd didn't do this to me! He couldn't. No matter what you did, son, Gawd didn't want you to die like this! I carried you in my body; I felt you growing; I birthed you in pain; I gave you life with my blood! Now, this. . . . Naw, naw Gawd! Somebody somewhere's got to tell me why you died like this. . . ." She lifted her loose wet face to the glaring, naked electric bulb. "Gawd, You didn't do this! You couldn't! And You got to do something to stop this from happening to black women's children! If I had to do it over again, I wouldn't have no child! I'd tear it out my womb! Women don't bring children into the world to die like this! Gawd, take Your sun out of the sky! Take Your stars away! I don't want Your trees, Your flowers no more! I don't want Your wind to blow on me when my son can die like this. . . . I'm standing 'fore Your throne asking You to tell me: What did I ever do wrong? Where's my sin? If my only son was to be killed, then tell me and I'd kill 'im. Not them white folks. . . . Lawd, we ain't scarred to die. BUT NOT LIKE THIS! Gawd talk to me. As long's I live, I'll be asking You to tell me why my son died like this. . . ." (75)

Wright's poignant discourse captures the absolute horror of a Black mother's profound loss of her only son, killed in a manner most inhumane. Here we have denial and desire as Chris' mother emotionally refuses to believe that this is the son that she gave birth to, as she desperately clings to her beloved son's body. The paradoxical trauma of a parent having to witness the death of a child becomes implicit. Like the sapling pointing a blunt finger accusingly at the sky, this hysterical Black mother asks God for an answer for Chris' brutal death. The electric light bulb becomes a symbol of the sun that registers its own horror of this gruesome death; the bulb is also symbolic of an unresponsive God whose silent presence is often frustrating to those Black individuals seeking answers to impossible questions concerning the racial violence that is often a daily aspect of their lives under Jim Crow segregation. Wright also gives a duality to this mother's question of responsibility, which functions as an accusation against God for allowing this lynching to happen. So horrific is the effect of this lynching that the idea of infanticide comes to this mother's mind. Similar to Toni Morrison's *Beloved*, where a whip-scarred Black woman, Sethe, has killed a daughter rather than have her children return to a slave existence, Wright has this emotionally distraught mother contemplating ripping new life from her womb. Tragically, infanticide becomes a better option than ongoing sexual violence or an extra-legal lynching where the Black body becomes a thing. The juxtaposition of this lynching and nature resonates with this Black mother's desire for God to take away the sun, the wind, the trees, the flowers, and the stars. The irony of these natural elements is that the lynched Black body is hung to the tree, the sun warms the dead body, and the wind sucks the dead flesh as the flowers become stained with Black blood; yet these elements of nature bring beauty, joy, and peace to human existence. Finally, before Doctor Bruce leads her away, this Black woman expresses an enduring call to God for a response for the loss of her son, Chris.

Wright's description of and discourse on Chris' battered body illuminates the theme of fear and desire for the Black body. As Fishbelly watches his father and the doctor circumspectly remove Chris' clothes from his "puffed flesh," he comes to terms with his own tenuous Black-male subjectivity within a white-supremacist culture. This lynching has removed any semblance of humanity: "The mouth, lined with stumps of broken teeth, yawned gapingly, an irregular, black cavity bordered by shredded tissue that had once been lips. The swollen eyes permitted slits of irises to show through distended lids" (76). Wright's focus on Chris' distorted mouth connects us to the nameless narrator of his poem and again illustrates consumption where the Black victim is forced to consume his own blood and teeth. Tyree's father and the doctor contemplate the loss of one of Chris' ears, scraped, sheered off. They concluded that Chris was dragged by an automobile and yet are surprised that there are no gunshot wounds. Then the doctor makes a profound and paradoxical statement that he cannot completely understand: "These *whites* suffered more than this boy. Only folks who *suffer* can kill like this . . ." (78). Chris' genitals are gone. Wright describes Fishbelly's trauma: "Fishbelly saw a dark, coagulated blot in a gaping hole between the thighs and with defensive reflex, he lowered his hands nervously to his groin" (78). More graphic than "Between the World and Me," where we recall the Black man's trousers "stiff with black blood," Wright makes it clear that the lynching of Black males comes down to the man's genitals, a source of sadistic sexual desire. Making the point that the whites "suffer" more than Chris moves us away from the victim to focus our gaze on the participants. That the whites involved in Chris' sadistic lynching and castration are deviant and pathological reinforces the concept that white supremacy represents a psychological disease. Doctor Bruce provides his analysis of this consumption:

> "I'd say that the genitals were pulled out by a pair of pliers or some like instrument," the doctor inferred. "Killing him wasn't enough. They had to *mutilate* 'im. You'd think that disgust would've made them leave *that* part of the boy alone. . . . No! To get a chance to *mutilate* 'im was part of why they killed 'im. And you can bet a lot of white women were watching eagerly when they did it. Perhaps they knew that that was the only opportunity they'd get to see a Negro's genital . . ." (78)

Again, Wright makes the profound point that lynching of Black males is simply not about fear but also represents white people's desire, especially white females who have an opportunity to have a vicarious relationship with the Black male's phallus. Doctor Bruce adds: "You have to be terribly attracted toward a person, almost in love with 'im to mangle 'im in this manner. They hate us, Tyree, but they love us too, in a perverted sort of way, they love us . . ." (79). Perhaps there exists no other profound paradox of racialized sexual desire than the killing and mutilating of the Black male body. The critical question in this gruesome autopsy that is not raised and difficult to answer: Where is Chris Sims' penis?

Similar to his story of the lynching of the African American young man, Chris, Wright's short story "Big Boy Leaves Home," depicts white males as sexual sadists who are afraid of African American men raping white women, and who are capable of shocking cruelty. Here, another young African American male, Big Boy, who hides in a nearby hole, hears the White males shout, "LES GIT SOU-VENIRS! . . . LOOK! He's gotta finger! . . . He's got one of his ears, see?" (*Uncle Tom's Children* 40) Here this young African American man's bodily subjectivity becomes dismembered and fragmented for easy consumption. During this Jim Crow segregation period, sexual relations between African American men and white women, whether consensual, forced, or fabricated, were met with the swift violence of extra-legal lynch law. As one scholar notes: "An inherent hatred, born of the white man's chagrin at finding male ex-slaves finally in a position to partially protect the women of their race against the habitual ravishment to which masters and overseers had subjected them, forms the basis for the sex perversion responsible for Southern lynchings" (Ginzburg 225–26). Conjuring the theme of miscegenation, Wright constructs a triangle of desire where the white woman, the African American male as a buck, and the white-male lynchers as protectors of white womanhood intersect. In the poem, the white whore could be viewed as a figure who mediates between the homosocial intersection of African American male as "beast" and the white males. Along with fingers, ears, toes, and bones, the African American man's genitalia would come under inspection, attack, and be subject to castration/consumption, as whites would often take home souvenirs.

In *Essentially Speaking*, Diana Fuss discusses the implications inherent in the sexualization of African American bodies: "It is not merely that to be a 'Negro' . . . is to possess a particular genetic or biological make-up; it is, rather to be biological" (75). African American men become defined as a "sexual body" and little else. Wright leads us to connect the whore with the victim: the whore smears the lipstick red on her lips, and the African American victim swallows his own blood. The whore has smeared the lipstick on at the lynching in her attempt to seduce white men to consume her, whereas the bloody mouth of the victim signifies the Christian ritual of communion where the true believers consume the symbolic body and the blood of Christ. Wright gives us "a kind of secular Eucharist, where, at least in Protestant theology, the sacramental elements of Christ's body and blood are substituted by wafer and wine, or in Catholic theology, these elements are transubstantiated into the actual body and blood of Christ" (Dyson 167). As a promiscuous individual, the "whore" signifies the stereotypical white-supremacist discourse where the African American man becomes defined as a salacious individual and a threat to white women. Also, as Trudier Harris points out: "Wright's assigning of the lipstick to a whore also imaginatively undercuts the claims white men usually made to the sanctity and 'purity' of Southern white womanhood. A man, who may or may not have had sexual contact with her, must die for a woman who sells her virtue for profit" (100). Thus the whore's red lipstick-stained mouth and the African American man's bloody mouth conjure up a synthesis between miscegenation and lynching, thereby suggesting consensual or nonconsensual race mixing as the ostensible motive for this brutally grotesque lynching. Rape-and-lynch psychosis is part and parcel of the pathology of white men projecting their insecurities onto their notion of the hypersexual African American man as well as their guilt in the raping of African American women, who they also viewed as hypersexual. Castration of the African American's Black phallus served a dual function in the redemption (displacement and projection) of the white-male psyche. With the removal and consumption of the Black phallus, racist white individuals felt that the society was theirs to control; Black men had few choices: acquiesce, flee, or be killed.

Paradoxically, many of these extra-legal lynchings in the South occurred in front of courthouses or churches with some core elements: white men with their guns, their knives, their dogs, and their sticks along with a lynch rope, faggots, chains, gasoline, tar, and feathers. In some cases, white children were let out of Sunday school to view the lynching spectacle. Wright reveals: "Scattered traces of tar, gasoline, restless arrays of feathers, and the lingering smell of gasoline" reveal that the Black victim was tortured before being burned alive. While the narrator is appalled by the horrible remains of the African American's Black body and the white people's tools of lynching, the sun equally is stunned and horrified by the injustice and pours "yellow surprise into the eye sockets of a stony skull." Wright's rendering of the sun's reaction to man's injustice to man echoes the absolute horror voiced by the sapling's blunt finger, which points to the sky accusing God of abandoning both man and nature. Indeed the lynching represents a symbolic and literal challenge to the existence of God as these racists destroy human life and nature. As a racial signifier, the use of the color yellow, as an amalgamation of Black and white, reinforces the theme of miscegenation suggested by the presence of the whore; many African American male individuals suspected of improper relationships with white females faced lynching. As Sandra Gunning sagaciously argues, sexual and political agency became increasingly linked to the African American male as rapist, and white manhood became linked to avenging any sexual transgression with a white woman:

> In turn, American society and civilization came increasingly to be figured as the
> white female body; silent, helpless, in immediate need of protection from the

black beast. Thus the protection of feminized whiteness in danger functioned as a primary argument of white supremacists to justify terrorism against black communities. Because whites could allege that the struggle was really one of racial survival, not democracy, black men would not simply be disenfranchised, they would rightfully be exterminated. (7)

Gunning's concept of a gendered American body politic reinforces the notion that African American men can never be true citizens because that means a symbolic embrace of the white woman. The presence of the white female is always symbolically present in the lynchings that African American writers describe.

Like Richard Wright's narrator, the nameless narrator in James Weldon Johnson's *The Autobiography of an Ex-Coloured Man* (1912) is immobilized. The ground grips his feet as he gives witness to a horrific lynching: "Some of the crowd yelled and cheered, others seemed appalled at what they had done, and there were those who turned away sickened at the sight. I was fixed to the spot where I stood, powerless to take my eyes from what I did not want to see" (187). Johnson's description of this African American man relates that he is "a man only in form and stature, every sign of degeneracy stamped upon his countenance. His eyes were dull and vacant, indicating not a single ray of thought. Evidently the realization of his fearful fate had robbed him of whatever reasoning power he had ever possessed (186–87). Even before this African American man dies a horrific death, he is reduced to a "thing." Illustrating the objectification of the African American body, Claude McKay in his poem "The Lynching" begins with the conventional association of African American lynch victims with the crucified Christ that I will later discuss with Langston Hughes's poetry and Robert Hayden's poetry but ends the poem with the final description of the corpse: "And little lads, lynchers that were to be/ Danced round the dreadful thing in fiendish glee" (37). Therefore, the "witnesses" that "rose and lived" and the narrator as a possible witness to his own violent death give testimony not to the legal process but reinforce the horrific extra-legal process of white racial violence.

Halfway through the poem the narrator expresses his profound sorrow and "cold pity" for the African American life that is gone; at this point, the poem takes a surreal turn as the narrator experiences the ritualistic violence of the lynch-burning. Wright's narrator states: "The ground gripped my feet and my heart was circled by icy walls of fear." With the wind muttering and the hounds yelping, "the darkness screamed with thirsty voices, and the witnesses rose and lived." Once only a stunned witness to the aftermath of this brutal lynching, now the narrator and the Black victim become one: "The dry bones stirred, rattled, lifted, melting themselves into my bones. The grey ashes formed flesh firm and black, entered into my flesh." This surreal metamorphosis morbidly allows the narrator to experience blow by blow, the torturing, maiming, beating, and lynch-burning that results in the creation of "this thing" that he has stumbled upon. Many lynchings of African Americans are fundamentally about flesh; Black men charged with rape or attempted sexual assault, viewed as criminals who have committed crimes against white flesh. White women are often characterized as some scared and protected space, and any African American male who violated this space in any form would meet with a brutal death. Like the nameless victim who has his flesh removed, the narrator becomes a thing, a part of nature. In many lynchings the victim was left exposed for days, and this would result in the bodily remains being consumed by animals, birds, insects, and other scavengers. White bones slumbering would be the result. Hence, African American people and nature, especially trees, come under white people's control.

Dry bones reinforce the theme that all African Americans are victims when any individual is lynched; dry bones will rise from the ashes and live in the consciousness of other Blacks. Dead Black men do tell tales. Wright brings back the dead, which were not, and cannot now be buried. As evidenced by the "hungry yelping of hounds" and the "thirsty voices" of the white lynchers, many African Americans face the possibility of being consumed by whiteness; here, hounds and humans lust for Black flesh. Slave catchers and lynch mobs would often use dogs to attack and consume the genitals of African American male victims. In order to foreshadow the graphically violent nature of communal consumption and sexual sublimation, Wright writes: "The gin-flask passed from mouth to mouth; cigars and cigarettes glowed, the whore smeared the lipstick red upon her lips/ And a thousand faces swirled around me, clamoring that my life be burned . . ." Once the whites' desire for blackness is publicly stated, the African American victim is stripped of his clothing (his status and dignity as a human being) and forced to consume himself as his teeth are battered into his throat until he swallows his own blood. This violent act of forced self-consumption causes the victim to lose his voice, as Wright relates that his screams are "drowned in the roar of their voices, and my black wet body slipped and rolled in their hands as they bound me to the sapling." This cannibalism, of the type referred to by anthropologists as autocannibalism, involves the victim being forced to consume his own flesh. The lynching of Claude Neal in Jackson County, Florida, on October 27, 1934, with more than 2,000 white individuals present, represents this autocannibalism type of torture.

> After taking the nigger to the woods about four miles from Greenwood, they cut off his penis. He was made to eat it. Then they cut off his testicles and made him eat them and say he like it. (I gathered that this barbarous act consumed considerable time and that other means of torture were used from time to time on Neal). Then they sliced his sides and stomach with knives and every now and then somebody would cut off a finger or toe. Red hot irons were used on the nigger to burn him from top to bottom. From time to time during the torture a rope would be tied around Neal's neck and he was pulled up over a limb and held there until he almost choked to death when he would be let down and the torture began all over again. (*Rituals of Blood* 198)

To make this bizarre lynching even more grotesque, Neal's skinned and mutilated body was photographed and copies were sold for fifty cents apiece; body parts of this lynching became prized possessions. Here we have a triple level of consumption of the tortured Black body: autocannibalism, visual consumption, and physical consumption. African Americans' Black bodies, as representative of some "strange fruit" and nature become one, elements to be controlled by whites; however, unlike nature, racial difference is inscribed on the body through skin color, hair texture, facial features, and especially the mythology concerning the African American male's genitalia. Considering the discourse of white supremacy, it is often the phallus between the African American male's legs that suggests the title "Between the World and Me." Lynching tools come graphically into play as the victim is first mutilated, then tarred and feathered before his "blood was cooled mercifully, cooled by a baptism of gasoline." Killing the African American male is never enough in these rituals; there is a sadistic element to this public spectacle. Wright's use of the word "baptism" indicts white-Christian theology and practices that crucify African American people, the same religious philosophy it used to demonize African American people, making them grotesque objects of physical, economic, and sexual exploitation. There is a stark contrast between the stump that has been charred and the victim's body that has been vaporized by the burning flames. Like Jesus who ascended to Heaven, this African American male crucified victim also leaps to the sky as his "pain rose like water," boiling his tree-like limbs. This ascension also recalls the Phoenix rising from the ashes. In Robert Hayden's poem "Night, Death, Mississippi," we view the intersection between religion and bloody violence in the lines: "In the sweet dark/Unbuckled that one then/ and him squealing bloody Jesus/ as we cut it off" (15). Hayden's use of the word "unbuckled" serves to define the Black man as a buck, a sexual threat as well as to suggest that the man's pants were unbuckled before he was castrated. Also, Langston Hughes echoes the same juxtaposition in his morbid poem "Song for a Dark Girl" in the lines: "They hung my black young lover/ To a cross roads tree." Here the word "cross" represents Christ's crucifixion as well as the intersection of Black and white made explicit by the speaker's question: "I asked the white Lord Jesus/ What was the use of prayer" (172). Accordingly, lynching becomes a malicious ritual, pregnant with physical, psychological, and economic violence, as other African Americans are put on local and national notice that they could face this extra-legal retribution for challenging white hegemony. Perhaps the message for African Americans is that they can be free, but they can never be Americans, a definition that often means being white. More often than not, the bloody Black bodies of tortured, disemboweled, mutilated, and burned African American individuals were tied to automobiles or trucks and dragged through African American communities or left hanging as warnings to other African American people. Discussing the newspaper accounts of lynchings, Patricia A. Schechter reveals: "These accounts portrayed white males as patriarchal protectors of white females against African American men, the so-called Black beasts or burly brutes [bucks] who function as dark foils for true (white) manhood" (292). In some cases this psychological trauma was effective, and other African American people such as Robert F. Williams, author of *Negroes with Guns* (1962), understood the critical need to arm themselves and keep their distance from whites because they knew it was one thing to make laws, and it was another thing to enforce those laws.[10] During this time period, white-supremacist (extra-legal) groups such as the Knights of the Ku Klux Klan, the Pale Faces, the Knights of the White Camelia, the White Brotherhood, and white legal authorities worked hand in hand to intimidate, harass, and murder African American people, especially those who challenged Jim Crow.[11]

The enduring effect of Wright's poem illustrates how this dehumanizing experience reduces an African American man into a naked, childlike state. This trauma is most evident in cases of sexual violence where the individual regresses back to a younger age in an attempt to come to terms with the assault. Wright's narrator states: "Panting, begging I clutched childlike, clutched to the hot sides of death. Now I am dry bones and my face a stony skull staring in yellow surprise at the sun . . ." By reversing the gaze, Wright creates the classic call and response structure where the victim responds to the total horror earlier expressed by the call of the sun's "yellow surprise." By ending the poem with an asyndeton, the omission of the last conjunction, we identify with the series of torturous events that this man experienced. Like the "restless arrays of feathers" used to torture this Black man, this body and this spirit will remain restless because the lynching at its core is antithetical to the America's body politic of democracy and humanity. In *Twelve Million Black Voices* (1941), Wright forcefully argues this point:

> We black folks, our history and our present being, are a mirror of all the manifold experience of America. What we want, what we represent, what we endure is what America is. If we black folks perish, America will perish. If America has forgotten her past, then let her look into the mirror of our consciousness and she will see the living past living in the present, for our memories go back, through our black folk of today, through the recollections of our black parents, and through the tales of slavery told by our black grandparents, to the time when none of us, black or white, lived in this fertile land. (146)

The history of lynching is one that enduringly mutilates the humanity of victims and so-called victors. Moreover, the larger issue that Wright forces readers to witness is the extent to which the Black individual, in his or her attempt to attain subjectivity within the racial hegemony, has to confront the violent characteristics of white supremacy with its gratuitous brutality. As James H. Madison maintains: "A lynching was a performance that sent a message of white supremacy, warning all blacks to stay in their place. It was a weapon of terror that could strike anywhere, anytime, against any African American" (14). Most African Americans, regardless of their status, color, religion, or their education, were vulnerable to racial violence; they were trapped by the brutal reality of lynching, psychologically forced to identify with any Black individual caught in the midst of this race-based horror. As Demarest explicates:

> When the speaker of the poem begins his walk alone, perhaps—the reader feels—enjoying the kind of personal contemplation that should be every man's birthright and that, for the artist is a necessity. The lynching wrenches him into a group identity he cannot deny, yet paradoxically, it reminds him also of his existential aloneness, his personal vulnerability. The question the poem ponders is how one can come to an understanding of himself, the meaning of his own mortality, when a racial situation constantly crushes in on him overwhelming thought and feeling. (238)

However, African American people, as biological and cultural hybrids, are not the only victims and disposable commodities; here, white people who commit these sadistic crimes diminish their own humanity and hybridity, becoming the incarnation of malfeasance. As John Reilly points out, Wright was an angry, potentially violent man, who, as he matured, "channeled a violent and terrifying outrage . . . which forces us to experience the truth about what man does to man" (75). Wright's prolific writing agenda, here and in much of his other literary works, is to remind African American people of the violence of white-supremacist culture and to force the white reading public into an awareness of the precarious African American situation. In the literary tradition of Frederick Douglass, Richard Wright transformed his life by writing himself into existence, an existence where Black-male subjectivity is central to his body of work. Equally important is the bold work of Ida B. Wells in her crusade against the lynching of African American men; the lynchings of three of Wells' friends in 1892 fueled this crusade. The three men, Thomas Moss, Calvin McDowell, and Henry Stewart, were owners of People's Grocery Company in Memphis, Tennessee, and their small grocery business had competed with white businesses. A group of angry white men attacked the People's Grocery, hoping to eliminate the competition, but the three Black owners fought back, shooting three of the white attackers. These three African American men were characterized as "brutes" and "criminals" who victimized "innocent" whites. The owners of the People's Grocery were arrested along with one hundred other African Americans and charged with conspiracy, but a lynch party broke into the jail and dragged the three men away, put them on the switch engine of a train headed out of the city, and lynched them (Giddings 17–18). During this year, there had been 255 lynchings, more than in any previous year (Hall, *Revolt Against Chivalry* 132). Ida B. Wells, who grew up in Holly Springs, Mississippi, owner and co-editor of the newspaper, *Free Speech,* wrote an article denouncing this brutal lynching and called for justice.[12] Like Wright's poem, Wells' words were profound and powerful in their impact on another Black-woman crusader for justice in face of lynching, Mary Church Terrell. Lastly, similar to the brutality and suggested phallic mutilation in Wright's poem, Calvin McDowell's body had fingers of his right hand shot to pieces and his eyes were gouged out.

Although Richard Wright's language specifies violence, wretchedness, and suffering from the beginning of this poem, Wright's prolific use of his poetic material makes quite clear that the "dry bones" will not rest. Those bones will speak to the urgency of the racial situation with which the poem is directly concerned. With the African American man reduced to a wounded body or dismembered as body parts, how do we remember this body? At its very core, the poem with the "stony skull staring" in its "yellow surprise at the sun" speaks to the issue of trauma. Indeed, the line that states: "There were torn tree limbs, tiny veins of burnt leaves, and a scorched coil of greasy hemp" reflects the grotesque image of the mutilated, tortured, burnt, and traumatized Black-male body. The burning of the Black body gives us another aspect of the cannibalism, that being how consumption connects to smell. As Orlando Patterson sums up: "The common observation that our sense of taste is strongly related to our sense of smell, and that tasting is in large part actually smelling, has now been scientifically proven" (*Ritual of Blood* 198). Hence, when the participants are suffused with the smell of the lynch victim's burning flesh, they are literally consuming and devouring the Black man's body through their nostrils. Ginzburg chronicles a lynching that makes this connection. Two African American brothers, Irving and Herman Arthur, were lynched and burned in Paris, Texas, in August 1920; their roasted bodies were chained to the back of an automobile and dragged through the streets and some shouted: "Here come the barbequed niggers" (139).[13] However, this individual trauma becomes, as in the case of Emmett Till, a collective trauma for the African American community. Discussing the enduring psychologically dialectic effects of trauma on the body, Judith Lewis Herman states:

> The knowledge of horrible events periodically intrudes into public awareness but is rarely retained for long. Denial, repression, and dissociation operate on a social as well as an individual level. The study of psychological trauma has an underground history. Like traumatized people, we have been cut off from the knowledge of our past. Like traumatized people, we need to understand the past in order to reclaim the present and the future. Therefore, an understanding of psychological trauma begins with rediscovering history. (2)

Individual African American trauma becomes racial trauma as the "dry bones" and "grey ashes" connect the dead to the living. Considering the thousands of African American people who have been lynched, there are many "dry bones" and "grey ashes" yet to speak to us of the holocaust against African American people. Like Billie Holiday's melancholy and masterful rendition of the protest song of lynching, "Strange Fruit," Wright forces us to understand this psychological trauma and the unspeakable horror of lynching, as this nameless African

American individual gains transcendent metaphoric value. With regard to the body, Wright illustrates that white people's desire for and consumption of the African American's Black body is sadistic and the desire can be done in horrific ways. Paradoxically, many enslaved Africans aboard the slave ships believed that white males were fattening them up in order to consume them; indeed, many refused to eat and were violently force-fed. In a comprehensive sense, white-supremacist culture under Jim Crow society, and currently, has attempted to leave many African American people morally vacant, economically empty, spiritually ripped, psychologically lonely, and in violent aspects it has undertaken Black bloodletting. Lynching, along with all aspects of racial violence and ingrained white supremacy, stands between the world and Black people. Racism in its most vicious form, despite its abnormality, has become natural to many white people. The narrator creates a disparaging oneness between the violence of racism and the world. Wright makes the point that racial violence and hegemonic aspects separate individuals from others, especially those who are different, and they are separated from the world. On this point, Philip Dray in *At the Hands of Persons Unknown: The Lynching of Black America* (2002), discussing the impact of *Black Boy*, states: "Particularly vivid were the book's descriptions of the numbing effect of daily racism, and the narrow line Black Southerners walked, never sure which whites to trust, never completely at ease because physical harm or even death might lie in the next misunderstood encounter with the white world. Lynching, both in its literal form and as an abstract, brooding threat, is a motif in virtually all of Wright's work" (366–67). Dray's point emphasizes the fact that for most Blacks a pervasive psychological discomfort was an everyday reality because violence was too often the result of some societal infraction. Lastly, there is the visual consumption of Black bodies in the form of photographic souvenirs of lynchings sold as postcards in the South. As Dray relates: "Until they were banned in 1908, these cards could be sent through the U.S. mail" (103). In these cards, white males stood next to the lynched-burned body of the African American individual, sending a message of their willingness to document their actions. Despite these photographic documents, the legal authorities claimed that the African American person was killed "at the hands of persons unknown." Clearly identified white males become reduced to unknown "things" just as the known lynched victim is reduced to a grotesque "thing."

Truly grotesque would be the exact words to describe the horrendous last mass lynching in American history. On July 25, 1946, the Moore's Ford "lynching" in Walton County, Georgia, involved the killing of two young Black men and two young Black women; they were killed by four volleys of gunshots by a large mob of white males. Since that summer evening, there have never been as many victims lynched in a single day in America. The quadruple murder of these two Black couples, Roger and Dorothy Malcolm and George and Mae Murray, involved the dark underside of miscegenation, extramarital affairs, and the double standards associated with race and gender.[14] After stabbing his 29-year-old white landlord,

Barnette Hester, 24-year-old African American Roger Malcolm ended up in the local jail. Despite rumblings of a lynching by enraged whites, Malcolm survived the jail stay, returning to the community on bond to await trial when it became clear Hester would survive the seemingly fatal wound. His release reignited the white racists. Rumors flew that Malcolm had been marked for death, and on July 25, 1946, it came not only to Malcolm but also his wife, Dorothy, and the other African American couple, George and Mae Dorsey. In her book *Fire in a Canebrake* (2003), Laura Wexler, reveals that the reason behind the stabbing was that Roger had discovered a sexual relationship between his wife, Dorothy, and the white landowner. Wexler states:

> But still others in Hestertown had heard that Dorothy had tried to fight off Barnette Hester, that he'd forced her to have sex with him. They'd heard she told him, "Quit bothering me, before the other hands know about this mess." They knew the tradition; they knew their mothers, sisters, and wives—or they themselves—had been forced to have sex on the mornings or afternoons when the white landlord sent the men in their family to the most distant field on the farm. Some even suspected Roger Malcolm was going to be killed so one or both of the Hester brothers could have easier access to Dorothy. (12)

Here the word "mess" suggests the issue of miscegenation and the echoes of slavery where the white slave master would use every device to have unrestricted sexual access to Black female slaves. Later, Wexler described Thomas Blanton Jr.'s conviction in the 1963 bombing of the Sixteenth Street church in Birmingham, Alabama, which claimed the lives of four young Black girls, and the conviction of Byron De La Beckwith, who assassinated Civil Rights leader Medgar Evers in Mississippi in 1963, in comparison to this mass lynching:

> The Moore's Ford lynching occurred nearly two decades before these crimes, and not a scrap of physical evidence remains. Even if someone were to confess to taking part in the lynching, it's likely the confession would be unprovable. Even if a suspected murder weapon were found in an antic or a basement, there are no bullets from the crime scene to compare it with. The Moore's Ford lynching, in short, is not a case to be solved. There will be no justice. (239)

Wexler's comments pronounce the sad truth involved with most of the lynchings that occurred in America; most of the white individuals involved in these sadistic crimes will never be prosecuted.

Richard Wright, in his brilliant literal and abstract manner, reminds and shocks his audience, using the graphic iconography of racial violence masquerading as racist white people's necrotic desire for African Americans' Black bodies. In terms of an existential philosophy, knowledge of one's death determines not only the shape of one's life but also the culture he or she lives in, especially within a Jim Crow culture. As Medgar Evers relates in a speech to the Los Angeles Branch of the NAACP in May of 1959 and another speech in Panama City Florida in September 1959, lynchings in America reveal racist white people's violent oppression of Black people to the world, especially those people seeking their own freedom. He also raises the question of America's legal responsibility to its African Americans:

> It is appalling to observe the unethical folly of men in government who think the outside world will continue to look up to America as a symbol of democracy, as long as the lynchings of Parkers and Tills and Lees and other Negroes ring out across this great continent and across the continent of Africa, Asia, and all the other countries who believe in freedom and justice and equality. . . . We are concerned about the fact that the lynchers of Mack Charles Parker are known to the F.B.I. and state officials, however, despite this knowledge not a single person has been arrested, which raises the question: Is it excusable to lynch a person to death and inexcusable to murder one? For when one is murdered, the guilty is immediately pursued, and if apprehended, arrested; but not so with the lynchers, they are still free, though they are known. (*The Autobiography of Medgar Evers* 154)[15]

"Between the World and Me" and all of Wright's works of fiction and non-fiction are critical in helping us understand the current racial violence that occurred, for example in the white-male police brutality in the cases of Black males Abner Louima, who was brutally sodomized with a wooden stick, Amadou Diallo, and Patrick Dorman (both shot to death by white-male police officers) in New York City, and the white extra-legal racial violence in the horrific murder and decapitation of the 49-year-old James Byrd Jr. in Jasper, Texas, on June 7, 1998. Byrd's murder was particularly heinous in that he was brutally beaten and log-chained to the back of a pickup truck by three white males, then dragged to his death.[16] All of these tragic incidents garnered national and international attention but generally did nothing to change the perception of African American males as dangerous criminals and drug dealers.[17] By making these untarnished African American males somehow responsible for what happened to them, many white people were reassured of their innocence and superiority. Paradoxically, the dominant white media's representations of African American men not only serve the interests of the dominant white society and help maintain existing economic institutions, but they also keep African American people from socioeconomic power and stature in American society, providing the rationale for the prison industrial complex and other educational institutions where African American males too often become disposable commodities. As Ishmael Reed puts it: "Thousands of Black citizens are convicted by the media, in most cases without even having been charged with a crime. Since the media are 50 years behind the South in the efforts to integrate, these Blacks are convicted by the new all-white jury: journalists, media critics, talk-show hosts, psychologists, TV columnists, and assorted quacks" (Quoted in *Skin Trade* 139). Richard Wright, whose major works consistently focus on Black-male subjectivity in a white-supremacist culture, makes the point that there is no grave that can keep Black people down, and our stories of terror and our narratives of triumphs over terror must be told if future generations are to understand how the past influences the present.

c h a p t e r   3

Miscegenation as Sexual Consumption

The Enduring Legacy of America's White-Supremacist Culture of Violence in John Oliver Killens' *Youngblood*

> The astonishing fact is the great indifference of most white Americans toward real but illicit miscegenation. . . . The illicit relations freely allowed or only frowned upon are, however, restricted to those between white men and Negro women. A white woman's relation with a Negro man is met by the full fury of anti-amalgamation sanctions.
>
> Gunnar Myrdal, *An American Dilemma: The Negro Problem and Modern Democracy*

Where is the historical evidence that even remotely suggests that African American people in the United States can ever trust the masses of white people, especially white males, to pursue the fundamentals of Jeffersonian democracy and Emersonian human decency? Where is the historical evidence that suggests that white people en masse will ever denounce, oppose, and eradicate white-male supremacy, white-male hegemony, and white-male privilege? Where is the historical evidence that suggests that women en masse will importune white males to dismantle the anti-humanist white-male supremacist culture? Where is the historical evidence that suggests that African American people, especially African American males, will not suffer from the capricious violence of white-male police violence brought on by racial apprehension and racial insensitivity?

In John Oliver Killens' timeless and racially explosive novel *Youngblood*, published on the heels of the Supreme Court's *Brown versus Board of Education* 1954 decision, Killens illustrates that physical, psychological, and economic violence directed at African American people, especially African American males, represents a fundamental aspect of America's white-male supremacist culture. Economic considerations did not prevent violence and disregard for law on the part of many white southerners in wake of the growing Civil Rights Movement. Killens describes the "New South" that required a significant and often troubling change in social relationships between Blacks and whites.[1] While the type of lynching that Richard Wright describes in "Between the World and Me" is decreasing, racial violence remains significant. As Jessie Daniel Ames pointed out in 1939, racial violence out of necessity took a new form:

> We have managed to reduce lynchings not because we've grown more law abiding or respectable but because lynchings become such bad advertising. The South is going after big industry at the moment, and a lawless, lynch-mob population isn't going to attract very much outside capital. And this is the type of attitude that can be turned to advantage much more speedily than the abstract appeal to brotherly love (J. D. Hall 169)

If we examine the lives of Laurie Lee and Joe Youngblood and their family in Crossroads, Georgia, from the turn of the 19th century to the Great Depression, it becomes evident that the enduring aspects of physical, economic, and psychological violence at the hands of racist white males were fundamental to the trauma that a large number of African American people experienced in the South. At the heart of this traumatizing racial violence is the issue of miscegenation, especially that between African American males and white females, despite the fact that consensual and nonconsensual miscegenation was a fundamental aspect of early America. Interestingly, Thomas Sowell states in his book, *The Economics and Politics of Race* (1983), that in the 1840s, more than 43 percent of white, out-of-wedlock babies were fathered by African American men (9). On the other hand, most white males, regardless of class status, have been socialized to have a crazed fearfulness of African American males consuming white female genitalia. Indeed, the central horror for many racist whites is the connection of white female genitalia and African American male genitalia. Furthermore, most white males (whether they act it out or not) have been socialized to consume the African American female's genitalia as part of their unhealthy sexual sojourn to white-male subjectivity. The sexual consumption of African American bodies and blackness is a fundamental aspect of America's violent culture of racial and gender hegemony.

In the passionate spirit of Charles Waddell Chesnutt, Richard Wright, and Chester Himes, three chroniclers of the violent nature of white supremacy, miscegenation, and racialized sexual violence, John Oliver Killens places his novel in the South during the Jim Crow segregation period, a period of violent socio-economic disenfranchisement, where many African American people boldly challenged an oppressive system designed to keep them in a landless slave-like status. The Ku Klux Klan, white-male police officers, white-male officials, and white-male landowners were central to the desire to maintain white-male wealth; indeed, there was a direct connection to socioeconomic construction of "white-ness as property" and the ongoing disenfranchisement and economic exploita-tion of African American people. African American writers like Killens bring a critical perspective to the issue of sadistic racial violence and at the same time bring an unparalleled optimism and redemption concerning the southern Afri-can American human condition in the face of white males' enduring mendacity, malfeasance, and malevolence. Central to Killens' analysis of African American people's socioeconomic subjectivity is the issue of miscegenation between Afri-can American males and white females. Whereas the sexual violence against African American women by white males was not viewed as a criminal act or cultural contradiction, any indication of a sexual relationship between an Afri-can American man and a white female was met with the full fury of white-male extra-legal violence in the form of a lynch-burning and castration ritual. Most African American males, especially those in the rural South, began to associ-ate white females with peril and acted in a manner that avoided any evidence or suggestion of intimacy. This was most evident in the 1955 brutal death of a 14-year-old African American boy, Emmett Louis Till, in Money, Mississippi; Till was tortured, mutilated, and shot after he whistled at a white woman. Till's brutal murder gave national and international attention to the racial bigotry and violence in the South.[2]

Before proceeding, it is important to define the philosophy of white suprem-acy. White supremacy represents a hegemonic philosophy, epistemology, and axi-ology that postulates that those who are non-white are biologically, intellectually, and culturally inferior. The origins of America's white-supremacist ideology can be found in Thomas Jefferson's *Notes on the State of Virginia* (1787) where he ten-tatively states that Black people are intellectually and culturally inferior to white people; he also articulates a fear of miscegenation.[3] Of course, this represents a paradox, considering his clandestine relationship with the light-skinned African American slave Sally Hemings and the children that he produced from his long-term relationship of pedophilia. With Jefferson being a wealthy white-male slave owner, the issues of race, gender, and economics become synthesized. Accord-ingly, white supremacy is about materiality, or as George Lipsitz argues in *The Possessive Investment in Whiteness: How White People Profit from Identity Politics* (1992), "Whiteness has a cash value" with profits mainly for those white males with physical resources; those white males without physical resources (property) only had the illusion of racial superiority. Discussing the materiality of white supremacy that continued during the Jim Crow period and that currently exists, Lipsitz explains:

Whiteness has a cash value that accounts for advantages that come through profits made from housing secured in discriminatory markets, through the unequal education allocated to children of different races, through insider networks that channel employment opportunities to the relatives and friends of those who have profited most from present and past racial discrimination and especially through the intergenerational transfers of inherited wealth that pass on the spoils of discrimination to succeeding generations. This whiteness is of course, a delusion, a scientific and cultural fiction that like all racial identities has no valid foundation in biology or anthropology. Whiteness is however a social fact, an identity created and continued with all-too-real consequences for the distribution of wealth, prestige, and opportunity. . . whiteness is invested in like property, but it is also a means of accumulating property and keeping it from others. (vii–viii)

George Lipsitz's argument is in accord with Cheryl Harris' perceptive analysis in "Whiteness as Property," where she argues that the legal structure of the United States reinforces the ability of whites to obtain and sustain wealth, whereas African American people are constantly disenfranchised.[4] Accordingly, white-male legal authorities play a prominent role in Killens' novel. The white males whom Killens characterizes as "crackers" (generally the poor white racists) were the individuals most likely to be engaged in acts of lynching and sexual assault on Black females. Thus the consumption of the African American male's phallus (castration or emasculation) and the consumption of the African American female's genitals (rape or sexual violence) are critical to the formation of white-male subjectivity; this sexualized consumption reflects a symbolic or literal decapitation, leaving the African American victim with no voice, no identity, no subjectivity, and no authority. In a symbolic sense, within a white-supremacist culture, African American individuals become decapitated, and decapitated bodies are easier to consume. Lynching represented the main form of intimidation used by the Ku Klux Klan and other white groups committed to white nationalism and white supremacy.

Systematic white-male violence directed at African American people, especially African American males during the Jim Crow segregation period, is deeply rooted in the brutal enslavement of African people. Although the destruction of human property (black bodies) was not very common during slavery, physical, psychological, and economic violence were fundamental aspects of slavery. After slavery, racial violence escalated to a tremendous level because of racist whites' desire to maintain their economic and political power at the expense of African American people. Lynching-burnings were the most common element of physical and psychological violence that helped to ensure economic subjectivity for white people. The critical social element that relates to the violence under white supremacy is the issue of miscegenation between African American males and white females. Any attempt by African American males to achieve social equality was seen by many white males as African American men seeking to have social or sexual relations with white females. White-racist violence directed at African American people illustrates both dread and desire. As Clovis E. Semmes perceptively argues in *Racism, Health, and Post-Industrialism: A Theory of African American Health* (1996), white people's apprehensions of and desires for the Black body represent the central dialectic of ethnocentrism and white supremacy:

> European oppression of Africans conjured up other distorted images of sexual fear. The African cultures did not have similar ambivalence about sexual intercourse and did not connect the activity to sin or evil. They and other groups who lived in tropical climates and who felt no shame in exposing their bodies were disturbing to the Europeans. The Europeans justification for chattel slavery stimulated already existing neuroses that resulted in likening Africans to apes. European slavers wanted to exploit the African body and therefore denied that the African had mental and human capacities. They fantasized that Black men were beasts with oversized sex organs and an insatiable lust for white woman. A resulting Eurocentric culture of domination transformed the fact of the vulnerability of African women to sexual abuse by white males into the view that African-American women were inherently immoral and sexually promiscuous. The myths of the Black man as a rapist and sexual brute and the Black woman as a whore became juxtaposed to the myths of mental inferiority and inherent cultural degeneracy. (107)

Most African American people began to understand this fundamental aspect of white cultural pathology and socialized their African American male children and nephews to always be on guard in their interactions with white females because they could be beaten or lynched. Notwithstanding this aspect of white-supremacist culture, Black females also had to always be on guard for sexual violence by racist white American males who believed that Black females should always be available for their often-sadistic sexual desires. In America, the killing of Black males and the rape of Black females have too often defined white masculinity. The lynching of Black males suggests that white males fear Black men, whereas the sexual conquest of Black females suggests that white males do not fear Black woman. Since 1859, some 5,000 Black individuals have been lynched for alleged or real acts against white supremacy. While the destruction of African American males mainly occurs on the psychological level, some Black females are, through enhanced social and employment possibilities in the service of white Americans, vulnerable to sexual violence or routinely viewed as sexual objects. As Jacqueline Jones astutely points out in her seminal book *Labor of Love, Labor of Sorrow: Black Women, Work, and the Family from Slavery to the Present* (1986), after enslavement, many African American women were routinely subjected to sexual violence by white males while in the domestic employ of whites.[5] The psychological and sexual violence that many Black women experienced while working for whites, whether spoken or unspoken, undoubtedly caused enduring trauma in their relationships with Black men, their children, and other family members.

Earlier, in John Oliver Killens's *Youngblood*, the issue of white-male sexual violence directed at African American females is poignantly illustrated. Like the extra-legal ritual of lynching directed at African American males, this sexual violence directed at African American females has a traumatic effect on the African American individual, her African American family, and her African American community. Historical documents reveal that white males were rarely if ever punished for any sexual violence (rape) or sexual misconduct against an African American female. On the other hand, historical documents do reveal that African American women were put on trial and punished if they killed a white male who attempted to rape them. Indeed, based on the racist stereotypical discourse concerning African American females as heathen, promiscuous, and licentious, the rape of an African American female by a white male was a ludicrous allegation, a cultural oxymoron. Notwithstanding this cultural absurdity backed by white legal dictates and authorities, Laurie Lee Barksdale, a light-skinned, 11-year-old African American girl, was assaulted in broad daylight by a lanky white man while she walked through an alley. Killens uses this incident to set the stage for the novel's repeated emphasis on racialized sexual violence:

> Nicely dressed, middle-aged white man with brown squinting eyes, mixed with whiskey-red. He mumbled to himself as he grabbed her plump buttocks. And he wouldn't let her go. Scared crazy with her heart in her mouth and blood flowing in the well of her stomach. Greatgodalmighty! She kicked him on his shins, she kneed him in his groin, but he wouldn't turn her loose.[6]

As this white man squeezes her "young breasts" he says: "Come on yaller bitch, you got something good and I know it. Ain't no needer keeping it to yourself" (5). Interestingly, the other white-male individuals look on and comment while this sexual assault occurs. They say: "Damn I reckin—Thassa fiery little nigger heffer" and "She sure is pretty." Only one of these white males says something in defense of this young Black female being assaulted by a drunken white pedophile. One white male states: "Leave her 'lone Mr. Hill, you old no-good hound" (5). The words "bitch" and "hound" illustrate the animalistic nature of the assault. Whites used hounds to track escaped slaves. Like a lynch-burning of an African American woman or man, this public act of sexual violence becomes a spectacle of sadistic sexual desire and consumption, where the African American female's body becomes a space for exploitation. By Killens describing the white man as nicely dressed, he establishes the paradox of this man's malevolent behavior. It is also interesting to note that this child attacker, Mr. Hill, calls Laurie Lee Barksdale a "yaller bitch." Of course, this pejorative signifier points to her light skin, but it also denotes the theme of miscegenation as sexual consumption and animalistic breeding, where African American females were routinely raped by white masters and white overseers. Slavery, an economic system that reproduced its own product for consumption, created light-skinned African American individuals who became desired by other white males and in some cases created a preference-by-pigmentocracy philosophy in the minds of many whites and some color-struck African Americans. In some cases, miscegenation would lead to incest because some white slave masters raped African American women and years later would rape their own daughters from these sexual encounters. To have a preference-by-pigmentocracy philosophy, or a hedonistic hegemony of color, is to validate the sexual violence that many African American women experienced. Discussing the dehumanized status of African American women during slavery, Dorothy Roberts argues:

> Racism created for white slave owners the possibility of unrestrained reproductive control. The social order established by powerful white men was founded on two inseparable ingredients: the dehumanization of Africans on the basis of race, and the control of women's sexuality and reproduction. The American legal system is rooted in this monstrous combination of racial and gender domination. One of America's first laws concerned the status of children born to slave mothers and fathered by white men: a 1662 Virginia statute made these children slaves. (23)

However, despite the violence that African American women experienced, they were characterized as oversexed females or wretches who seduced white males. Interestingly, many white women who discovered that their husbands were forcing themselves on African American female slaves would attack the slave rather than confront their husbands. Within a Marxist context, this behavior suggests that many white women were "slaves" to their own white husbands who owned African American slaves.

The white male's use of the words "something good" denotes that Laurie Lee has something enjoyable that can be consumed; in this case the "something" is her breasts and her genitalia. Hence Laurie Lee's sexual assault recalls the sexual violence of the past where most African American females were almost powerless, although many resisted.[7] By raking her fingernails down his long scrawny face and drawing blood, Laurie Lee escapes a sure public and bloody rape but not before he upped her skirt and urinated on her thighs. The drunken man's urine on Laurie Lee's tender thighs allows us to consider the worst possibility of this attack, that being this white man's semen greasing her thighs. The fact that he was able to urinate on her thighs reveals that his penis was exposed and that he was serious in his desire to rape Laurie Lee in public. "Running and crying most of the way home—Through the heart of Crackertown, across the railroad track and through Tucker's field, she reached Colored town. She stopped running and crying, and she leaned against an evergreen tree, and she looked at the shanties scattered over the valley, but her eyes saw nothing" (5). On her way home, the deep-seated psychological trauma begins to seep in as Laurie Lee views an axe and considers: "She should chop off her legs. Whack them off clean up to her belly" (5). This disturbing desire for amputation and self-mutilation in response to the sexual assault has four important aspects. First, it suggests that amputation and self-mutilation represent a way to avoid further attacks of sexual violence. That Laurie Lee desires to chop off her legs "clean up to her belly" reveals that the target of this sexual assault (her genitalia) has somehow been desecrated and that she has no desire to develop and maintain her sexual identity, and by extension, her reproductive possibilities. At the literal level, Laurie Lee's desire suggests a horrific bloody suicide. Second, it suggests a sense of powerlessness that her family, especially her African American father, will not be able to seek any legal action against this attack; hence, some white authorities will view the act as if the African American female victim somehow caused the attack. If the father did take any extra-legal action against Mr. Hill, he would most likely be beaten or killed along with the family driven out of their home. Third, it suggests that, under the system of white supremacy, the African American body cannot be redeemed by any other act. Fourth, psychological distress connects to Judith Lewis Herman's sagacious argument in *Trauma and Recovery: The Aftermath of Violence from Domestic Abuse to Political Terror* (1997), about the dialectical aspects of trauma. Herman states: "The conflict between the will to deny horrible events and the will to proclaim them aloud is the central dialectic of psychological trauma. People who have survived atrocities often tell their stories in a highly emotional, contradictory, and fragmented manner, which undermines their credibility and thereby serves the twin imperatives of truth-telling and secrecy. When the truth is finally recognized, the victim can begin their recovery" (1). Instead of some bloody act of self-mutilation, Laurie Lee strips off her clothes and she "scrubbed the skin off her young brown body with washing powder and lye soap. Her legs and her thighs were on fire. Standing in the tub now, naked and trembling. One thing sure, she wouldn't tell the folks" (5). This act of purification attempts to erase both the physical and psychological violence of this attempted rape and its humiliating effects. When Big Mama asks Laurie if she is alright, Killens explicates the dialectical aspect of Herman's theory: "She started to say, nothing Big Momma, but her voice choked off and her eyes filled up and she couldn't hold it back. Steamed up and boiling right over. Telling it now, bit by bit, then fast and fiercely, pouring it angrily out of her system" (7). After being comforted by her grandmother, a stern warning is issued to Laurie Lee, "Don't say nothing to your Papa about it, please, sugar pie. Do, he'll go outer here and get himself kilt, sure as gun's iron!" The paradoxical paradigm here is that, in a patriarchal society, a fundamental right is for a father to be able to protect his children from harm and to seek some sort of redress for wrong doing, but in a Jim Crow society, African American men had virtually no legal privileges or social opportunities to protect their women and their children from the sexual violence of white males and false allegations of rape by white females. America represents a white patriarchal culture and it appears that one of the greatest threats to this patriarchy is an African American patriarch; clearly many racist white men fear African American men.

Killens illustrates that even when some African American individuals interact with each other, and when some whites interact with African Americans, the issue of miscegenation is used to inflict psychological damage. Two friends of Laurie Lee and Joe Youngblood's son Robby Youngblood are engaging in some verbal dynamics and playing the dozens over skin color. Fat Gus asks Shinny Johnson: "Did your dear old mother have her fist balled when she slept with that white policy man, you half-white, shit-colored sonabitch?" (112). This contemptuous statement causes Shinny to pick up a rock with the intent to hit Fat Gus, but Robby makes a statement against skin-color hegemony: "Ain't no difference—black, yellow or brown—All of us Negroes. One color ain't no better than the other. We need to stick together, don't care what color" (112). Interestingly, when Robby and Fat Gus are seduced to fight each other for the entertainment of two white men, the issues of skin color and illicit miscegenation are used to create antipathy and intra-racial conflict between the two boys. One of the white men, Mr. Brad, encourages Fat Gus to beat Robby: "Come, fat-black, stop assing around. Knock the shit out of that little yaller bastard! Draw his goddamn blood! He think he bettern you cause his skin a little lighter. His mammy muster been messing with the policy man" (72). In a scene that echoes Ralph Ellison's "Battle Royal" episode in *Invisible Man* (1952), two African American boys are paid to fight each other in a demonstration of how some white males have a strong desire to view African Americans drawing blood from each other.[8] Two African American males fighting for the amusement of these white males recalls the slave experience where black individuals were constantly exploited for white people's pleasure. As Claude Anderson explains, this was just another form of exploitation for whites' enjoyment:

> On Sunday and special days, like New Years, Christmas or Easter, slaveowners enjoyed watching demonstrations of blacks' physical prowess in special sporting events. Blacks participated in various kinds of sports or other contests to entertain or for personal profit for their masters or themselves. Some of the more popular sporting events were wrestling, chopping or picking cotton, shooting marbles, pitching horseshoes, coon hunting, or foot racing against dogs and horses. (177)

At some point, Robby understands how they have been tricked to do real harm to each other. With a bloody lower lip, Robby "wanted desperately to stop fighting. Wished that Gus would suggest it. Hating these crackers and every last one of them should be dead and in hell. Hating Gus for letting the white men talk him into fighting so easily" (73). The lynchings of African American males, the rapes of African American females, and African American males fighting each other serve as sadistic entertainment for racist whites, especially white males. Laurie Lee Youngblood discovers the boxing scene and with a seething anger denounces the white men: "Two grown men. I guess you mighty tickled. You want some fun, pick on your own damn kind! You ought to be ashamed but I don't reckin you got that much mother-wit. Uncivilized savages! Low-down, filthy pecker-wood trash!" (73). Laurie Lee Youngblood's antagonism against these two white males resides with the present and the past as she perhaps recalls her own sexual assault when she was a young girl. Robby and Gus also experience Laurie Lee's wrath, especially Robby. She tells them: "Neither one of you ain't got the sense you were born with" (73). In both of these scenes, concerning the discourse of pigmentocracy and references to consensual miscegenation, we understand how Killens brilliantly makes the point that interracial conflict can produce intra-racial conflict. The Machiavellian divide-and-conquer philosophy represents a fundamental trope of white supremacy, and the issue of skin-color hegemony, as a result of miscegenation (whether it is consensual or in the form of sexual violence), reinforces racial hegemony. Killens' diction and characterizations of the white males also suggests that consensual miscegenation on the part of whites does not mean that they do not have a white-supremacist perspective. Consensual consumption of African American bodies does not preclude the possibility that racism still exists.

Along with other racist acts by white males that demean, emasculate, and symbolically castrate African American men, this inability to protect ones' children recalls that period of enslavement and the natal alienation that existed with African American parents and their children. During this period of America's white-supremacist culture, African American men are not allowed to be fathers and African American women are not allowed to be mothers.[9] As Orlando Patterson adeptly argues in *Slavery and Social Death: A Comparative Study* (1982), the power dynamic has three aspects: "The first is social and involves the use of threat of violence in the control of one person by another. The second is the psychological facet of influence, the capacity to persuade the other person to change the way he [or she] perceives his [or her] interests and his [or her] circumstances." The third is the cultural facet of authority, "the means of transforming force into right, and obedience into duty" which, according to Jean Jacques Rousseau, the powerful find necessary "to ensure them continual mastership." (1–2). These three aspects of power are evident in Laurie Lee's response to the two boys fighting for the amusement of whites, as well as to her previous sexual assault, and her grandmother's response of trepidation for Laurie Lee's father. Hence, this scene synthesizes the psychological and physical violence of white supremacy with disastrous economic violence to this African American family, especially if the father takes any action. Clearly, slavery was the most extreme form of violent domination, approaching the limits of total power from the viewpoint of the master, and of total powerlessness from the viewpoint of the slave, but the legacy of this violence is evident during Jim Crow segregation. African Americans were always vulnerable to white violence. After slavery, African American people, especially African American males, were more likely to be killed because they were no longer property. Killing property (African American people) is unproductive for business, but the killing of lone African American individuals to intimidate the masses of African American people can further the interest of white males, especially those who used African Americans as sharecroppers, a system of relentless exploitation that kept African American people in a perpetual economic slavery.

With the two children of Laurie Lee Barskdale and Joe Youngblood, John Oliver Killens again addresses the issue of miscegenation in order to illustrate interracial conflict producing profound intra-racial conflict. Jenny Lee and Robby Youngblood have an experience that has the potential to tear the Youngblood family apart. On her way home from school, walking down Planters' Alley, Jenny Lee is confronted by four white boys who throw her to the ground and begin to sexually assault her. Although Jenny attempts to "bust one of them peckerwoods wide open," it becomes clear that there are too many of them. Crying and talking at the same time, Jenny relates to her mother, Laurie Lee, that the white four boys were "Yelling—yelling nigger pussy—nigger pussy" (165), while their hands were under her dress. When Laurie Lee attends to her daughter, she discovers the scratches on her skinny thighs and that her "drawers had been ripped and torn" (165). Here we see that these four young white males have been socialized to violently consume "nigger pussy" as some pathological rite of passage to white-male subjectivity. While this attack occurs, Robby comes along and fights the white boys, but he is the only individual who is arrested. Of course, this traumatic scene of Jenny Lee's sexual assault recalls the mother's sexual assault. While it is unlikely that Laurie Lee has told her young daughter about her own violent sexual assault, this malicious sexual violence causes the mother to relive her own traumatic experience, where she had the desire to chop off her legs. Herman's theory of the dialectic of trauma is again evident in the hysterical manner that Jenny Lee reveals the attack. Herman states: "The psychological distress symptoms of traumatized people simultaneously call into existence the attention to the existence of an unspeakable secret and deflect attention from it. This is most apparent in the way traumatized people alternate between feeling numb and reliving the event" (1). Herman's theory helps us understand the complicated psychological aspects of the transgenerational transgression of trauma that African American people, especially African American women, have experienced as a result of white-male sexualized violence because "an understanding of psychological trauma being with rediscovering history" (2). When we consider the historical aspect, that the status of the enslaved African American child's status was determined by the status of the mother, African American females in American represent a subversive threat. As Marlene Nourbese Philip explicates in *Genealogy of Resistance* (1997): "The Black woman comes to the New World with only her body. And the space between. The European buys her not only for her strength, but also to service the Black man sexually—to keep him calm. And to produce new chattels—units of production—for the plantation machine. The Black woman. And the space between her legs. Is intended to help repopulate the outer space" (20). Hence, whereas the white woman's space becomes protected, the African American woman's space becomes a virtual thoroughfare for both African American males and white males. The trauma to Jenny Lee's genital space does not end with the violence that African American females experience; the agenda of white supremacy is the enduring socioeconomic disenfranchisement and psychological destruction of both African American females and males. Unlike Laurie Lee, Killens does not reveal any self-destructive thoughts that Jennie Lee may experience, but the arrest of her brother may result in the sublimation of any self-blame.

With Robby Youngblood defending his younger sister, Jenny Lee, from the sexual attack of the four white boys and his subsequent arrest by white-male legal authorities, Killens relates how white law represents a fundamental aspect of America's white-supremacist culture of violence. While Robby is arrested for "fighting white boys," the four white boys are allowed to go home, despite the fact that they initiated a violent sexual assault on Jenny Lee Youngblood. Indeed, they go home confident in their whiteness, but perhaps frustrated and still longing for the taste of "nigger pussy." A synthesis of Laurie Lee Youngblood's sexual assault and Jenny Lee Youngblood's sexual assault conveys that for racist white males, "nigger pussy" and "nigger bitch" are how they view most African American females. These racist signifiers also juxtapose disgust and desire. The legal message represents some disturbing critical aspects of white-supremacist culture. First, the sexual assault on an African American female by white males does not represent a legal or cultural transgression. Second, African American males cannot defend African American females from sexual assault when white males are involved, and if they do they will be beaten, arrested, or worse. This aspect reinforces the slave experience where African American males were unable to protect African American females from the sexual assaults of the white slave masters and other white males. Third, the testimony of African American individuals in court is worthless when it comes to accusing white males of any wrongdoing, especially when it involves an African American female. What becomes clear here is that, then and now, "white law" generally services the socioeconomic interests or white males, especially wealthy white males. Without any trepidation of legal or social consequences, many white males viewed African American females like Laurie Lee and Jenny Lee (and their genitalia) as public spaces to express their sexual desires. Then and now, African American women become viewed too often as sexual objects.

Laurie Lee Youngblood's visit to the Georgia courthouse (the sign "Justice For All" is displayed outside the building) to obtain her beloved son Robby

Youngblood results in unspeakable psychological, physical violence, and profound natal alienation between mother and son. Even before Laurie Lee gets to see her son, the psychological violence begins as a white-male police officer transforms her to "eye candy" as Laurie Lee "could feel him watching her as she walked down the corridor, looking at her supple body, at the quick, pleasant-for-him-to-watch movement of the pair of hips inside of her dress. Her face burned in anger. It wasn't the first time. Many white men had done so in the past, even more boldly" (167). Here the white police officer, Shinny McGuire, tells Laurie the offense, "'Gotcha boy down here—fighting white boys—Little white boys coming home from school—Serious offense, Laurie—Don't be you and Joe's youngun wouldn't let him off so easy—Y'all some mighty good colored folks and we don't wanna see your boy git into no trouble—I go git him now.' His greenish-blue eyes had been traveling everywhere except into Laurie's face" (168). Again Laurie becomes "eye candy" as Skinny McGuire's taxonomic gaze consumes her. Worse still, Laurie Lee becomes symbolically decapitated while her daughter, Jenny Lee, and her sexual assault become invisible. The four "little white boys coming home from school" become characterized as innocent individuals, while Robby becomes characterized as the out-of-control and brutal Black buck.[10] Knowing the tragic fate of those African American males who are characterized as brutes, the central trepidation for Laurie Lee Youngblood is that Robby would be sent to the reformatory like her brother, Tim Barksdale, who had been ruined by reform school after fighting white boys:

> Tim went to the reformatory for rockbattling white boys and breaking old man's McWhorter's window. They kept him there for two whole years and when he came out he was as mean as a bulldog. Tim Barksdale had been the sweetest boy in the world before that reformatory got hold of him. . . . Greatgodalmighty they made that nice boy ugly and mean and heartless and don't care, and when he got out he wouldn't listen to anybody. (10–12)

Laurie Lee Youngblood's thoughts of her brother are central in her concern for her son: "Just wasn't like himself, when he came out of that reformatory place . . . the memory of Tim reared up before her and the reformatory itself, the mean, hateful-looking, dirty gray buildings, the Negro-hating people who ran the place, almost entirely filled up with Negro boys" (168–69). Like sharecropping and the peonage system, the reformatory system functioned to exploit African American people and to keep uncontrollable African Americans "in their place." These fearful thoughts enter Laurie Lee's mind as Shinny McGuire hands her a buggy whip. Laurie Lee must whip her son Robby in front of Shinny and another white man as a trade-off for not sending him to the reformatory. What is also implicit here in Killens' characterization of the reformatory is the issue of sexual violence at the reformatory. These oppressive conditions would lead the white-male guards to rape the African American boys, who would in turn rape other

African American boys. Like Eva Peace in Toni Morrison's *Sula* (1973), who kills her beloved son Plum (a heroin addict and a veteran of World War I) because he desires to crawl back into her womb,[11] Laurie Lee Youngblood refuses to take Robby back into the womb and is forced to teach him a bloody and painful lesson of a Black mother's enduring love for her child in the face of vicious racism. The paradox of this voyeuristic scene is violently profound as Killens relates Laurie Lee's complex desires and frustrations:

> She would rather have bared her own body to the lashes of these white men than to do this thing to her son. . . . She raised her arm again and she felt like taking the whip and lashing these white men until every bit of breath left their bodies. She wished every white person in the world were at this very moment under her power. She would lash the life out of them one by one with a smile on her face. . . . Her boy's eyes narrowed, almost closing, his lips curved and set, giving forth a grunt now, as each blow knifed his body. She saw Joe at the mill wrestling with a barrel of turpentine. She felt a contemptuous anger towards him. He had it so goddamn easy. Just lifting those heavy drums, while she lashed their son in front of white men for defending his sister against a bunch of little no-good crackers trying to rape her. (171–72)

As Laurie Lee Youngblood makes her son's back a bloody mess of flesh, her seething anger grows not only for the white men who are forcing her to do this, but also for her husband, Joe, a dark and muscular six-foot-four African American man—because he is ignorant of this traumatic ordeal, but equally important is the fact that he would be powerless to effect any change in the outcome of this whipping. Laurie Lee's anger towards her husband reveals that African American men were generally powerless in this Jim Crow society and those who resisted were brutally beaten, imprisoned, or killed by lynching. Here, white males are psychologically forcing Laurie Lee to assume the role of a white sadistic master who beats his African American slave for some violation of the rules of the plantation. The critical difference is that this mother loves her son so much that she is willing to brutally beat him in order to save him from a worse destruction at the reformatory.

At the reformatory, Robby Youngblood's destruction would be both an enduring physical and psychological destruction. Even more disturbing is the possibility that Robby could be raped at the reformatory. Like his maternal uncle Tim, Robby would emerge from the reformatory as a broken and emasculated African American man, who would be an economic and psychological liability on his African American family and his African American community. However, it is difficult for Robby to understand why his mother is whipping his naked back into a bloody pulp of flesh as these white males gaze and encourage Laurie Lee to whip him harder and harder until Robby's agonized screams fill the room. Laurie Lee's humiliation and shame in being forced to whip her son, who protected his sister from sexual violence, represents one of the most disturbing scenes in the canon of African American literature, and the journey back to some form of redemption for mother and son will be a difficult process because Robby feels a deep-seated betrayal. Here the paradox is profound: a mother compelled to whip her son for stopping the rape of his sister. More important than the individual is the crushing effect this traumatic incident has on the Youngblood family and the legacy of Big Mama, who taught her children to resist and fight against white supremacy. Laurie Lee recalls Big Mama's words: "Honey, don' choo never let em walk over you—don' choo do it—Fight em honey—Fight em every inch of the way, especially the big rich ones. . . . They lynch us, they starve us and they work us to death, and it ain-na gonna change till you young Negroes gits together and beat some sense into their heads. So fight em, sugar pie. Aah Lordy, honey" (10). Paradoxically, here the benevolent and moral fight leaves the entire Youngblood family psychologically scarred, and like the traumatized Sethe in Toni Morrison's *Beloved* (1987), Robby is left with a whip-scarred back. As Keith Gilyard rightfully argues in *Liberation Memories: The Rhetoric and Poetics of John Oliver Killens* (2003): "That she acquiesces to authorities and beats Robby is a crushing defeat for her family . . . Laurie Lee made the right call, but the decision offers her no immediate solace"(14). The issue of solace is made more emphatic when Laurie Lee orders Robby to say that he will not fight with white boys; implicit in this statement is that he will not resist white people's evil actions. Worse still, the message to Robby, and by extension all African American males, is that he does not have the right to defend his sister from a sexual assault by white males who wanted to consume his sister's "pussy." Robby's heroic defense of his sister Jenny could place in him in a position where the "Negro-hating" white males and other African American boys like him could sodomize him and turn him into a "yella bitch" for relentless sexual consumption. Robby Youngblood's symbolic emasculation and castration, facilitated by his mother, are complete, and the healing and restoration of his African American male subjectivity will take time.[12] Thus Killens gives us the linear transgenerational transgression of sexual violence, where Laurie Lee is almost raped by a white male; her daughter Jenny is almost raped by four white males; and Laurie Lee has to whip her son Robby to save him from being raped by white males and other African American males.

The characterization of the white woman, especially the southern white woman, is fundamental to white supremacy as it relates to sexual violence and miscegenation. The historical perspective is that white women must be protected at all cost; symbolically, the white woman has been placed on the proverbial pedestal in honor of her status of purity and innocence. Accordingly, racist whites viewed the African American male as the single most dangerous threat to white females because of the absurd idea that most African American males lusted after white females. In *Youngblood,* Ossie Jefferson relates his father's racism and his historical position on the southern white woman:

That was the southern code. . . . He had heard Pa shout nigger nigger nigger a million times and what a threat they were to southern white womanhood and southern womanhood had to be protected and southern womanhood and southern womanhood and southern womanhood, and first and last southern womanhood till he had believed that this was the one principle John Jefferson would never go back on. (240–41)

It is this position of the status of white women that causes John Jefferson to become hysterical with anger after his white wife, Martha Mae Johnson, bruised and bleeding, is carried home in the arms of Little Jim, a tall and lanky African American man. Although his wife informs him that a white man, Charlie Wilcox, lied to her about her husband being hurt and then attempted to rape her, John does not believe her and vows to kill Little Jim, who brought his wife home because her leg was broken. John's response is clearly in line with the rabidly racist white males depicted in Thomas Dixon's novel *The Clansman* and in D. W. Griffith's film *Birth of a Nation* (1915): "I don't believe it was Charlie Wilcox at all. You just trying to protect that nigger. I always knowed you was stuck on him. . . . Come on boys, let's go nigger hunting." (244). John's statement reflects the stereotypical concept that African American men lust after white women and also the idea that some white women desire African American men. Charlie's views on miscegenation are reinforced when the sheriff and the preacher harass Martha Mae about what happened to her and accused her of being a "nigger lover" in her attempt to protect Little Jim by equivocating about Charlie Wilcox as a potential rapist. Like a relentless winter storm, the white preacher sternly warns a psychologically frail Martha Mae:

"There's only one truth. . . . And that is—Every nigger man alive is after raping a white woman, and God wants you to help put a stop to it. If you don't repent and tell the truth, you going to hell and tarnation. I'm going to pray for you in Church on Sunday and ask God to forgive you if you tell the truth this evening. But effen you don't open up your soul to God and me, I'm gonna preach you straight into the jaws of hell." (249)

Here, Killens sagaciously positions white law and white religion as critical in their support of white-supremacist culture and those doctrines having ideologies and axiologies that are fearful of miscegenation between African American males and white females. The psychological weight of white supremacy becomes too much for Martha Mae, and she reverses herself by telling the "right story." She tells her son, Ossie: "I just made up that story about Charlie Wilcox to protect that black skunk, Little Jim, cause I knowed you was so crazy about him. That oughta teach you how not to be a nigger-lover" (250). "Nigger-lover," with its connotation to miscegenation as sexual consumption, only applies to whites who have some concern for the socioeconomic plight of African American people. Killens uses this term repeatedly throughout the novel to convey those whites who either do not have a white-supremacist agenda (attitude) or who show any sympathy to African Americans. For example, when Officer Skinny McGuire shows a little compassion to Laurie Lee Youngblood after she brutally whipped her son, Robby, the white plainclothesman states: "Officer of the law—Goddammit, Skinny, I believe you turning into a chickenshit nigger lover" (175). However, if a white male attempted to rape an African American female, this would just be seen by legal and religious authorities as a white male having some innocent amusement; within a cultural context, this individual would not be considered a "nigger-lover." The possibility that a white man could be a rapist of a white woman represents an outrageous concept to the husband, the sheriff, and the preacher. Like an out-of- control fire, John Jefferson (of course the last name Jefferson conjures up Thomas Jefferson and his miscegenous relationship with the Black slave Sally Hemings) and a group of "nigger hunters" go to the home of Little Jim. Mr. Mack relates the massacre to Ossie: "Boy I'm telling you that was a sight to see. Just as soon as one of em would run out of the house, we would knock em off like a bunch of black birds. Killed every last nigger of them. The way I figger, it was an eye for an eye and a tooth for a tooth." (252). Like the bloody violence of 1923 experienced in the Florida town of Rosewood, a white woman's prevarication results in a deadly tragedy. Based on the false allegation that a white female was beaten by an African American man, this African American town was destroyed and hundreds of African American people were killed by white mob violence.[13] The 1922 destruction of the African American town of Wallstreet, OK, has a similar history; here a false charge of a young white female being raped led to the destruction of this wealthy African American community.[14]

The final scene of miscegenation as a sexual act of consumption involves the 15-year-old Robby Youngblood and a 13-year-old white girl, Betty Jane Cross Junior. Robby works at her parents' house and they are one of the wealthiest white families in Crossroads, Georgia. Robby does things such as raking the leaves, doing yard work, chopping wood, and taking in coal and splinters, but his presence at the girl's home has sparked the white girl's sexual desire. On a number of occasions, Betty Jane seeks out Robby for conversation and companionship. One particular incident involves Betty Jane showing Robby the hair under her arms and then removing her panties to reveal her genitals with "her triangle of dark, yellow hairs, dirty pubic hairs." (91) Understanding the absolute danger that this naïve white girl represents, Robby asks her: "'What you trying to do—make me lose my job?' He hated her because she was white and dangerous and she had the color of skin that everything and everybody had taught him to hate ever since he could remember" (91–92). Here again, Robby becomes caught up in another paradox of miscegenous sexual desire and consumption; he wants to keep the job, but he does not want to get involved with this white girl because he knows that he could be beaten and lynched. Although she is careful to avoid Robby when her mother is around, Betty Jane seems unaware of any serious problems with regard to her seductive actions. Like most white children, Betty Jane has been socialized to view herself as having privileges based on her racial identity. When Robby first meets Betty Jane, he "wondered about the yellow-haired girl, hoping he wouldn't have any trouble out of her" (67). Later, the innocent sexual explorations on Betty Jane's part escalate to the point where she follows Robby into the African American chauffeur's room. Here the adolescences of two individuals, one African American male and one white female, collide within the context of American's white-supremacist culture, where the African American male is characterized as an oversexed Black brute lusting after a white female. Despite the cultural danger signals exploding in his head, Robby Youngblood

> reached out toward her and took her into his arms and he kissed her awkwardly and clumsily on her wet pink lips and he felt her body tremble and her knees buckled like something had hit her and both of them almost fell to the floor—Even at that late moment he heard a warning voice like a white danger signal—but it was all too late—with his manhood asserting itself all over his body, and his inexperienced hand wandering and blundering and discovering new wonders and Rob! Rob! Rob! A smothering gasp, and her arms tightening around his neck, as the door to Mr. Jim Bradford's room opened noisily, bring them quickly back to this world. (312)[15]

Betty Jane's mother is horror-stricken as she views her young white daughter in the arms of this young African American male. In her mind, this innocent incident of sexual desire quickly turns into an attempt by Robby Youngblood to rape her daughter. The sight of the girl's mother has a profound effect on Robby: "He could feel the lyncher's rope around his neck choking off his life. He swallowed the hard bitter spittle in his mouth" (312). Considering the film *Birth of a Nation*, for most whites during this period the only possible reason for a white female to be close to an African American male is because he intends to rape or sexually assault her. This incident of youthful sexual interest and exploration reaches a crescendo when Mrs. Cross Junior goes to the home of the Joe and Laurie Lee Youngblood with the allegation that Robby has attempted to rape her daughter and requests that they place Robby in the reformatory. Robby firmly denies the charge of sexual violence, and it soon becomes clear to Laurie Lee Youngblood that there was no rape and that Mrs. Cross Junior has not gone to the police and will not report the incident out of embarrassment and shame for her daughter's sexual desire for Robby. Once Laurie Lee fully understands the true circumstances of this alleged miscegenous situation, she unleashes a devastating verbal tirade that deconstructs this white woman's gendered and racialized class status along with Mrs. Cross' illusion of white racial subjectivity:

> "You're just like the rest of the cracker women, aren't you? You're worst than the rest. That's what you are. Cause you know better. You sell your body and soul to

hell with your eyes wide open just to live in the biggest house in town—to wear pretty clothes and strut Miss Ann." The meanness and bitterness emptied out of Laurie like a pot boiling over. "I'm black but I'm free and you're a slave. You understand? Mr. Cross Junior's beautiful white slave. You're a slave and a whore to every white man in the state of Georgia." (320–21)

Killens' diction echoes the scene of Laurie Lee's sexual assault by the white male, Mr. Hill; in this scene Laurie Lee becomes a "pot boiling over" and in telling Big Mama about the assault we encounter the same analogy. Hence, the sexual assault and the false charge of rape against her son are systematic of a white-supremacist culture, where both African American females and males are vulnerable to racial violence. Laurie Lee Youngblood's perceptive analysis of reversing the Hegelian master and slave dialectic captures the true essence of white women's illusion of subjectivity with regard to white men. Laurie Lee's analysis also suggests the Faustian paradigm where Mrs. Cross has "made a deal with the devil" of white-male supremacy and becomes symbolically decapitated and consumed in the process. Hence, white women only have the illusion of subjectivity and only in relationship to the white phallus. However, Laurie Lee does not stop here; she deconstructs the systematic role that many white women play in the killing of African American males due to their prevarications about Black males:

"You know my boy didn't rape your daughter. The white man has taken all of your dignity from you. Isn't a drop left in you. And now you ready to sacrifice the dignity of every poor black man in the United States. The blood of every Negro ever been lynched is on your lily-white hands, and you ready to make my boy one in that number. If you think I'm help you, you're a liar and the truth isn't in you." (321)

Laurie Lee Youngblood's didactic discourse leaves this white woman confused, shaken, and hysterical. Here, Laurie Lee denounces the complicity and the silence of white women in the lynching of African American males who were often killed because of rumors or fabrications associated with sexual relations with white females. Those white women who support white supremacy are essentially "raped" of their dignity and self-worth by white-male hegemony. Better still, racist white males become characterized as bloodsuckers who prey on the dignity of white women. Perhaps this is the first time that an African American woman has told her the truth about herself and her devious part in the furtherance of white supremacy and its violent aspects, which attempt to disenfranchise and destroy African American people. As Keith Gilyard points out, life for African American people in Crossroads, GA, is an almost-daily confrontation with racist white people: "[H]ardly a day goes by without Blackfolk having to resolve some crisis created by whites. Days upon days are wrapped in threat and death. Barely a conversation transpires without 'boy,' 'sir,' 'nigrah,' 'cracker,' 'nigger,' or 'peckerwood.' In the midst of these polarities, the author drives home the message that Black redemption can only come through Black unity" (12–13). Every member of the Youngblood family experiences some horrific traumatic incident that shapes their psyche and their relationships with other members of the family. What becomes clear in *Youngblood* is the transgenerational transgression of trauma associated with the phenomenon of post-traumatic slavery syndrome. Accordingly, the icy winds of white supremacy have created a perpetual winter in the lives of African American people, but there are those individuals who resist those icy winds with a rock-like fortitude that inspires others to defy evil. As Addison Gayle explicates in the foreword to *Youngblood:*

> Existential man may be a product of the paradise lost, but his journey must be toward reclaiming that paradise, not for himself alone, but for all. Such a journey is undertaken by the Youngbloods and the gallant men and women of their community. It is a journey whose byroads, to be sure, are strewn with evidence of human viciousness, with fear, trepidation, and death. Still, it is a journey made by human beings who realize that manhood and womanhood are achieved not so much from reaching or not reaching a prescribed goal as by the courage displayed in moving toward it. (ix)

Gayle's analysis highlights the fundamental humanity in Killens' novel. African American people are struggling to make better lives for themselves and for future generations; however, some of their sacrifices may not be realized in their lifetimes, but the example of struggle is critically important. Killens makes the point that "youngbloods" need to see their elders take a stand against philosophies and practices of white supremacy.

The final trauma in the novel involves Joe Youngblood being shot after he challenges Mr. Mack, a racist white paymaster, over his pay at the mill.[16] Joe's often demeaning and physically strenuous work at the mill represents another form of consumption in that he and other African American men are treated like animals. Joe ultimately dies as a result of his wound, but his death inspires many African American people and a few whites to come together to transform the community.

What we discover in John Oliver Killens' historical novel *Youngblood* is the pervasive issue of miscegenation as sexual consumption within the context of the physical, psychological, and economic violence of America's white-supremacist culture. Many white people's unfounded apprehensions and racist anxieties of miscegenation between African American males and white females have resulted in an untold number of lynchings of African American men, whereas the voluminous sexual assaults on African American women by white males have generally gone unpunished. Hence, the lynchings of African American men and the rapes of African American women become central to white-male subjectivity under America's white-supremacist culture. Killens' novel can be viewed as a historical indictment of the sexual pathology of those racist whites, especially racist white males who have projected their own psychotic and sadistic sexual desires onto African American people and who have acted out their desires by engaging in the sexual consumption of African American bodies. However, despite the often-traumatic challenges that Laurie Lee and Joe Youngblood's family face, there is a profound courage and redemption that allow this African American family to survive a relentless system of white violence. Sexual violence in the form of rape becomes Killens' central focus. This African American family faces the transgenerational transgression of trauma associated with the horrors of racial discrimination, but they are never crushed; indeed, they teach whites and other African Americans profound lessons in the fundamental redemptive aspects of humanity. While miscegenation no longer remains a significant issue of racialized sexual consumption, the issue of miscegenation, especially between African American males and white females, continues to be the critical force in the formation of America's public policies concerning education, employment, and housing. John Oliver Killens' *Youngblood*, as a novel of redemption in the face of malicious racial malevolence, issues an audacious call for all those youngbloods and those whites who believe in the fundamental principles of Jeffersonian democracy and Emersonian human decency to respond to the enduring and malevolent plague of white supremacy.

 chapter 4

Miscegenation, Monstrous Memories, and Misogyny as Sexual Consumption in Gayl Jones' *Corregidora*

Perhaps she remembers her great great grandmother who wanted to protest but only rolled her eyes and willed herself not to scream when the white man mounted her from behind.

Andrea Williams, "Something to Talk About"

Early on in Gayl Jones' *Corregidora* (1975), Ursa Corregidora, an attractive light-skinned African American blues singer, is accidentally pushed down a flight of stairs by her drunken husband, Mutt Philmore Thomas. She is about a month pregnant at the time and loses her ability to have children ("make generations"). She visits her male physician, who sympathetically inquires: "Is Mr. Corregidora with you?" Ursa's self-affirming and yet negating response is: "That's *my* name, not my husband's" (author's emphasis).[1] This rather straightforward yet profound question to Ursa and her terse response provide narrative structure, synthesis, and signification to Jones' chilling novel. In this modern-day slave narrative, nonconsensual miscegenation and racial memory represent sexual consumption of Black female bodies, bodies consistently violated by a violent misogynist, a 19th-century Portuguese slave-holding white male who fathered both Ursa's grandmother and her mother.[2] Paradoxically, Ursa, boldly claiming the name of a deceased white slave master, goes to the doctor with Tadpole McCormick, who is not her husband, but her drunken husband, Mutt Thomas, is responsible for her being at this doctor's office. This question and Ursa's brusque response fore-shadow the enduring sexual tensions in the novel. The termination and the con-tinuity of Ursa's psychological trauma reside in her reproductive lack, evidenced by this follow-up visit to her hysterectomy; Ursa's future is marked by slavery's past. Discussing her exploitative genealogy of miscegenous sexual consumption in unambiguous language and raising the question of the future generation, Ursa Corregidora tells Tadpole McCormick ("one of them Hazard Kentucky niggers"), the owner of Happy's Café:

> "Corregidora. Old man Corregidora, the Portuguese slave breeder and whore-monger. (Is that what they call them?) *He fucked his own whores and fathered his own breed. They did the fucking and had to bring him the money they made. My grandmama was his daughter, but he was fucking her too.* She said when they did away with slavery down there they burned all the slavery papers so it would be like they never had it. . . . My great-grandmama told my grandmama the part she lived through that my grandmamma didn't live through and my grandmama told my mama what they lived through and we were suppose to pass it down like that from generation to generation so we'd never forget. Even though they'd burned everything to play like it didn't never happen. Yeah, and where's the next generation?" (9; emphasis added)

The enduring sexual violence in the form of fondling, rape, incest, and forced sexual relations (breeding and prostitution) that many Black women experienced during slavery in North America and South America is fundamental to Jones' enduring theme of post-traumatic slavery syndrome, and its transgenerational transgression of trauma, the harmful psychological effects on Black women and men and on their children. As Haki R. Madhubuti maintains: "Rape is the viola-tion and negation of the spirit, soul and physical presence of women" (105). By claiming the name of the slave master, Ursa either allows Old Man Corregidora to symbolically lay claim to her genitals or attempts to assume ownership of past memories so that she can rearticulate them through the blues. However, since Jones positions this scene at the doctor's office, the theme of sexual violence is emphasized. In *Black Feminist Thought* (1990), Patricia Hill Collins remarks, "rape and other acts of overt violence that Black women have experienced, such as physical assault during slavery, domestic abuse, incest, and sexual extortion, accompany Black women's subordination in a system of race, class, and gender oppression" (177). Indeed, the past in the form of long-term memory represents living history in the life of 20-year-old Ursa Corregidora, as she struggles with current forms of male hegemony and male oppression, while in her mind she painstakingly relives her maternal family's legacy of sexualized racial violence at the hands of a brutal slave-master pimp, a plunderer of Black female flesh.

Structurally, the novel is infused with rhetorical, logical, and epistemological paradoxes; these paradoxes are represented in slavery's past as well as in the present-day African American life, where racism, sexism, and color hegemony flourish like overgrown weeds. As stated by Rosalie Colie, the preeminent scholar of paradoxes: "paradoxes play back and forth across terminal and categorical boundaries—that is, they play with human understanding" (7). Jones' narrative of human understanding is accomplished through italicized narration that functions as Ursa's consciousness, as dreams, memories, interior monologues, and the storytelling of Ursa's great-grandmother, grandmother, and mother. Accordingly, this chapter will examine how Gayl Jones' theme of racialized sexual violence, or more specifically, nonconsensual miscegenation (exclusively between white males and Black females) during the traumatic enslavement period on Old Man Corregidora's Brazilian plantation, functions as both literal and metaphorical consumption of the reproductive Black female body, her genitals, and her womb. Equally important, this sexualized consumption manifests in the lives of countless Black men and women who carry their psychosocial pasts to their present relationships with each other. Miscegenation, memory, and misogyny will structure and frame my critical examination of the narrative's illustration of the themes: the living charge to Ursa to "make generations," to reproduce children who will bear witness and testify to the legacy of slavery; Ursa's inability to fulfill the living charge because of the accidental fall that left her without the ability to reproduce children; Ursa's efforts to adapt to a new responsibility, the restoration of her spirit; and lastly, Ursa's confrontation with the sexual and psychosexual tensions that are the result of both her heritage and her immediate personal relationships with Black men, Mutt Thomas, and Tadpole McCormick. Being wombless, in the face of the legacy of making generations (Black women speaking through their bodies), represents the novel's fundamental paradox and psychological tension in Jones' meditation on miscegenation, memory, and misogyny.

Since the narrative is from Ursa's point of view, a summation of the novel is necessary. As her response to her physician indicates, Ursa Corregidora retains her family's last name from the "the old man Corregidora," a breeder of slaves; her maternal ancestry consisted mostly of slaves who served as prostitutes and concubines. Ursa's mother was conceived on the Brazilian plantation, but her mother, Ursa's grandmother, escaped the plantation in terror of her life, after she infuriated Old Man Corregidora during an act of fellatio conjoined with the threat of oral castration. The mother later returns to secure her daughter and brings her to the United States. Ursa's mother has a brief, dysfunctional, and violent marriage with an African American man, viewing this relationship as her fulfilling the living charge to "make generations." Ursa inherits this biological injunction, but a dispute with her drunken husband, Mutt Thomas, about her singing the blues, results in her fall down the stairs, a miscarriage, and an operation (a hysterectomy) that renders her infertile. Her consequent inability to bear children ineffably traumatizes her; it makes her feel less of a woman and also contributes to her sense of guilt that she is somehow failing the generations of women in her family who have always been told to "make generations" to bear witness to their former slavery under Corregidora, a Brazilian plantation master. Convalescing from the hysterectomy, Ursa stays with Tadpole McCormick, the owner of the club where she sings. The conversation with both the physician and Tadpole occur during that stay. During the course of the novel, Ursa divorces Mutt and marries Tadpole, then leaves Tadpole and reconciles with Mutt, but the narrative constantly revolves around Ursa's mental reflections of slavery and the experiences of Old Man Corregidora, especially the sexual violence. Indeed, the narrative structure consistently reinscribes Jones' theme of the Black female as a victim of racialized sexual violence, and this is done by using the structure of the blues to interlock critical scenes. Like miscegenation, the blues represents a discourse of hybridity. Jones' recording of the past follows a literary tradition embodied in the literature of Zora Neale Hurston.

Racialized sexual violence in Zora Neale Hurston's *Their Eyes Were Watching God* suggests the intertextual conversation that Gayl Jones engages in with *Corregidora*. What is significant in thinking about these two novels is the oral tradition and folklore. Janie Crawford hears grandmother's narratives of the past; white males raped Nanny Crawford and her daughter, Janie's mother. Janie's memories of her maternal ancestors along with her own memories are shared with her friend, Pheoby Watson, who will in turn share Janie's narrative. A critical part of the narrative of Janie's grandmother (Nanny Crawford) is the idea that, "De nigger woman is de mule uh de world." This folkloric statement comes out of the story of God placing down a load and the white man tells the Black man to pick it up and carry the load; the Black man picks it up, but he hands it to the Black woman to carry. Like Ursa Corregidora, Janie Crawford experiences the load of racialized male hegemony in her marital relationships with Logan Killicks, Joe (Jody) Starks, and Vergible "Tea Cake" Woods. As we will discover in Jones' novel, Hurston's Janie is not only a product of miscegenation, but she is a site of miscegenous sexual desire for those Black males who have a preference for light-skinned Black females. Discussing the issues of colourism on an international level, Carol Camper explains:

> Colourism is one legacy of colonization. The invasion of women's bodies is always a device of war. The creation of a mixed European and local "class" helped ensure division and conflict among the indigenous people. This has happened all over the world. The mixed race progeny often were given access to things their unmixed sisters and brothers would never have. The lighter-skinned people were also indoctrinated into the colourism hierarchy and believed themselves to be superior, creating their own history as oppressors and justifiable mistrust which is still having impact on our lives today. Even in countries no longer under white rule, the colour hierarchy is often still intact. (xx)

Along with her maternal memories from Brazil, Ursa Corregidora will experience the blues of racialized male hegemony in her two marriages. Equally important is the issue that both Janie Crawford and Ursa Corregidora are both childless, but Ursa's memories are more critical to her role as blues singer.[3] This lack of fecundity suggests that some elements of the Corregidora family narrative will be permanently gone because Ursa represents the end of the master Corregidora narrative; at the same time, a new narrative is possible through Ursa singing the blues.

Understanding the structure of the blues provides a deeper sense of Gayl Jones' creative intent and "flat-footed truths."[4] In addition to its harmonic structure, the blues has three recognizable features: (1) the so-called blue note, (2) an a-a-b three-line lyric structure, and (3) a particular pattern of call and response. The term *blue note* refers to any pitch between adjacent notes in the 12-tone Western system of equal treatment (as represented by the black and white keys on the piano). The blues structure consists of two different lines, with the first line being repeated to form a three-line a-a-b pattern. The following lines from Howling Wolf's 1951 recording of *How Many More Years* demonstrate this structure:

a. How many more years do I got to let you dog me around?

a. How many more years do I got to let you dog me around?

b. I just as soon be dead, sleeping six feet under ground.

Each line is typically sung over the first half (first two bars) of a four-bar line. After each lyric (the call), an instrumental response is commonly played, also consisting of approximately two bars. The tension created by the two-bar call-and-response pattern of vocal and instrumental sounds; by the repetition of the first lyric line, which delays the resolution in line b of the lyric idea; and by the variable placement of the so-called blue note defines blues as a style of music. Ursa's explanation of her family's history to Tadpole McCormick reflects a blues trajectory:

> My great-grandmother told my grandmama the part she lived through that my grandmama didn't live through and my grandmama told by mama what they both lived through and my mama told me what they all lived through and we were supposed to pass it down like that from generation to generation so we'd never forget. Even though they'd burned everything to play like it didn't never happen. (9)

Here we have an example of the transgenerational transgression of trauma passed down by storytelling. Of course in this process of telling and retelling there exists the possibility that parts of the narrative, as improvisational discourse, could be lost or restated in a different manner than was previously stated. This narrative blues structure is also most evident in those scenes illustrating literal scenes of sexual violence and memories of sexual violence, especially those with the slave master, whose physical description echoes horror and violence: "Tall, white hair, white beard, white mustache, an old man with a cane and one of his feet turned outward, not inward, but outward. Neck bent forward like he was raging at something that wasn't there. Mad Portuguese" (10). Shortly afterward, Jones renders a description of his stroke when Ursa' great-grandmother states:

> "Yeah I remember the day he took me out of the field. . . . He would take me himself first and said he was breaking me in. Then he started bringing other men and they would give me money and I had to give it over to him. Yeah, he had a stroke or something and that's what turned his foot outside. They say he was praying and calling in all his niggers and telling them he'd give them such and such a amount of money if they take it off him but they all said they didn't put it on him. He got well, though, and didn't die. It just turned his foot outside and he behaved like he always did. It did something to his neck too because he always go around like he was looking for something that wasn't there. I don't know how he finally went, because by then I was up in Louisiana, but I bet he didn't go easy. Yeah, he have that took afterward. I stole it because I said whenever afterward when evil come. I wanted something to point to and say 'That what evil look like.' . . . Yeah, he did more fucking than the other men did. Naw, I don't know what he did with the others." (11–12)

Old Man Corregidora's stroke suggests some divine or magical intervention in the violence to which he subjects his Black slaves, especially the women.

During the period of slavery and its inexpressible horrors of sexual violence, miscegenation represented a fundamental paradox in terms of racial relationships between Blacks and whites. Miscegenation suggests a complex duality, yet the dynamics of racial contact and sexual desire were stronger than prejudice, theory, culture, law, or belief. Because of the doctrine of white supremacy and economic concerns, legal measures were enacted to prohibit intermarriage. While this ensured that the children of enslaved Black women would follow the condition of their mothers, mulatto children of white women were free but were generally bound to long terms of indentured servitude. And while there was widespread miscegenation between white males and Black women, miscegenation between Black men and white women was generally met with severe hostility and violence. This duality resulted in miscegenation being mainly restricted to white men and Black women; relations between Black men and white women became the one taboo, which, when transgressed, often led to the lynching of Black men. Also, since the Middle Passage, the sexual violence that Black woman experienced has been considered a "gesture of symbolic castration" of the Black man (Ain't I a Woman 57). It is critical to note that miscegenation is a physical act that requires sexual contact but not intermarriage.

In addition, it is critical that in that absurdist world of mixed races, miscegenation continued beyond the binaries of Blacks and whites and whites and mulattoes. Miscegenation also may be said to occur when there is intimacy between unmixed Africans and mulattoes, and between mulattoes and other mulattoes. A significant number of the slave-era Blacks who were sold into prostitution were mulattoes. Freeborn light-skinned Black women often became the willing concubines of wealthy white southerners. Two novels of racial passing, Charles Chesnutt's *The House Behind the Cedars* (1900) and James Weldon Johnson's *The Autobiography of an Ex-Coloured Man* (1912), illustrate light-skinned Black women who have consensual sexual relationships with wealthy white southerners.[5] This system, called "placage," involved a formal arrangement for the white suitor to financially support the Black woman and her children in exchange for her long-term sexual services. The white men usually met Black women at "Quadroon Balls," a genteel sex market. As Ursa's genealogical discourse to Tadpole conveys, a bitter and strange fruit associated with miscegenation is the taboo of incest. With the predatory, tooth-and-claw environment of slavery, most Black women had little defense against the sexual advances of white males; some white slave masters would have sexual relations with their own slave mulatto daughters. This sexual displacement or dissonance in the minds of many white males is possible because Black people were viewed as inferior individuals and somehow less than human, despite the sexual desire implicit in miscegenation and incest.

As a blues singer, Ursa Corregidora represents the legacy of those Black women who migrated to the North to escape Jim Crow segregation. While many Black women worked in factories or in domestic service, there were some women who found good employment in the entertainment industry. In *Black Pearls*, Daphne Harrison discusses this period:

> Young black women with talent began to emerge from the churches, schools, and clubs where they had sung, recited, danced, or played, and ventured into the more lucrative aspects of the entertainment world, in response to the growing demand for talent in the theaters and traveling shows. The financial rewards often out-weighed community censure, for by 1910–1911 they could usually earn upwards of fifty dollars a week, while their domestic counterparts earned only eight to ten dollars a week. Many aspiring young woman went to the cities as domestics in hope of ultimately getting on stage. While the domestics' social contacts were severely limited mainly to the white employers and to their own families, the stage performer had an admiring audience in addition to family and friends. (21)

Ursa finds employment in an industry that pays significantly more than domestic work, but the elements of sexual violence and sexual abuse are still present, traumatic echoes of slavery's past.

Corregidora (the name is a feminization of the Portuguese word "corregidor" and refers to the wife of a petty judge or judicial official) is especially shocking because it illustrates the theme of miscegenation in some of the most graphic and disturbing scenes in African American literature. Judging is critical to the narrative because of the charge to "make generations," generations who can give oral testimony to the horrors of enslavement, especially the sexual abuse of Black women. However, the word "Corregidora" also incorporates the sense of its French root *corregir*—"to correct." A fundamental paradox in the novel is that Old Man Corregidora himself never speaks in the novel; his actions speak for him. Through her memories and by singing the blues, Ursa Corregidora attempts to correct a horrific past by making it more comprehensible to herself and the audience that hears her sing. Like many Black women who left the church, Ursa uses the blues as a therapeutic means to deal with slavery's past. Discussing the significance of history, Karl Marx in *The Eighteenth Brumaire of Louis Bonaparte*, states: "Men [and woman] make their own history, but not spontaneously, under conditions they have chosen for themselves; rather on terms immediately existing, given and handed down to them. The tradition of countless dead generations is an incubus to the mind of the living" (13). Toni Morrison, who edited *Corregidora*, explains in an interview with Robert B. Stepto that the novel illustrates "the weight of history working itself out in the life of one, two or three people: I mean a large idea brought down small, and at home, which gives it a universality and a particularity which makes it extraordinary" (*Conversations* 29). Accordingly, history and representation of historiography are fundamental to this novel of psychological realism.

Sexual and psychological abuse of Black women takes its violently repulsive form in miscegenation between the Old Man Corregidora and his Black female slaves. What Jones characterizes in this Portuguese seaman–turned–slave-owner is not just an unmitigated control of his Black male and female property but a tyrannical psyche where sadistic sexual violence and physical violence were common. Like the arrogant and physically brutal Tom Buchanan in F. Scott Fitzgerald's *The Great Gatsby* (1925), who articulates his apprehensions of miscegenation, Corregidora is described as "a big strapping man then. His black hair was straight and greasy. He was big. He looked like one a them coal Creek Indians but if you said he looked like an Indian he'd get mad and beat you" (11). Paradoxically, Corregidora appears to be unconscious of his physical appearance, especially his pigmentation. Obsessed with miscegenation, this slave owner appears to be a product of miscegenation. Another sexual paradox is his relationship with his white wife. Ursa recalls being told by her grandmother that: "His wife was a skinny stuck-up little woman he got from over in Lisbon and had her brought over here. He wouldn't sleep with her, so she made me sleep with her, so for five years I was sleeping with her and him. . . . Then she started looking real bad and then died on account of the climate. But they had me sleeping with both of them" (13). Similar to many white slave owners or slave traders, the presence or absence of the white female does not preclude white males from having sexual relationships with Black female slaves. Black slave women were also frequently pregnant. Fundamental to the institution of slavery was Black women supplying future slaves. All possible methods were used to encourage slave women to reproduce.[6] Young Black girls were encouraged to have sex in preparation for their future role as breeders. When they did have children, Black women's fecundity was viewed as proof of their insatiable sexual desires. Deborah Gray White argues:

> Major periodicals carried articles detailing optimal conditions under which bonded women were known to reproduce, and the merits of a particular "breeder" were often the topic of parlor or dinner table conversations. The fact that something so personal and private became a matter of public discussion prompted one ex-slave to declare that "women wasn't nothing but cattle." Once reproduction became a topic of public conversation, so did the slave woman's sexual activities. (29)

As stated earlier, Corregidora fucked his own whores and fathered his own breed, but this was done within a culture of sexual exploitation. Again Ursa remembers part of the story:

> "Naw, he wasn't the first that did it. There was plenty that did it. Make the women fuck and then take their money. And you know sometimes the mistresses was doing it too so they could have little pocket money that their husbands didn't know about. And getting their brothers and their brother's friends and other mens they know, you know, and then they make theyselves right smart money for their purse." (23).

In this culture of sexual exploitation, Black females are preyed upon by both white males and females, as the Black female's genital space becomes a thoroughfare, especially for all white males in the family and their male friends. Quite simply, Old Man Corregidora's sadistic actions can be associated with rape-trauma syndrome. Rape-trauma syndrome, a form of post-traumatic- stress disorder, is a psychological reaction to rape involving feelings of shock and shame. Victims who experience this syndrome are reluctant to acknowledge rape; paradoxically, since sexual violence was so fundamental to slavery, it might be difficult for the victim to define the assault as a rape.[7] Great Gram defines the sexual assault as fucking, but fucking becomes analogous to a rape. Returning to the issue of sexual violence, Jones relates a horrifying incident of miscegenation as racialized consumption:

> "The master shipped her husband out of bed and got in the bed with her and just as soon as he was getting ready to go in her she cut off his thing with a razor she

had hid under the pillow and he bled to death, and then the next day they came
and got her and her husband. They cut off her husband's penis and stuffed it in
her mouth, and then they hanged her. They let him bleed to death. They made
her watch and then they hanged her." (67)[8]

Despite the reality of the effects of her castrating the white phallus, this Black
woman boldly protected her vaginal space and the dignity of her relationship
with her husband. She claimed her body. Overkill of Black individuals in the
form of grotesque torture and mutilation was meant to send a message to the
masses of Black people. This particular killing is reflective of autocannibalism.
Like the tortured Black victim in Richard Wright's "Between the World and Me"
who is forced to consume his own blood and teeth before they pour gasoline on
him and set him ablaze, the killing of this husband and wife involves them being
forced to consume each other. The Black man's penis is forced into her mouth
and the woman is also forced through her eyes to consume the death of her husband, whereas the Black man is forced to consume his wife's death. A clear message here is that the Black woman slave does not own her genitals. There is a
particular white outrage that this Black slave woman would protect her vaginal
space for her husband's penis and deny the white master's penis. As in John Oliver Killens' *Youngblood* (1954), there is the racialized assumption that the Black
female bodies should always be available for white male's consumption, either literally through sexual violence or symbolically through the taxonomic male gaze
that reduces the Black woman to eye candy.

Jones reinforces the consumption of the Black woman by suggesting how
Black females are stereotyped as the Jezebel, the innately promiscuous, even predatory, woman. This Jezebel stereotype was used during slavery as a rationalization for sexual relations between Black women and white men, especially sexual
unions involving slavers and slaves. The Jezebel was depicted as a Black woman
with an insatiable appetite for sex; she was not satisfied with Black men. Slavery-
era Jezebels, it was claimed, desired sexual relations with white men; therefore,
white men did not have to rape Black women. Since slave women were property,
there was the notion that legally they could not be raped. Frederick Douglass'
personal narrative contradicts this notion; in *My Bondage and My Freedom*, he
states that the "slave woman is at the mercy of the fathers, sons or brothers of her
master" (60). Clearly, Black women were at the mercy of white males because of
the fundamental power relationship; rape, promises of less work, or gifts were all
used by white males to achieve their sexual desires.

Corregidora's miscegenous consumption of Black female bodies is equally
disturbing, especially with regard to his preference-by-pigmentocracy philosophy.
Under a philosophy of white supremacy, there is a hegemony based on color,
where dark-skinned individuals are less acceptable than light-skinned individuals. Corregidora's behavior defies the color hegemony and yet reinforces this
schism: "He liked his womens black, but he didn't even wont us with no black

mens. It wasn't color cause he didn't even wont us with no light black mens, cause there was a man down there as light as he was, but he didn't even wont us with him, cause there was one girl he caught with him, and had her beat, and sold the man over to another plantation, cause I think he just wont to get rid of him anyway" (124). Here, it appears that Corregidora's miscegenous sexual desire is simply about male privilege, but later we hear that he states: "Don't let no black man fool with you, do you hear? I don't wont nothing black fucking with my pussy" (127). Corregidora does allow "his own color to mess with" her "all they wont to" (127). Interracial conflict and hegemony leads to intra-racial conflict and hegemony where dark-skinned individuals are marginalized, but to privilege light-skinned individuals means to validate the racialized violence that produced so many of these individuals. Another element concerning Corregidora fucking his whores, and creating his own breed, is the issue of incest. While miscegenation, especially between Black men and white women, represents America's greatest taboo, incest represents a rather universal taboo in most societies. White slave owners compounding sexual violence with the act of incest makes the dehumanization of enslavement even worse, because the fundamental humanity of African American people is ignored. Contemplating a new song, Ursa contemplates Black people's trauma:

> Their survival depended on suppressed hysteria. She went and got her daughter's womb swollen with the child of her own father. How many generations had to bow to his genital fantasies? They were fishermen and planters. And you with the coffee-bean face, what were you? You were sacrificed. They knew you only by the signs of your sex. They touched you as if you were magic. They ate your genitals. And you, Grandmama, the first mulatto daughter, when did you begin to feel yourself in your nostrils? And Mama when did you smell your body with your hands? (59)

This repressed hysteria reappears in Ursa, and she can be considered a hysterical subject who struggles to find subjectivity through the blues. Slavery was fundamentally about the denial of Black people's humanity. When this fundamental humanity of a people is ignored, it makes it easier to abuse and sell the children from these nonconsensual sexual relationships. Beyond that, this passage suggests to what extent there was a de-gendering process where Black people were reduced to orifices. In her seminal essay "Mama's Baby, Papa's Maybe: An American Grammar Book," Hortense Spillers deconstructs slavery and its impact on gender:

> First of all, the New World, diasporic plight marked a theft of the body—a willful and violent (and unimaginable from this distance) severing of the captive body from its motive will, its active desire. Under these conditions, we lose at least gender difference in the outcome, and the female body and the male body become a territory of cultural and political maneuver, not at all gender-related

or gender specific. But this body, at least from the point of view of the captive community, focuses on a private and particular space, at which point of conver-gence biological, sexual, social, cultural, linguistic, ritualistic, and psychological fortunes join. This profound intimacy of interlocking detail is disrupted, how-ever, by externally imposed meanings and uses: 1) the captive body becomes the source of an irresistible, destructive sensuality; 2) at the same time—in stunning contradiction—the captive body reduces to a thing, becoming *being for* the cap-tor; 3) in this absence *from* a subject position, the captured sexualities provide a physical and biological expression of "otherness"; 4) as a category of "otherness," the captive body translates into a potential for pornotroping and embodies sheer physical powerlessness that slides into a more general "powerlessness," resonat-ing through various centers of human and social meaning. (259–260)

What is critical to consider in Spillers' analysis is that a form of "social death" takes place under this dehumanizing system of enslavement. Black females become enmeshed in the involuntary production of human capital, and it is here that the paradoxical possibility exists, of procreation as both sexual love and the perpetuation of brutality.

Ursa's relationships with Black men also connect to the issue of miscegena-tion. Like Janie in *Their Eyes Were Watching God,* there are a number of instances that suggest that some Black men are attracted to her because of her light-skinned complexion and her hair texture. Too often in America, light-skinned Black women are more desired than dark-skinned Black women; this color hegemony comes directly out the discourse of racial superiority. In Janie's third marriage, with Tea Cake, the issue of her light skin causes conflict. Mrs. Turner, a light-skinned Black woman states: "Ah got white folks' features in mah face" (136). Zora Neale Hurston relates Mrs. Turner's philosophy as it explicates intraracial color hegemony:

> Mrs. Turner, like all other believers had built an altar to the unattainable—Cau-casian characteristics for all. Her god would smite her, would hurl her from pin-nacles and lose her in deserts, but she would not forsake his altars. Behind her crude words was a belief that somehow she and others through worship could attain her paradise—a heaven of straight-haired, thin-lipped, high-nose boned white seraphs. The physical impossibilities in no way injured faith. . . . So she didn't cling to Janie Woods the woman. She paid homage to Janie's Caucasian characteristics as such . And when she was with Janie she had a feeling of transmutation, as if she herself had become whiter and with straighter hair and she hated Tea Cake first for the defilement of divinity and next for his telling mockery of her. (139)

Mrs. Turner attempts to have Janie develop a relationship with her brother and as a result Tea Cake physically abuses Janie. Worse still, other Black men validate Tea Cake's domestic violence. For example, Sop-de-Bottom states: "Lawd! wouldn't Ah love tuh whip uh tender woman lak Janie! Ah bet she don't even holler. She jus' cries, eh Tea Cake?" (141)[9] Like Janie, Ursa is also a light-skinned Black woman who attracts the attention and gazes of Black men. Ursa's relationship with her husband, Mutt Thomas, becomes confrontational due to her singing the blues at a club. Indeed, Ursa begins the narrative at the point of conflict: "I was singing in Happy's Café around on Delaware Street. He didn't like for me to sing after we were married because he said that's why he married me so he could support me. I said I didn't just sing to be supported. I said I sing because it was something I had to do, but he never understood that" (3). More specifically, Mutt states: "I don't like those mens messing with you" (3). The unified gaze of these other men threatens Mutt's own taxonomic gaze and his patriarchal control of Ursa's body. This "mess" creates an unstable element (in Mutt's mind) of the role of Ursa as a wife and a blues singer, who is constantly the object of the collective male and female gaze. Jones' use of the word "mess" also connects to the mass lynching, in 1946, of four Black people in Walton County, Georgia, where a Black man, Roger Malcolm, stabbed a white man, Barnette Hester, because he believed that this white man was having sexual relations with Roger's wife, Dorothy. As a blues singer, Ursa is constantly in conversation with her audience. Like Jody Starks, who represents a controlling reconfiguration of a white slave master, Mutt Thomas desires to control Ursa Corregidora, and especially the possibility that her singing may produce evidence of his abuse. Their separation and alienation from each other remain charged by sexual tension. Mutt's voice echoes constantly in her dreams, memories, and reflections. Here we understand the similarity between Old Man Corregidora, who did not want any Black man fucking his whores, and Mutt, who views Black men watching Ursa sing as "messing" with her. "Messing" suggests miscegenation; Ursa, as a product of miscegenation and as a site of miscegenous sexual desire (light-skinned), symbolizes the white female. Both metaphorically and literally, Ursa Corregidora becomes a site of miscegenation with Old Man Corregidora in her. With Old Man Corregidora having fucked Ursa's ancestors, there is a symbolic sense that his phallus is still in the collective genital space of every Black female descendant that he has produced, whether they remember or deny the past. Corregidora created his mixed breed, a breed that would symbolize whiteness. In African American discourse and culture, light-skinned Black females are often named "white girl," "red bone," "high yellow," "mulatto," and "yellow girl."[10] Consequently, with Ursa as a symbolic representation of the white female, we have a number of desires in conflict: Ursa's desire to sing the blues, Mutt's desire to control Ursa by not allowing her to sing the blues, and the desire of those in the audience who want Ursa to sing the blues. Discussing the tensions in the blues in *Blues Legacies and Black Feminism: Gertrude "Ma" Rainey, Bessie Smith, and Billie Holiday* (1998), Angela Davis argues:

What gives the blues such fascinating possibilities of sustaining emergent feminist consciousness is the way they often construct seemingly antagonistic relationships as noncontradictory oppositions. A female narrative in a women's blues song who represents herself as entirely subservient to male desire might simultaneously express autonomous desire and a refusal to allow her mistreating lover to drive her to psychic despair. (xv)

Accordingly, the blues becomes a metaphor for the collective oral narratives of African American people who have survived the holocaust of enslavement and who are enduring the current plague of white supremacy. Ursa's essential need to sing the blues represents a challenge and a confirmation of history: "I wanted a song that would touch me, touch my life and theirs. A Portuguese song, but not a Portuguese song. A new world song. A song branded with the new world" (59). This desire suggests an attempt to heal herself and to heal the scars of slavery, a need to testify and transform a discourse. Equally important, the blues helped to create the radical Black feminist movement, who, like other feminists, also redefined the source of theory. As Robin D. G. Kelly argues, this movement "expanded the definition of who constitutes a theorist, the voice of authority speaking for black women, to include poets, blues singers, storytellers, painters, mothers, preachers, and teachers" (154). And as a blues singer, Ursa's personal trauma of not being able to "make generations" compounds the painful history of a people subjected to a relentless system of violent sexual exploitation.

Ursa Corregidora's memory represents not only the collective narratives passed down to her from her great-grandmother, her grandmother, and her mother but also the collective memories of Black people in the Americas during the holocaust of slavery and its enduring aftermath. As Adam McKible states: "Ursa's family name perpetuates a memory that contradicts the 'truth' of the past. Because slavers destroyed evidence that could later incriminate them, only the oral history surrounding Ursa's name preserves the knowledge of the indignities experienced by her foremothers" (232). Let us return to the doctor's question: "Is Mr. Corregidora with you?" We can say without a doubt that the memories associated with the slave-owning Corregidora are with Ursa. This question speaks to the fact that Ursa Corregidora has not taken Mutt Thomas' last name and that she symbolically belongs to the slave owner who raped her maternal ancestors; this creates a triangular sexual configuration involving Ursa, Old Man Corregidora, and Mutt or Tadpole. Clearly, the past is present and it is determining Ursa's future. Ursa has their memories, but never her own (100). Equally significant, without any memories of her Black father, Old Man Corregidora becomes a symbolic father figure. An often-repeated part of the story, which Ursa must accept as the truth, relates to the evidence. Great Gran tells her:

"When I'm telling you something don't you ever ask if I'm lying. Because they didn't want to leave no evidence of what they done—so it couldn't be held against them. And I'm leaving evidence. And you got to leave evidence too. And your children got to leave evidence. And when it come time to hold up the evidence, we got to have evidence to hold up. That's why they burned all the papers, so there wouldn't be no evidence to hold up against them." (14)

Like Old Man Corregidora's actions, there are a number of paradoxes in Great Gran's charge. They can burn papers, but they were reluctant to burn all the property, Black bodies. Black bodies speak the truth, the evidence. However the evidence is not simply "making generations," but individuals or generations who will tell the Corregidora story. Gran emphasizes memory: "The important thing is making generations. They can burn the papers but they can't burn conscious. Ursa. And that what makes the evidence. And that's what makes the verdict" (22). Implicit is the long-standing conflict between the written word and the oral tradition, especially since Black people could not testify in a court of law against a white individual. However, white individuals like Old Man Corregidora, through miscegenation, created the evidence and memories to be held up against them. What becomes clear in Jones' narrative are the tensions between private space and public space. Old Man Corregidora's world of private consumption of Black flesh leads him to the public or communal consumption of Black bodies through prostitution.

Another aspect of Ursa Corregidora's memory is the nature of the narratives she must remember, especially in light of her inability to "make generations." At the same time that Ursa deals with the loss of her pregnancy and the termination of her marriage with Mutt Thomas, she has the memories of sexual violence and physical violence that she constantly replays in her mind. Ursa tells her friend Catherine (Cat) Lawson: "From the day he throwed me down those stairs we not together, and we not coming back together" (25). Here we have Ursa's view that what happened was not an accident, but a deliberate act of violence, an act that sends her to Tadpole who allows her to stay with him. Cat informs Ursa that this is a vulnerable position, especially since she has sexual options beyond being barren:

> Listen, honey, I'm a tell you something seem like you don't know or play like you don't know. Right now's not the time for you to be grabbing at anything. Any woman to be grabbing at anything. Out of fear. I don't know what. Ask yourself how you feel about Tadpole before all of this happened. I know he's being good to you, but this is a rush job. Just thinking about the two of y'all getting together is a rush job. You know what I mean? He's looked at you and seem like you scared somebody else won't. You a beautiful woman. They be many mens that . . . (26)

Cat's analysis of Ursa' apprehension is only half correct, in one aspect, because Ursa's concern of not being wanted by other men only represents the present and not the past, when she has been charged with "making generations." Now being without a womb, Ursa cannot fulfill the maternal legacy that she has been given; this has a devastating psychological effect on her and the memories, because she will not be able to leave evidence in the proscribed manner. Within a blues context, the discourse between Ursa and Cat is significant because the female blues singers would often share stories about abusive partners or advise their sisters how to conduct themselves in relation to such men. However, here we have the role reversal, where the blues singer is being given advice by a spectator (friend) on how to conduct herself after an abusive situation.

Ursa's generational and natal loss places her in a vulnerable position, where she is subjected to both sexual and psychological violence. Following Cat's advice, she leaves Tadpole's club and stays at Cat's place across the street from the club. Here, Ursa, unable to sing the blues, begins living the blues. Like the structure of a blues song with a slightly improvised variation, we hear Ursa's repeated refrain: "If that nigger loved me he wouldn't've throwed me down the steps . . . If that nigger loved me he wouldn't've throwed me down the steps." (36). The repetition of the first and second lines of a blues song is emblematic of the narrative structure, especially in the manner in which Ursa gives us narration. While sleeping at Cat's place, a young female, Jeffrine (Jeffy), begins feeling Ursa's breasts. Ursa shoots awake and knocks her to the floor "calling her a goddamn bull" (39).[11] What is similar to slavery's past here is that Ursa's great-grandmother was forced to sleep with Old Man Corregidora's wife. Ursa's vehement anger must be placed in the context of the memories that she has been given along with her own memories concerning her sexuality. While playing doctor with a little boy across the street, Ursa was lying down on a board and the boy lifts her dress; her mother sees this. Ursa's mother exaggerates the event: "Don't you know what that boy was doing? He was feeling up your asshole" (42). Throughout the novel, Ursa' memories and her own sexual experiences frame the present. Ironically, Cat Lawson knew Jeffy was like that but never tells Ursa Corregidora. Cat, "drowsy, and hurt and angry," never takes any responsibility for what happens and gives Ursa her own blues narrative response. In response to Ursa's calls, Cat repeatedly responds: "I told her to sleep on the floor. . . . I told her to sleep on the floor" (40). At some point, Cat scolds Jeffy and threatens her with sexual violence: "If you bother her again I'll give you a fist to fuck. . . . said if you do you got my fist to fuck" (47). Ursa's tone and attitude suggest the extent that "Mr. Corregidora" is with her. Overhearing their conversation, Ursa realizes that Cat knew about Jeffy because they were lovers. Ursa's thoughts on the "consequences of fucking" are the results of this experience with Jeffy and Cat; Ursa begins to consider the psychological aspects of her transformed sexuality, gender roles, and thinks about the possibilities if the tragic incident between Mutt and herself were reversed:

> It wasn't so much how much fucking I was going to do now, I was thinking, but the consequences of that fucking. Shit. Cat telling me about the consequences

of him [Tadpole] loving me. Shit. What the hell did that mean? Maybe it's just a man can't stand to have a woman as hard as he is. If he couldn't support her in money, he'd be wanting to support her in spirit. And what if I'd thrown Mutt Thomas down those stairs instead, and done away with the source of his sex, or inspiration, or whatever the hell it is for a man, what would he feel now? At least a woman still got the hole. (40–41)

The consequences of Ursa's fucking are profound: the simple aspect is that loving Tadpole would mean a permanent end to her relationship with Mutt. However, Ursa's deeper argument resides with the stringent structure of patriarchy that many Black men like Mutt support and advance. While many African American males understand how deeply racism affects them, there is not enough understanding of the impact that gender marginalization has on Black women, who also face the pernicious psychological, physical, and economic aspects of America's racism. "Double jeopardy," the effect of racism and sexism on Black women, is the term that Ursa suggests in her discourse of gender reversal. Ursa's hardness resides in her desire to sing the blues; indeed this desire represents a need. Connecting desire to sexuality, Robin D. G. Kelly states:

Desire and sexuality, and their relationship to revolt, have always been central themes in the music, but were too often avoided by well-meaning defenders of the race concerned about reinforcing stereotypes of Black promiscuity. Surrealists, on the other hand, had a long-standing interest in sexual liberty and power of the erotic, which must have rendered the blues all the more attractive. (164).

Like Ursa's mother, it seems that Mutt has only a vague sense of the critical impact Ursa's memories and the transgenerational effect they have on her reflective need to sing the blues. Ursa's mother characterizes blues music as "devil music" (146) and says, "listening to the blues and singing them ain't the same" (103). Paradoxically, Ursa's mother, and her mother, and her mother have created Ursa by the memories they have shared. Trapped in a past that is not her own, Ursa's life is a blues song because as she states: "It helps me to explain what I can't explain" (56). Memories passed on to Ursa are difficult to contemplate, and the blues help her to explain the unexplainable, speak the unspeakable.

Ursa Corregidora's brief relationship with and marriage to Tadpole McCormick become another blues narrative synthesized by her memories. As Cat Lawson has foreshadowed, there would be some consequences to fucking Tadpole. Ursa further contemplates the consequences: "It seems as if you're not singing the past, you're humming it. Consequences of what? Shit, we're all consequences of something. Stained with another's past as well as our own. Their past in my blood. I'm a blood. *Are you mine, Ursa, or theirs?*" (45; author's emphasis). Fundamental to Tadpole's relationship with Ursa is a simple power dynamic; Tadpole owns Happy's Café, where Ursa sings. Under slavery, the relationship between the slave master and his slaves was based on power supported by physical and psychological violence. No matter what type of relationship developed between the slave master and the slaves, the power dynamic tended to erase any sense of subjectivity that the slave possessed. Tadpole's initial, seemingly genuine, concern for Ursa's tragic fall transforms to a desire that is essentially sexual; Ursa becomes reduced to a vagina. Going back to Tadpole after discovering that Cat and Jeffy are lovers, Ursa submits to sexual relations with Tadpole and she decides to begin singing at Happy's Café again. "Then I started singing about trouble in mind. Still the new voice" (50). Having no place to go, Ursa's decision to have sexual relations seems to be a payment rather than out of some real desire for Tadpole. Shortly after Ursa and Tadpole are married, conflict develops in terms of sexuality. Tadpole defines their sexual encounters as "fucking." One particular painful incident highlights the growing sexual tension:

> He dug his finger up my asshole. I contracted against him. "You fucking me. Yes, you fucking me." He finger my clit again, but it was painful now. "It hurts," I fretted. He took his hand away. I kept moving with him, not feeling it now. I waited till his convulsions were over. His sperm inside me. Then we lay back together, exhausted, ready to sleep. (75)

Even in this sexual act, Jones gives us the call and response structure of the blues. Tadpole repeatedly asks Ursa what he is doing to her; he desires a validation of his fucking. In a sense Tadpole is engaged with three of Ursa's orifices: her mouth, her vagina, and her anus; this recalls how Black female slaves were inspected when they were on the auction block and how they were subjected to oral, vaginal, and anal sex on the slave plantation. At the same time that Ursa is having painful and perhaps dehumanizing sexual relations with Tadpole, she experiences Mutt's discourse in her head. Ursa attempts to deny him, but Mutt says: "What do you mean you don't know me? I was in your hole before he even knew you had one" (75). Here, Ursa's past sexual relations (memories) with Mutt create a present discourse. Another possibility is that Ursa engages with a dialogue with Old Man Corregidora ("Is Mr. Corregidora with you?"). This would explain why Ursa states: "Don't talk to me. I don't know you" (75). Two triangles of sexual desire are constructed: one with Tadpole, Mutt, and Ursa, and the other with Tadpole, Old Man Corregidora, and Ursa. Memories associated with Old Man Corregidora, as well as her memories of Mutt Thomas, haunt Ursa Corregidora as she experiences nonfeeling and frustrating sexual relations with Mutt Thomas. "He was inside, and I felt nothing. I wanted to feel, but I couldn't" (82), states Ursa during another sexual encounter with Mutt. At some point sex becomes labor as Mutt states: "Work Ursa" (83). "I am working," Ursa responds and finally desperately pleads "Tadpole, I can't, I can't" (83). Ursa's further reflections on Mutt reveal a synthesis: "Shit, I know how it is. Mens just hanging in there trying to get some. It's the Happy Café awright.

Mens just hanging around so they can get something." (84). Mutt's reference to Ursa's genitals suggests a crude consumption of "something" that Ursa is selling. The synthesis is that, in Mutt's perspective, Happy's Café becomes analogous to Corregidora's whorehouse. At this point, Ursa's inability to experience feelings while having sex may be both physical and psychological; Ursa's feelings are connected to her inability to make generations.

Seeking some relief in singing the blues, Ursa decides to sing at the Spider club, owned by Max Monroe, in addition to singing at the Happy's Café, but this leads to another sexual confrontation and more sexual tension. Tadpole's refrain to Ursa's desire is, "You your own woman. You your own woman" (85). The statement by Mutt reinforces Ursa's response to the doctor that her name is Corregidora and that it is not her husband's name. There is a presence and an absence in the naming here. Ursa's absence at Happy's Café leads to the presence of a 15-year-old female, Vivian, who ends up in Tadpole and Ursa's bed. When Ursa confronts them, Tadpole's arrogant defense is that he "wasn't doing nothing but sucking on her tiddies" (88). Tadpole continues his vicious verbal attack: "Her tiddies do more for me than your goddamn pussy hole do. . . . She got more woman in her asshole than you got in your whole goddamn cunt" (88–89). Tadpole's debasing tirade has a crushing emotional affect. Like the situation with Cat Lawson, Ursa Corregidora finds herself in a vulnerable position because her sexual relations are infused with memories. Deeply hurt, Ursa goes to the Drake Hotel and decides to obtain full-time work at the Spider nightclub. However, Ursa, at the Spider club, comes under another sexual attack when Max first places his hand on her shoulder and then attempts to put his hand between her breasts. Jumping up and almost spilling coffee on Max, Ursa keeps saying "naw." Among other men who seem to eroticize Ursa, Max's behavior suggests the manner in which many light-skinned Black women become stereotyped.[12]

As Carol Camper argues: "The other stereotype of mixed race women is that of moral and sexual degeneracy. It is as if our basic degeneracy as women of color is magnified by White ancestry. Our so called 'Whiteness' increases our 'beauty' along with our awareness of it, driving us to a frenzy of bitter abandon so agreeable and piquant to our White male pursuers" (xvi).

Max ends his inappropriate behavior but does not seem to understand how uncomfortable it makes Ursa. Immediately after this sexually charged incident, Ursa remembers an experience as a child that echoes the uncomfortable experience with Max. Waiting outside a beauty parlor for her mother, Ursa is approached by a man holding his hand out. He states: "Gimme what you got. What you gonna gimme? Gimme what you got" (95). Ursa gives us her mother's interpretation that "he was reaching for me down between my legs. I thought he was holding his hand out" (95). Again, we obtain a synthesis of the present and the past with regard to Ursa's body as a site of miscegenous sexual desire; we cannot dismiss the possibility that Ursa's light-skinned complexion and hair "like rivers" (81) cause her so much sexualized attention as a young girl and as an adult. With memories of Mutt (a name that reinforces the hybrid notion of the Black individual as some "indeterminate breed" and a name that suggests mulatto and signifies miscegenation) sashaying constantly in her mind, Ursa begins another conversation with her first husband. Their conversation begins with Mutt attempting to ascertain if Ursa has lost the blues. Ursa responds: "Naw, the blues is something you can't lose" (97). The long back-and-forth conversation comes down to sexual desire. Mutt's repeated refrain is: "I still want to fuck you . . . I still want to fuck you . . . Let me get behind you." At some point, they disagree on how the fucking will occur and Mutt says: "Then fuck you" (98). Mutt encourages Ursa to forget the past except theirs, "the good feeling," and ends with "Let me get up in your hole, I said. I want to get up in your goddamn hole" (100). Like a lusty white slave owner, Corregidora, Mutt Thomas essentially attempts to reduce Ursa Corregidora to an orifice where he deposits his sperm. Recalling a disturbing description in Alice Walker's *The Color Purple* (1982), for some men sexual relations seems analogous to some mindless activity. In *The Color Purple*, Celie's marriage to Mr. reflects a decapitating level of degradation. Celie, describing her loveless marriage, states: "Mr.____come git me to take care of his rotten children. He never ast me nothing bout myself. He clam on top of me and fuck and fuck, even when my head bandaged. Nobody ever love me, I say" (112).[13] Here Celie is being consumed by the intense labor of caring for a husband and his three children, the beatings from her husband, as well as through the sexual violence.

Despite the sexually charged encounter with Max, Ursa's deep-seated pain finds expression in her singing voice, now richer with the exquisite anguish she has experienced. Not surprisingly, Max comments on Ursa's voice and gives an analysis that reflects some of her memories: "You got a hard kind of voice. . . . You know, like callused hands. Strong and hard but gentle underneath. Strong but gentle too. The kind of voice that can hurt you. I can't explain it. Hurt you and make you still want to listen" (96). What becomes evident is a remarkable evocation of an injured woman engaged in the struggle to regain her psychological balance. Ursa represents a blues singer bent but not broken by her personal trauma of childlessness, a singer who uses a blues sensibility to give voice to who she is and a woman who sings the blues to help her explain what she cannot explain. Max's analysis suggests the improvisational nature of the blues and the oral tradition that Ursa is expected to pass down, memories that can hurt and memories that can heal.

We obtain a clear understanding of Ursa Corregidora's rejection of the idea of forgetting the past when we discover the relentless way in which Ursa as a young girl has been subjected to the memories of her great-grandmother, her grandmother, and her mother. These memories are given to Ursa in a systematic manner that makes it difficult for her to function without a recollection of these "monstrous" memories:

The three of them at first and then when I was older, just the two of them, one sitting in a rocker, the other in a straight-back chair, telling me things. I'd always listen. . . . They kept to the house telling me things. My mother would work while my grandmother told me, then she'd come home and tell me. I'd go to school and come back and be told. When I was real little, Great Gram rocking me and talking. And still it was as if my mother's whole body shook with that first birth and memories and she wouldn't make others and she wouldn't give those to me, though she passed the other ones down, the monstrous ones, but she wouldn't give me her own terrible ones. . . . And still she told me what I should do, that I should make generations. (101)

What is striking here, beyond the deliberate triangular matrilineal intent of passing on these monstrous memories, is the selective aspect of the memory transference because oftentimes it is the silences that speak more powerfully than the utterances. For Ursa, the utterances are profoundly disturbing, and the silences, especially her mother's silences in regard to her existence, are equally disturbing. Ursa's mother's relationship with Ursa's father represents a troubling legacy of intra-racial violence within Black communities. This is made clear when Ursa's mother tells her: "You carry more than his name" (103). Ursa understands that her mother has disturbing memories beyond those handed down to her from her grandmother and mother.

Although extremely disturbing, the theme of misogyny, particularly toward Black women, represents a pervasive issue in *Corregidora*. When we consider the inhumanly brutal physical and psychological violence that Black people have been subjected to during the enslavement period, it is necessary to consider hate juxtaposed with desire. In the novel, the malicious hatred of Black women and their reproductive ability is central to the trope of miscegenation as sexual consumption. Furthermore, misogyny is also evident in Gayl Jones' characterizations of Black women's relationships with other Black men.

Old Man Corregidora's abominably abusive behavior represents a fundamental paradigm of misogyny; his behavior represents a mixture of sexual desire (control) and antipathy for women. Historically, Black women, because of race and gender prejudice, have been subjected to the cruelest forms of patriarchy. In *The Creation of Patriarchy* (1986), Gerda Lerner describes patriarchy as the "manifestations and institutionalization of male dominance over women and children in the family and the extension of male dominance over women in society in general (289). By characterizing all of his sexual relations as "fucking," Jones illustrates Corregidora's dehumanizing of women who become objects of his sadistic desire. Sexual trauma would be a manner to classify the experience of his Black female slaves. With Corregidora's wife sleeping in a separate room, he sexually terrorizes Ursa's Great Gram:

He grab hold of me down between my legs and said he didn't want nothing black down there. He said if he just catch me fucking something black, they wouldn't have no pussy, and he wouldn't have none neither. And then he was squeezing me all up on my pussy and then digging his hands up in there. We was up in his room. That's where he was always bring me when he wont to scold me about something, or fuck with me. Him and his wife was living in separated rooms then. Then he was just digging all up in me till he got me where he wonted me and then he just laid me down on that big bed of his and started fucking me. (125)

The isolation of his separate room facilitates Corregidora doing anything and everything he wants to Ursa's grandmother; the scolding represents the psychological violence, and the fucking presents the physical violence. The "digging up in" this Black woman has a certain inhuman quality that suggests him digging into the earth with some tool or instrument; here, those instruments will be his fingers and his phallus. Old Man Corregidora's dehumanization of Black females is in accord with the cultural and economic cultural dictates during this period; this misogyny and dehumanization of the Black female began at the inspection: "Cause that's all they do to you, was feel up on you down between your legs see what kind of genitals you had, either so you could breed well, or make a good whore. Fuck each other or fuck them. Tha's the first thing they would think about, cause if you had somebody was a good fucker you had plenty money on the side or inside" (127). This auction-block inspection was without a doubt one of the most dehumanizing aspects of the enslavement of Black people because these were public spectacles where men, women, and children gathered to see the inspection, selling and buying of Black bodies. And the fucking produced Black bodies to be sold or made to fuck. On this point, Ursa's grandmother states:

Yeah, Mama told me how in the days he was just buying up women. They'd have to raise up their dress so he could see what they had down there, and he feel around down there, and then he feel their bellies to see if they had solid bellies. And they had to be pretty. He wasn't buying up them fancy mulatto womens though. They had to be black and pretty. They had to be the color of his coffee beans. That's why he said he always liked my mama better than me. But he never said nothing about what it was she did to him. What is it a woman can do to a man that make him hate her so bad he wont to kill her one minute and keep thinking about her and can't get her out of his mind the next? (173)

Here the enslavement of Black people is placed purely as a sexualized desire as Jones through her language connects sexual desire to a consumable commodity, coffee.

Another aspect of the misogyny of Black women is the wholesale whoremongering. With the status of the child being determined by the status of the mother, this policy ensured a continuous stream of wealth for white slave owners. Through sexual relations with white slave owners or with other Black male

slaves, the children remained property. Black women were "cultivated" by forcing them to have sexual relations with cultivated white men in private rooms.
On the other hand, other Black women were forced to lie naked and they "sent
trash into them" (124). Also, there was a communal fucking where "some of
these others, they had to been three or four or five whores fucking in the same
room" (124). Here Black women have no subjectivity and are reduced to sexual
bodies for consumption. Fundamental to healthy sexual relationships is a level
of intimacy and mutual respect; none of these elements of integrity is present in
these situations. Like the mass lynchings of Black males, here we have the mass
fucking of Black women. Paradoxically, Black women have been characterized as
whores by white-male individuals who have socialized them to be whores. Projecting their sexual aggressiveness and sexual desires onto Black women removed
any accountability of white males for the sexual violence that Black women
experienced. As Great Gram relates, even Black women who had husbands or
mates on the plantation would be subjected to sexual violence:

> Any of them, even them he had out in the fields, if he wanted them, he just ship
> their own husbands out of bed, and get in there with them, but didn't nothing
> happen like what happened over on that other plantation cause I guess that
> other plantation served as a warning, cause they might wont your pussy, but
> if you do anything to get back at them, it'll be your life they be wonting, and
> them beatings and killings wasn't nothing but sex circuses, and all them white
> peoples, mens, womens, and childrens crowding around to see. . . . (125)

The deadly message or ultimatum to enslaved Black women: give us your pussy
or face a degrading public beating and/or a humiliating death. Forcing a Black
woman to forsake her genitals is so disturbing because this is where her generations are created; it is the most precious and most sacred space of the female
body, the source of female power. There can be few things more psychologically
difficult than being forced to have sexual relations, especially if pregnancy is the
result. With the deep level of shame involved in being pregnant after a rape, it
is easy to see why so many Black women would consider suicide and infanticide.
In *Killing the Black Body: Race, Reproduction, and the Meaning of Liberty*, Dorothy
Roberts reminds us: "For slave women, procreation had little to do with liberty.
To the contrary, Black women's childbearing in bondage was largely a product
of oppression rather than an expression of self-definition and personhood" (23).
Indeed, the ability for self-definition and personhood is fundamentally impossible. Beyond the personal trauma is the aspect that Black women are forced to
reproduce children who were not their own, and these children also became victims of sexual abuse, creating a vicious cycle of sexual exploitation. With Great
Gran referring to these public spectacles of violence as "sex circuses," this connects physical violence to the lynching as a sexualized ritual of human consumption. Men, women, and children watching Black people being tortured were in

fact consuming these black bodies with their gazes often while they enjoyed the food and beverages that would be provided at a picnic or other festive events. The sexual violence that white people inflicted on Black people created tensions between Black males and females because Black males were often powerless to protect Black females. This inability to protect Black females became exacerbated after slavery when Black males had a difficult time trying to provide for their families.

Ursa's mother's relationship with her husband, Martin, painfully exemplifies the theme of misogyny in the novel. She tells Ursa that she met him at a place where she used to have lunch. "He was a good-looking man, I guess. Yeah, your daddy was a good-looking. Tall and straight as an arrow. Black man. You know, kind of satin-black. Smooth satin-black. You come out looking more like me than you did like him, I mean about the color. You got long legs like he had" (112). What is amazing here is that Ursa Corregidora (of course she does not have his last name) is hearing about her father for the first time in her life. At this point, she knows more about Old Man Corregidora than she knows about her own Black father, Martin (his full name is not given). The color contrast between Ursa's parents represents a challenge to Old Man Corregidora, who never allowed Great Gram to have sexual relations with a Black man. Great Gram states that she was denied seeing a man because Corregidora said "a black man wasn't nothing but a waste of pussy, and wear me out when it came to the other mens" (124). Ursa's mother states that her relationship with Martin began with him continuously looking at her: "I never was out looking for no man. I had to go there, had to go there and sit there and have him watch me like that. Sometimes he'd be cleaning the counter and watching me, you know how mens watch you when they wont something" (112). In a sense, while Ursa's mother goes here to have a meal, she becomes consumed by his gaze, a male gaze that seduces her to submit to a visual consumption. This issue of consumption becomes reinforced when Ursa's mother feels compelled to return to the diner and eats dinner, but in order to conceal her routine visits from her mother and grandmother, she consumes dinner again when she returns home. Overconsumption of food causes Ursa's mother to feel as if she is pregnant and the first time they have sexual relations, Ursa's mother becomes pregnant. However, before this occurs, Ursa's mother reveals that she experiences a sexual desire that totally consumes her:

> He kept asking if he could touch me certain places, and I kept saying yes. And then all of a sudden it was like I felt the whole man in me, just felt the whole man in there. I pushed him out. It was like it was just that feeling of him in there. And nothing else. I hadn't even given myself time to feel anything else before I pushed him out. But he must have . . . I . . . . still that memory, feeling of him in me. I wouldn't let myself feel anything. It was like a surprise. Like a surprise when he got inside. Just that one time. (117–118)

Ursa's mother tells her, "It was like my whole body wanted you, Ursa. Can you understand that?" (117). This statement of maternal need reflects Ursa's mother manifesting the imputed desire of "making generations," given to her by her mother and grandmother.

Ursa's mother's pregnancy brings conflict and violence. Conflict begins once the pregnancy becomes evident and when Great Gram visits Ursa's father and talks to him. And then Ursa's mother states: "I begged her not to, but he came and married me and then . . . he left me" (118). When Ursa is two years old, Ursa's mother visits him one final time at some boarding house in Cincinnati. He calls her "bitch" and says it again, "bitch." His anger escalates over being forced to marry her and living in that house for two years. In a description that echoes Old Man Corregidora's vile behavior, Ursa's mother explains Martin's misogynistic behavior:

> He squeezed tighter. I kept trying to get away, but then he started slapping me all over the face. One time it was like he was going to go for some place else, like he was going to go straight for my cunt, or for my belly, or some place like that, but then he stopped himself, and just kept slapping me all over my face, twisting me, and slapping me all over my face. I didn't think I'd get out of there. I didn't think I would. I started to scream. And then I said, Naw, to myself. I said, Naw, I wasn't going to scream for no nigger, and having people coming up there and make me feel worse than I did already. I said, Naw, I wasn't going to scream for no nigger. (119)

This statement suggests Martin's outrage in his having made a generation, Ursa. And Ursa's mother reluctance to scream for assistance reflects the historical fact that Black women were afraid to report sexual or physical violence by a Black male because they feared that they would be lynched; here the fear is that the Black man would be beaten by the police. Also, this description conveys a symbolic decapitation where he attempts to slap her face off. In their important study *Off with Her Head: The Denial of Women's Identity in Myth, Religion, and Culture* (1995), Howard Eliberg-Schwartz and Wendy Doniger posit a theory of female subjectivity that is useful in understanding Jones' characterizations of the Black female journey into womanhood, specifically, and of the more general loss of speech, identity, and power due to the psychological, economic, and physical violence of white supremacy. Discussing their theory of female decapitation, Eliberg-Schwartz and Doniger argue:

> The female head is a particularly rich and important site in the symbolization of gender and in the linking of gender to the transcendent values of specific cultural or religious systems. For the head, which is potentially separable from the body, poses special dilemmas when it belongs to a woman . . . the other half of woman: the anatomical part of the female body that gives women a

voice and an identity and that thereby threatens to unmake and disrupt the classic gender distinctions that have linked men to speech, power, identity, and the mind. If the head is typically thought of as masculine, then what is to be made of the female head? Our contention is that the objectification of woman as a sexual body necessarily requires coming to terms with the presence of her head. (1)

Decapitation becomes a way of solving the problem because removing the female head relieves the woman of both identity and voice and reduces her to a mere sexual and reproductive body. Moreover, the female body becomes objectified and reconfigured where the eyes become breasts, the nose a navel and the mouth a vagina; the female head becomes part of a woman's genitalia. This eroticization of the female head extends to the woman's body and thus turns the head into a seductive and sexually provocative organ. Moreover, female decapitation becomes an equal-opportunity process where men with a taxonomic gaze can decapitate women and where women who internalize patriarchal hegemony can decapitate other women and simultaneously decapitate themselves. What becomes surely disastrous here is that some men are unable to view women as individuals with identity, power, and voice, and some women are unable to view themselves and other women with these qualities. Female decapitation severely marginalizes women and thus weakens individuals, families, communities, and nations. In a sense, decapitation represents any marginalizing process whereby an individual loses his or her identity, voice, and subjectivity. Here the violence is designed to leave marks on her face, and it gives the notion that she represents property to be used or abuse in any manner that the "master" sees appropriate. Slapping a woman's face is an attempt to make her sexually unavailable for another man at least temporarily; leaving physical marks on a woman is analogous to branding an animal. During slavery, slaves who escaped and who were captured were often branded or mutilated by their masters. In America, slaves who were captured after they escaped were branded with an "E" or an "R" on their cheek to denote that they had escaped or they had run away.[14] Like rape, physical violence is about power and control; Black men during the enslavement period were generally unable to protect Black women and their children. This emasculating aspect produced a legacy of guilt, frustration, and shame.

Martin's deep-seated shame resides in his inability to provide for his wife and child, Ursa. Like Jody Starks and Tea Cake who slap Janie Crawford, Martin expresses his seething contempt for Ursa's mother. Martin's frustration perhaps resides in the two years that he lived with Ursa's mother, the grandmother, and the great-grandmother. It is possible that the stories of Old Man Corregidora had a negative affect on Martin. On one particular occasion, Ursa's grandmother was powdering her breasts and Martin views this intimate scene. When she sees him watching her, she lets out a hateful diatribe: "You black bastard, watching me. What you doing watching me, you black bastard?" (130). And Martin's response:

"he kept calling her a half-white heifer"(130). In a symbolic sense, the grand-mother through sexual relations with Old Man Corregidora has become white, and this voyeurism is symbolic of the Black man consuming her naked flesh, an act that Old Man Corregidora has repeatedly forbidden. What is particularly dis-turbing here is that Ursa's mother relates that her grandmother knew that he was watching her while she powdered her breasts. This scene suggests the extent to which the grandmother has internalized the racialized discourse of Old Man Corregidora where she exposes her breasts (white powder, of course, makes her light-skinned breasts even whiter) to a Black man who should never have sexual relations with someone like herself. Black women represent "wasted pussy" for Black men. With this in mind, Ursa's mother continues to relate the horror of her visit to Martin's room: "He hated me, Ursa. I know he did. I was holding myself all on my face, and I know I was going to be black and blue all over, it hurt so bad I was just hugging my face" (119). Martin hates Ursa's mother. The level of misogyny is profound, but it needs to be understood (never justified) within the context of slavery and its aftermath of Jim Crow segregation, which has created a transgenerational transgression of trauma in the lives of most Black people. We never know the particular legacy of Martin's family, but based on Ursa's memo-ries we can theorize that there has been a history of psychological, physical, and economic violence with regard to Black males. For example, Great Gram reveals a synthesis of Corregidora's sexual desire for Black female slaves and the physical violence directed at Black males. Old Man Corregidora is fucking Great Gram at the same time that overseers with their hounds are tracking a young Black male who has escaped the plantation in his desire to join the Palmares, a Brazilian group of rebel slaves:

> Wasn't nothing but seventeen. And he had this dream he told me about. That was what he wanted me for, was to tell me about this dream. He must've trusted me a lot, though, cause I could've been one of them to run back to Corregidora with it. . . . And I kept feeling all the time he was running, he kept thinking I'd told something and I didn't. And then there I was kept crying out and ole Corregidora thinking it was because he was fucking so good I was crying. "Ain't nobody do it to you like this is it?" I said, "Naw." I just kept saying Naw, and he just kept squeezing on my ass and fucking. And then somehow it got in my mind that each time he kept going down in me would be that boy's feet running. And then when he come, it meant they caught him. . . . (127–128)

Again the rubric of white males fucking Black women and killing Black men is repeated as Old Man Corregidora confuses screams of anger and frustration for screams of desire. His ejaculation represents a synthesis of control over two Black bodies. Better still, his ejaculation represents a literal and a symbolic rape of two different Black bodies. Misogyny and misanthropy become juxtaposed by Corregidora's sadistic sexual abuse masquerading as patriarchal power.

Martin's actions and Old Man Corregidora's actions become juxtaposed in the final part of Ursa's mother's tragic narrative of domestic violence. After he concludes slapping Ursa's mother, Martin grabs her purple pants and the elastic waistband breaks; she catches them before they fall down. At this point, he tells her: "Get out. . . . Go on down the street, lookin like a whore. I wont you to go on down the street, lookin like a whore" (120–121). Like Old Man Corregidora, Martin out of his own sadistic rage reduces Ursa's mother to a sexual object to be consumed and discarded. Being discarded, Ursa's mother is forced into the street with a badly beaten face as she struggles to keep her purple pants from falling down. Using the color purple foreshadows Alice Walker's treatment of slavery's legacy in the lives of Black men and women in her novel *The Color Purple;* here the abusive male character Albert repeatedly beats and humiliates his wife, Celie. Celie tells Shrug about her sexual relations: "He git up on you, heist your nightgown round your waist, plunge in. Most times I pretend I ain't there. He never know the difference. Never ast me how I feel, nothing. Just do his business, get off, go to sleep." Shug's response, "Why Miss Celie. You make it sound like he going to the toilet on you" (77), captures the sexual humiliation. Black-on-black violence is often a result of white-on-black violence because interracial conflict often creates intra-racial conflict. At some point, Ursa's mother reveals the real reason for the conflict between her grandmother and Martin; Martin had the courage to ask the question: "How much was hate for Corregidora and how much was love?" (131). As disturbing as this question is for these Corregidora women, there is a profound possibility that this dialectic frames the charge of "making generation" as well as the near obsession that these women have of telling the stories of Old Man Corregidora's sexual abuse. Ursa's great-grandmother states: "He fucked her and fucked me. He would've fucked you and your mama if y'all been there and he wasn't old and crooked up like he got" (172). This statement of Old Man Corregidora's incestuous sexual desire transcends generations and here hate and love are analogous to hate and desire. Martin's question also connects us to the doctor's question "Is Mr. Corregidora with you?" Ursa's memories are not simply about the sexual horrors, but also about the sexual desires. The doctor's question suggests that the white man, Corregidora, is metaphorically fucking Ursa when she has sexual relations with Mutt and Tadpole. Better still the question suggests that there is some sexual dissonance between Ursa and Mutt, and Ursa and Tadpole. Ursa's mother's private memories that include misogyny bring a sense of satisfaction to Ursa, but the revelation of these memories causes her to consider her own life. Ursa reflects: "I was thinking that now that Mama had gotten it all out, her own memory—at least to me anyway—maybe she and *some man* . . . But then, I was thinking, what had I done about my own life? (132). This sharing serves as a cathartic moment for both women; Ursa's mother shares the brief and tragic end of her marriage and Ursa obtains information about her mother's private memory. Like her mother, Ursa Corregidora's current life is in a void, having divorced Tadpole

McCormick and being divorced and estranged from Mutt Thomas as well as being estranged from her best friend, Cat Lawson.

As Ursa Corregidora reflects on her life, there appears to exist a culture where Black females are not respected, indeed a level of developing misogyny. Indeed there are a number of incidents in Ursa's life as a child and as an adult that suggest a culture of misogyny. For example, Ursa shares with her friend May Alice an experience when a boy named Harold comes to her house with some other boys: "'Let us in, Ursa,' Harold had said. 'Let us in so we can give you a baby. Don't you want a baby?'" And then: "'Henry said when you was five you let him see your pussy,' Harold said . . . 'He said you let him feel all up in your ass'" (138). Here there is a level of complicity among the boys that suggests their desire for them to take turns fucking Ursa in her "pussy" and in her "ass." Also, there is the story that the young Ursa hears about the Melrose woman who committed suicide because of pregnancy. In hushed tones, Ursa hears her mother and grandmother discuss the woman's death:

> "They thought it must've been some man, you know, got her pregnant or something, but she wasn't pregnant."
>
> "Had to been some man," Gram said, "I ain't never known a woman take her life less it was some man." (133)

This culture of animosity of Black women extends to the legal process where the death of a Black female receives little attention and little respect. At Mr. Deak's store, Ursa overhears some Black men talking about the suicide:

> You know they ain't gon take they time to find out nothing about a nigger woman. Somebody go down there and file a complaint, they write it down all right, while you standing there, but as soon as you leave, they say, "Here, put it in this nigger file." That mean they get to it if they can. And most times they can't. Naw, they don't say put it in the nigger file, they say put in the nigger woman file, which means they ain't gon never get to it. (134)

There is also the story of May Alice, who was deserted because of pregnancy; her story is analogous to Ursa's mother who experiences a similar fate. Typical of many blues songs sung by Black women, the racial and gender dynamics in America position Black females as the nigger's nigger. In America's white-supremacist culture, the only thing worse than being a nigger is being a nigger woman. Jones suggests that Black life is cheap, but Black female life is even cheaper. Combined with the narratives of sexual abuse and sexual exploitation during slavery, this devaluation of Black females by other Black people formulates a disturbing self-image for a young Ursa Corregidora. Another incident of the misogyny occurs on the day of Tadpole's and Ursa's marriage; Ursa and Cat have a conversation that attempts to resolve Jeffy's sexual advance to Ursa, but Ursa is rather cold towards

Cat. However, here Cat tells Ursa a story of her own sexual abuse while working as a domestic for Mr. and Mrs. Thomas Hirshorn. Ursa describes the incident:

> She was a young woman, about my age. She lived in during the week and every morning at six o'clock she had to get up and get Mr. Hirshorn's breakfast because he was the supervisor in a plant, and his wife stayed in the bed sleeping. . . ."You pretty, Catherine, you know that? You pretty, Catherine. A lot of you nigger women is pretty." She kept thinking he was drunk, and wished he'd stayed in the room with his wife till she called him like she always did. But he kept sitting, thumping on the table watching her, her bare arms in a housedress. "You ought to let me watch you straighten your hair sometime. Beatrice said you were in there straightening your hair." She was saying nothing and then she'd got the can of coffee grounds down and was opening it to pour in the pot, he was behind her, touching her arm, and she dropped the can, and it banged and rolled across the kitchen floor spilling grains. He jumped back, and she was stooping trying to clean it up when his wife came in. (65–66)

With his wife in the bedroom, this lusty white man attempts to assault Cat before he consumes his breakfast. Somehow he thinks calling Cat Lawson "pretty" and a "nigger" is a compliment. Furthermore, the desire to see Cat straightening her hair articulates a deep-seated desire for a level of intimacy that would be reserved for a husband or lover. When the wife comes into the kitchen she asks: "What happened, Tom?" Her husband responds: "That clumsy nigger. I won't have time to eat breakfast this morning, sweetheart." Then the wife states: "You made a mess" (66). Like Old Man Corregidora, Tom Hirshorn seeks to consume some nigger pussy before he has his coffee. Again Jones' use of the word "mess" relates to the theme of miscegenation as sexual consumption of the Black female body, white men messing with Black women. Cat's scene with Tom recalls Ursa's scene with Max; in both incidents, Ursa and Cat are sexually assaulted and coffee is spilled; the coffee connects us to Brazil and the sexual consumption orchestrated by Corregidora. Equally important, Jones' naming strategy (Cat) reinforces the idea of a white male consuming nigger pussy.[15] Similar to life during slavery, the Black female and the white wife both become polarized rather than understanding the social constructions of race and gender that benefit Tom's subjectivity. Like the white woman who desires to have Janie's grandmother whipped for having sexual relations with the slave master, this white woman places the blame on Cat. For Cat and many Black women, the urban environment becomes just another "slave market." As the supervisor in a plant (plantation), Tom's behavior reinforces and reinscribes the materiality of white supremacy that generates wealth through the exploitation of Black bodies and Black labor. Beyond this incident, Cat relates: "You don't know what it's like to feel foolish all day in a white woman's kitchen and then to come home and feel foolish in the bed at night with your man. I wouldn't a mind the other so much if I didn't have to feel like a fool in the bed with my man" (64). Cat's discourse (she trembles after she relates these incidents) on her past personal experiences seeks to explain why she is currently a lesbian, but Ursa is rather unsympathetic in her response: "You over your hysteria now?" Despite her own troubles with Black men, Ursa finds in difficult to identify with a woman who has sexual relations with another woman, especially with the lover of a woman who attacked her while she was sleeping. Another critical aspect of the relationship between Cat and Ursa is that Cat's pussy is free of any maternal mandates (she can have sex with a man or woman, even a young girl like Jeffy) and Ursa's pussy is tied to slavery's past. Cat's pussy belongs to pussy and Ursa's pussy belongs to the phallus. Perhaps the wombless Ursa is envious of Cat because she has a functioning pussy with a womb and can make generations if she chooses. A fundamental aspect of slavery was for Blacks not to openly show any affection because of the apprehension of loved ones being sold. Black mothers and fathers realized that showing affection toward their children could result in them being sold. The fear of loved ones being sold was a fundamental trauma that Black people faced during the generations of enslavement. For many generations, Ursa has been so consumed with the concept of making generations that it is impossible for her to identify with any sexual relationship where this is not possible, even though she is incapable of bearing children. Cat eagerly waits for a sympathetic embrace, but Ursa never embraces her. However, Ursa by her own unspoken words understands exactly what Cat feels in the sexual tensions that keep Black men and women from enjoying intimacy:

> Yes I know what it feels like. I remember how his shoulders felt when he was going inside me and I had my hands on his shoulders, but I also remember that night I was exhausted with wanting and I waited but he didn't turn toward me and I kept waiting and wanting him and I got close to him up against his back but he still wouldn't turn to me and then I lay on my back and tried hard to sleep and I finally slept and in the morning I waited and still he didn't and I wanted but the clock got him up and he went off to work and I lay there still waiting. I was no longer even angry with waiting. I just lay there saying don't make me use my fingers, and then I got up too. Yes, I could tell her what it feels like. *Do I have to wait until in the morning? Don't punish me this way. What's a husband for? Don't you feel like a man?* And wanting to cry and not wanting him to see me turning over against the wall until sweat came out of my eyes but never wanting him to hear me cry. (64–65; author's emphasis)

Ursa does not name the Black man with whom she experiences this sexual frustration, but it is clear that she feels that this is psychological violence or punishment that forces her to consider satisfying herself. If Mr. Corregidora is with her, this would explain her disconnect with her Black husbands. Ursa's desire to cry but not wanting him to hear her cry represents the dialectic associated with trauma. Again Judith Lewis Herman's theory of trauma is helpful here. Herman states: "The dialectic of trauma gives rise to complicated, sometimes uncanny alterations of consciousness, which George Orwell, one of the committed truth-tellers of our century, called 'doublethink,' and which mental health profession-als, searching for a calm, precise language, call 'dissociation'" (1). Ursa finds herself in a subordinate position of a slave, affirming the cry of her master in the ritualistic embraces that take place during this and other sexual encounters with Black men. Similar to the blues, the ritualized cry and response between the cries and the respondent can be analogous to that of a master and slave. Like the sadistic and brutal Old Man Corregidora, this Black man (most likely Mutt Thomas) uses sex as a weapon to punish Ursa. This sexual frustration is compounded by Ursa's inability to have children, which makes her feel shame, guilt, and anger.

It takes twenty-two years of feelings of anger and shame, but Ursa Corregi-dora ultimately becomes reunited with her first husband, Mutt Thomas. While still singing the blues at the Spider, Ursa reencounters Jim, Mutt's cousin; he acts to mitigate the trauma between Mutt and Ursa, and his reappearance at the con-clusion of the novel foreshadows Mutt's appearance. However, before this occurs we get a long back-and-forth conversation between Ursa and a drunken male in the audience. The discussion involves singing and singers, but the man's con-versation comes down to a "nasty" sexual proposition: "'I bet you got some good pussy. . . . Tell me if you ain't got some good pussy. . . . I know you got some good pussy,' he said as if he were giving a verdict" (71). Ursa does not expect this and does not initially respond, but at some point she states that what he said did not make her mad, and she tells him to take it easy. Throughout the novel, Black women, especially Ursa, are reduced to the derogatory signifier of female genita-lia, pussy. Pussy becomes a consumable commodity. Although disturbing, there is some psychological and social acceptance on Ursa's part that this is the way too many Black men feel about Black women. Singing the blues, where the issue of sexuality would be addressed, causes the Black female singer to become an object of sexual desire. For some men, when the blues singer opens her mouth, there is the sense that she is opening her legs, especially when there is the sense that she does not have a steady man or husband. This recalls Mutt's anxiety over Ursa singing the blues at Happy's Café because of the manner in which the men look at her; there is the sense that no husband would allow his wife to sing the blues. Jim, with a call-and-response analysis of the blues, sums up Mutt's feelings: "You show your ass to these men and then when they try to get on it, you say Uh-uh, uh-uh" (179). Of course, this analysis is antithetical to Ursa's need and desire to sing the blues; for Ursa, singing the blues is directly related to the memories that have been squeezed into her psyche. Using Houston Baker Jr.'s formulation in *Blues, Ideology, and Afro-American Literature* (1984), Ursa stands as a site of interpretation at the intersection of cultural, historical, and subjective elements. According to Baker: "The [blues] singer's product constitutes a lively scene, a robust matrix, where endless antinomies are mediated and understanding and explanation find conditions of possibility (7). Knowing that Mutt will come to the club, Ursa becomes excited and she sings to him. Mutt wastes little time; he says: "I want you to come back" (183). Ursa's simple reply is "Yes." Back in Mutt's room, we receive the answer to the question of what Ursa's great-grandmother did to Corregidora that made it hard for him to forget her. Ursa gets between Mutt's knees; Mutt relates his surprise: "'You never suck it,' he was saying. 'You never would suck it when I wanted you to. Oh baby you never would suck it. I didn't think you would do this for me'" (184). It finally comes to Ursa that oral sex is what her great-grandmother performed on Old Man Corregidora and during this sex act she bit his penis. *Corregidora* concludes with Ursa making connections with her most significant memories and wondering:

> I didn't know how much was me and how much was Great Gran and Corregidora—like Mama when she had started talking like Great Gran. But was what Corregidora had done to her, to them, any worse than what Mutt had done to me, than what we had done to each other, than what Mama had done to Daddy, or what he had done to her in return, making her walk down the street looking like a whore? (184)

Here we have a conflation of the past and the present as represented by Ursa's memories. A synthesis of Ursa's memories leads to some redemption between her and Mutt. Moreover, holding true in the fundamental definition of a paradox, the pervasive theme of miscegenation as sexual consumption becomes reversed as Ursa orally consumes Mutt's semen, a descent on the phallus that represents a paradoxical trajectory of pleasure with a looming possibility of pain.

What becomes clear in Gayl Jones' *Corregidora* is that the body is the manifestation of one's ideas and the manifestation of one's memories. Jones emphatically makes this call-and-response point when Ursa remarks that, "they squeezed Corregidora into me, and I sang back in return" (103). This articulation makes it clear that throughout the novel, Jones establishes Ursa's identity as intricately bound to and interwoven with the details of her family's history, a complex horrifying history kept vivid and current through the conscious oral recitation by a great-grandmother, a grandmother, and a mother. Commenting on the novel, Gayl Jones explains:

> The language, the linguistic patterns that run throughout have been with me all along. The history, the past, not so much in terms of personal past but a collective past, is something that was relatively recent. At the time I was writing, I was doing a lot of reading in slave history in South America—Brazil—and I guess my mind was trying to make connection between the difference there and here in North America. . . . One of the things that I was consciously concerned with was the technique from the oral storytelling tradition that could be used in writing. A story is told to someone in the same way when Ursa sings.

She picks someone out to sing to. The book has layers of storytelling. Percep-
tions of time are important in the oral storytelling tradition in the sense that
you can make rapid transitions between one period and the next, sort of direct
transitions. (Roseann Pope Bell 283–285)

The doctor's question—"Is Mr. Corregidora with you?"—resonates that the past
will always be present in Ursa's memories because the truth of slavery resides
in the name. By keeping the slave master's name, Ursa maintains the oral storytelling tradition that keeps the past alive in the present. Furthermore, Jones
constructs a constant transition between the slave master Corregidora and Ursa's
husbands, Mutt Thomas and Tadpole McCormick. Old Man Corregidora is with
Ursa at the physician's office simply because Mutt Thomas is not there, because
of his violent action that causes Ursa to be barren. Tadpole becomes a surrogate
Corregidora; yet Old Man Corregidora comes between all of Ursa's relationships
with Black men. Mutt Thomas would have been with Ursa Corregidora if this
accident had not happened, but they would not be at this doctor's office. However early in the novel, neither Mutt Thomas nor Tadpole McCormick could
ever be totally with Ursa Corregidora because memories of Old Man Corregidora
are so deeply embedded in Ursa's psyche. Their presence (Mutt's and Tadpole's)
with Ursa was always negated by the past embedded in Ursa. Like her great-
grandmother and her grandmother, Ursa symbolically represents one of Old Man
Corregidora's women, but Ursa has the potential to transform herself by singing
the blues, making her body a speakerly text of multiple discourses. Ursa's subjectivity has always been at the crossroads of traumatic and competing discourses.
Even without a womb, Ursa becomes a creative repository, or to use Mae G. Henderson's trope, the "*womblike matrix* in which soundlessness can be trans-formed
into utterance, unity into diversity, formlessness into form, chaos into art, silence
into tongues, and glossolalia into heteroglossia" (36; emphasis added). Singing
the blues becomes Ursa's life-sustaining strategy as she continues to deal with
the loss of making generations as well as an attempt to reclaim her sexuality and
subjectivity in a society where the marginalization of Black women remains a
disturbing yet fundamental aspect of America's racial and class hegemony. Ursa's
tragic "fall" from the Corregidora matrilineal line leads to a restructuring of the
past. The break with the doctor's question and Ursa's response reside in the final
scene of reconciliation between Ursa and Mutt. Perhaps Ursa can be with Mutt if
she can channel those memories into narratives that do not reduce Black women
to sole victims of sexual violence. A larger point is that racial hegemony appears
as a particularly disturbing aspect etched in North, Central, and South American
history, an indelible and brutal legacy. Through singing the blues, Ursa can construct her own master narratives in manners that do not reinscribe and reinforce
the dominant male hegemony where a Black woman's freedom is often viewed in
sexual terms, even when it's viewed through the prism of economic freedom. Bernette Golden, commenting on the novel, praises Jones for having "opened the

emotional baggage, locked and sealed, that Black women carry" (82). With audacious clarity, Gayl Jones has given us a novel that stands as one of the innovative
renditions of the modern-day slave narrative. Albert Murray, another blues novelist, succinctly sums up the innovative nature of this novel, which remarkably
Gayl Jones published at the age of 26:

> Once the writer accepts the obligation which comes with knowledge of the
> chaos which underlies all human life, he [or she] must also accept another. He
> [She] must presume to go beyond established categories. As with the self-elected
> dragon slayer who would save his [or her] fellow citizen, he [or she] must choose
> his [or her] weapons and proceed as a one-man [or one-woman] expeditionary
> force into the unsafe territory of the outlying regions. (225)[16]

By positioning the European/American site of interracial conflict and its enduring legacy in Brazil, Jones allows us to comprehend the national and international
consequences of white supremacy, nativism, xenophobia, and the consequences
of the relentless exploitation of Black females who were forced to reproduce children who became commodities for physical and sexual consumption.[17] Some
revisionist scholars would propose that the evils that white people have subjected Black people to during the enslavement period and beyond were marginal
at best. Jones not only dispels that incongruous notion, but she crushes that idea
into the dust with an explosive novel that lingers in the mind. Considering what
Jones has given us, perhaps there is no match for the evil that Black people in the
Americas have been subjected to by white people, especially white males. Articulating her desire for a broader literary worldview rooted in folklore, Gayl Jones in
an interview with Charles Rowell, says she would "like to be able to deal with the
whole American continent in my fiction—the whole Americas—and to write
imaginatively of blacks anywhere/everywhere" (Rowell 40). Accordingly, like
John Oliver Killens, Toni Morrison, Michael Harper, Gloria Naylor, John Edgar
Wideman, and Octavia Butler, Gayl Jones positions herself as writer who is willing to expand and explode the traditional boundaries established and maintained
by too many African American writers. As a modern-day dragon slayer, Jones,
through a meditative blues narrative structure, exposes how slavery's horrific past
continues to impact the psychological lives of Black people in the Americas by
giving us Ursa Corregidora's personal perspective on her maternal family's tragic
journey to regeneration and redemption. Like many Black individuals impacted
by the horrors of slavery's past, Ursa Corregidora represents a survivor who carries the deep scars of white people's sadistic sexual violence during slavery. In
Gayl Jones' *Corregidora*, the family story truly shapes each and every generation
as healing and redemption become possible as Ursa Corregidora continues to sing
the blues with the love and emotional support of her husband, Mutt Thomas.

chapter 5

Moving Past the Present

Racialized Sexual Violence and Miscegenous Consumption in Octavia Butler's *Kindred*

> So it appears that the subjection of blacks was the basis of both individual and collective security. This anxiety about impending dissolution and engulfment found expression in an organization of space that arranged, separated, and isolated bodies to forestall this feared and anticipated intrusion. Bound by the fetters of sentiment, held captive by the vestiges of the past, and cast into a legal condition of subjection—these features limn the circumstances of an anomalous misbegotten, and burdened subject no longer enslaved, but not yet free.
>
> Saidiya V. Hartman, *Scenes of Subjection: Terror, Slavery, and Self-Making in Nineteenth-Century America*

Octavia Butler's *Kindred* (1979) is haunted by history, family lineage, and a specter that involves both. However, it would be accurate to say that *Kindred* is haunted by the history and memory of nonconsensual miscegenation, specifically, the pervasive rape of Black women by white slave masters. Like Gayl Jones' *Corregidora*, Octavia Butler's *Kindred* takes us into uncharted literary territory as Butler traces the intense psychological, physical, and cultural challenges of Edana (Dana) Franklin, a 20th-century African American woman. Edana is periodically transported back to the antebellum South in order to ensure her own existence by repeatedly protecting a distant white-male relative, her slave-owning great-grandfather, Rufus Weylin. Butler depicts myriad abuses of slavery—the backbreaking field work, persistent verbal abuse, and whippings—yet the primary themes that emerge are the dramatization of the horrors of miscegenation as sexual consumption, which has lost its reality for many individuals, including Dana and her white husband, Kevin, and the ways in which the development of white-supremacist attitudes and behavior are products of social conditioning. In a general sense, Butler connects her surreal novel to Frederick Douglass' *Narrative of the Life of Frederick Douglass, an American Slave Written by Himself* (1845), because Douglass describes his life as a slave and the arduous journey towards subjectivity and freedom. Douglass vividly relates the psychological and physical violence that slaves were routinely subjected to: neglect, abuse, loneliness, and relentless work defined their lives on the slave plantation. On the other hand, Harriet Jacobs' *Incidents in the Life of a Slave Girl* (1861), with a more concentrated emphasis on gender, describes the relentless sexual abuse that most Black females were subjected to by their white slave masters. These slave narratives represent the evidence of the slavery experience and they help to provide the judgment on the recognizable story of white men raping Black women, and narratives of homosexual rape.[1] The significant number of light-skinned Black individuals speaks to the wholesale rape of Black females by white males.

Butler's story line in *Kindred* is straightforward yet complex in its content and narrative structure. In June 1976, Dana Franklin, an African American woman, while celebrating her 26th birthday with her white husband, is telekinetically and psychokinetically transported from their new home in southern California to the antebellum South, in Maryland. These repeated journeys into slavery's past are connected to the life-threatening experiences of her great-grandfather Rufus Weylin, a white slave master's son; every time Rufus is in mortal danger, Dana is transported to the South to save his life. Equally significant, the problem for Dana is that she becomes just another slave on the Weylin plantation during her time there, until those times when her life is in danger and then she returns to her present life in California. During these journeys, Dana understands that Rufus is a white relative who fathers the child named Hagar with the Black slave Alice Greenwood. Hagar initiates Dana's family line. Essentially, Dana repeatedly saves Rufus' life so that she will exist but also encounters the physical and psychological violence of being a slave on a plantation. During Dana's trips to the past, only a few minutes or hours go by in 1976; yet these short time spans can equal months in the alternate time of the antebellum South. Butler's point in this time span reveals that any impact that Dana seeks to have on Rufus is negated by years of absence. On one occasion Dana's husband is also transported back into the past for a period of five years; Kevin's involvement in the lives of slaves makes the antebellum South appear as cruel and unjust to him as it does to Dana. Dana's final return to the South on July 4, 1976, reveals Alice's suicide as a result of Rufus' threat to sell their children (he makes the threat to force Alice to stay with him). Also, Rufus articulates his desire to rape Dana; this places Dana and Rufus in danger. In defense, Dana stabs Rufus as he attacks her; this mutual danger causes Dana to be transported back to the present with the loss of an arm, as Rufus clings to her. Dana and Kevin become permanently united in the present; yet they will always retain the knowledge of the past.

Dana's present life of miscegenation signifies on the miscegenation during the enslavement period. Nonconsensual miscegenation, during the enslavement period and beyond, represents one of the most degrading experiences for Black women. As bell hooks convincingly argues in *Ain't I a Woman: Black Women and Feminism* (1981), sexual violence was fundamental to the psychological and physical abuse that many Black women experienced:

> It was only in relationship to the black female slave that the white slaver could exercise freely absolute power, for he could brutalize and explore her without fear of harmful retaliation. Black female slaves moving freely about the decks were a ready target for any white male who might choose to physically abuse and torment them. Initially every slave on board the ship was branded with a hot iron. A cat-o'-nine-tails was used by the slavers to lash those Africans that cried out in pain or resisted the torture. Women were lashed severely for crying. They were stripped of their clothing and beaten on all parts of their body. . . . The nakedness of the African female served as a constant reminder of her sexual vulnerability. Rape was a common method of torture slavers used to subdue recalcitrant black women. The threat of rape or other physical brutalization inspired terror in the psyches of displaced African females. (18)

Rape and brutalization continued in the slave markets and of course on the slave plantations, as the sexual violence on the slave ships served as an indoctrination that would transform the African, free human, into a slave. Pregnant Black women on the slave ships were ridiculed, mocked, and treated contemptuously by the white-male crew. Indeed, the Black women who arrived pregnant represented the continuous sexual violence that they and many generations of their miscegenous children would experience. Once on the slave plantation, Black women were vulnerable to white slave masters, white and Black overseers, and the white-male relatives of the owner of the plantation. African women received the focus of the brutal treatment not only because they could be victimized through forced sexual relations, but also because they were needed as cooks, wet nurses, and housekeepers. *Kindred* functions as more than the repository of the horrors of slavery; Butler reenacts sexual violation and thus figures the persistent problems common to survivors of trauma. Her focus constitutes a challenge to Alice and Dana, who endure sexual violence or its threat while they were enslaved directly, and especially to Dana, who confronts a past she cannot forget. Indeed, it is Dana's forgetting that subjects her to traumatic return; confrontation requires a concentrated attempt at remembering.

Butler lays the foundation for the tensions in Dana Franklin's returns to the Weylin southern plantation by illustrating the family tensions in Dana's miscegenous relationship with Kevin before and during the marriage. In both Dana's and Kevin's families there are individuals who are opposed to interracial marriages. Dana registers surprise at Kevin's marriage proposal. Dana states: "As I spoke, it occurred to me that one of the reasons his proposal surprised me was that we had never talked much about our families, about how his would react to me and mine to him."[2] Set during the mid 1970s, this period reflects the Black Nationalist consciousness, where Black pride and an enduring love and respect of one's people were fundamental aspects of the culture. Accordingly, any Black person who dated or married a white individual was viewed as a self-hating individual and a traitor to the Black race, especially a Black woman because of the history of sexual violence. Most Black men who dated or married white women did not seem to receive the same level of animosity and scrutiny that most Black women received. Perhaps the reason for this gender imbalance resides in the fact that most of the sexual violence during the enslavement period that was documented in the slave narratives involves white males assaulting Black females. Dana informs Kevin, "But I'm afraid my aunt and uncle won't love you" (110). When Dana does inform her aunt and uncle of her plans to marry Kevin, she encounters some problematic acceptance and hostile rejection. From Dana, Kevin learns, "I think my aunt accepts the idea of my marrying you because any children we have will be light. Lighter than I am, anyway. She always said I was a little too 'highly visible'" (111). Dana's aunt's view of this marriage reflects a preference-by-pigmentocracy philosophy, where light-skinned individuals are viewed as superior to dark-skinned individuals. More disturbing, as noted in Gayl Jones' *Corregidora*, is the fact that placing superior value on light-skinned Black individuals seems to validate the sexual violence that many Black women experienced during the enslavement period that produced these light-skinned individuals. Dana further informs Kevin that, "She doesn't care much for white people, but she prefers light-skinned blacks" (111). On the other hand, Dana's uncle is adamantly opposed to Dana's marriage:

> He . . . well, he's my mother's oldest brother, and he was like a father to me even before my mother died because my father died when I was a baby. Now . . . it's as though I've rejected him. Or at least that the way he feels. It bothered me. He was more hurt than mad. Honestly hurt. I had to get away from him. . . . He wants me to marry someone like him—someone who looks like him. A black man. (111)

Dana's uncle's hurt is understandable, considering what is known about slavery and how white slave masters raped and molested Black women. His hurt is specific in terms of the personal rejection that he feels as well as the perception of Dana's rejection of Black people's journey from slavery to freedom. With Dana's mother dead and her father having died when she was a baby, Dana's aunt and uncle become her parents. Like many slave narratives, Dana's life reflects natal alienation, a disconnection between the child and his or her parents. The child may grow up to experience some cultural alienation based on the abandonment through death, divorce, or separation. Hence, to some of her family members, Dana's marriage to Kevin represents a personal and a collective betrayal. Notably absent here is any discussion of Kevin's family (his parents are dead, killed in an automobile accident) and their reactions to his desire to marry a Black woman; this narrative absence suggests a host of possibilities, including the concept that there would be white individuals who would understand why Kevin would want to have sexual relations with Dana but would not understand why he would want to marry her. Buz, a disheveled worker at the plant where Dana and Kevin work, makes the crude miscegenous comment, "Chocolate and vanilla porn!" (56) when he passes by them. There is the belief that white-male subjectivity is based on having sexual relations with a Black female, but this sexual contact is outside of any marital relationship.

Butler makes the point of foreshadowing Dana's excursions to the antebellum South by characterizing her present relationship with Kevin in terms of slavery's discourse. Dana recalls the employment agency where she worked as "a casual labor agency—we called it a slave market" (52). However, as Dana relates, the agency was the antithesis of a plantation because the people running the place did not care if individuals showed up for work that they offered. The desperate individuals included winos, poor women with children attempting to supplement their welfare checks, teenagers looking for their first jobs, and old people who got fired too often. Those who found no work were reduced to selling their blood at one of the storefronts near the agency. Dana's revelation that she sold her blood once foreshadows the bloodletting that she experiences when she travels into the past on the Weylin plantation. Like work on a slave plantation, the agency sent people to do almost any and everything imaginable, such as cleaning toilets, stuffing newspapers, taking inventory, washing dishes, and sweeping floors. Upon meeting Kevin for the first time, Dana recalls him asking her: "Why do you go around looking like a zombie all the time" (53). As a writer, Dana spends a lot of time writing and goes to work to do the mindless tasks. Butler's use of the word "zombie" significantly connects to slavery in the sense that Black people were required to do mainly what they were told and never ask any questions. The sexual aspect of this is that white slave masters viewed Black females as sexual zombies, individuals were expected to have sexual relations without protest, and if they did protest they would be beaten and raped.

The theme of miscegenation as sexual consumption is symbolically illustrated in Dana Franklin's relationship with Rufus Weylin. Indeed Butler's phrase that sums up the Southern slave culture of miscegenation is "white men preying on black women" (119). Like Gayl Jones' *Corregidora*, Octavia Butler's *Kindred* demonstrates how sex is used as a weapon. Dana's first journey to the antebellum

South begins in 1976, the year of the United States' Bicentennial, a celebration of American freedom and independence (of course Black people were slaves when America was founded). Like Avatara "Avey" Johnson in Paule Marshall's *Praisesong for the Widow* (1983), who becomes dizzy and nauseous on her Caribbean cruise,[3] Dana Franklin becomes nauseous and dizzy before she is transported back to the South. Dana soon discovers that she is near a riverbank and then hears the cries of a drowning white child. After administering artificial respiration, she is attacked by the boy's mother, who believes she was trying to kill him. When Rufus' father points a gun at Dana, she once again feels illness and faints; Dana immediately finds herself back at home in Los Angeles, yet she is covered with the mud of the riverbank. Of course, Dana's husband is bewildered and awestruck by his wife's disappearance and return (wet and covered in mud) as he tries to make sense of this bizarre phenomenon. This episodic pattern continues throughout the novel as the time Dana spends in the South on the Weylin plantation dramatically increases. However, it is the relationship between Dana and Rufus that continues to suggest the theme of miscegenation as sexual consumption. As Rufus grows into manhood, Dana, throughout the time-travel episodes, maintains her age as she attempts to influence him with regard to his vile racist and sexist perspectives on Black people. Like his stern father and most white-male slaveholders, Rufus considers all Black people to be property; they are there to serve the needs and desires of white people. By continuously saving Rufus' life (as a child and as an adult), Dana becomes a surrogate mother (mammy) figure and a trusted confidant to this white male. Here Butler illustrates a fundamental paradox of slave life in America: white slave masters are extremely dependent on Black people for labor, but they routinely abuse, rape, and torture their slaves, making their lives absolutely miserable as whites enjoy the social and economic benefits. Black labor creates tremendous wealth and privileges for slave-owning whites, and Black women working in the slave master's house provided enormous social and sexual benefits. Tess, a slave on the Weylin plantation who is passed from Tom Weylin to his overseer, Edwards, sums up the life of a Black female slave: "You do everything they tell you . . . and they still treat you like a old dog. Go here, open your legs, go there, bust your back. What they care! I ain't s'pose to have no feeling" (182). By bringing Black women to work in the house, this provided white slave masters opportunities to develop relationships that would lead to these women later being raped or sexually molested. Discussing the status of the slave woman, Harriet Jacobs states: "She is not allowed to have any pride of character. It is deemed a crime in her to wish to be virtuous" (29). Similar to many cases of sexual violence, the Black female victim becomes the criminal as she is forced to drink from the cup of sin, shame, and sorrow.

The symbolic miscegenous bonding during Dana's spontaneous journeys into the past allows the reader to come to terms with the fact that slavery's past influences the racial present; the bonding between Dana and Rufus foreshadows the sexual violence that ensues. Dana's life-saving actions toward Rufus Weylin begin the formation of an emotional bond that will lead to Rufus' obsession with having Dana stay on his plantation. As Dana states: "Rufus's fear of death calls me to him, and my own fear of death sends me home" (50). On the second trip to the South, Dana has to save Rufus when he plays with fire and sets the draperies ablaze. Here they have an extended conversation where Dana learns some general and specific information about slavery. She learns that Rufus' father is Tom Weylin and that he uses a whip on Rufus, the same "kind he whips niggers and horses with" (26). The name "Weylin" triggers Dana's memory; she asks Rufus about a slave girl named Alice. Although she cannot recall the slave girl's last name, Dana states: "The memory was coming back to me in fragments" (27). Typical to most slaves, the last name is always a problem; in most cases a slave was given the last name of his or her master. The buying and selling of slaves would result in a constant change in the last name. As seen in Gayl Jones' *Corregidora*, naming of slaves became problematic when a slave master raped a Black female slave and then raped the female's daughter, and then raped the daughter of the Black female's daughter. Paradoxically, Rufus states, "Alice is my friend" (27). Rufus also states: "She's no slave either. . . . She's free, born free like her mother" (28). Ironically, the status of any Black person, either free or a slave, was always tenuous. As the novel states: "Blacks were assumed to be slaves unless they could prove they were free—unless they had their free papers. Paperless blacks were fair game for any white" (34). Recalling the common African American tradition—the family Bible contains the genealogy—Dana begins to solve the puzzle of her existence on the Weylin plantation: "Grandmother Hagar. Hagar Weylin born in 1831. Hers was the first name listed. And she had given her parents' name as Rufus Weylin and Alice Green-something Weylin" (28). However, some rather strange or perhaps naïve questions come to Dana's mind as she contemplates her ancestors:

> Alice Greenwood. How would she marry this boy? Or would it be marriage? And why hadn't someone in my family mentioned that Rufus Weylin was white? If they knew. Probably, they didn't. Hagar Weylin Blake had died in 1880, long before the time of any member of my family that I had known. No doubt most information about her life had died with her. At least it had died before it filtered down to me. There was only the Bible left. (28)

Here Dana's lack of knowledge of the realities of American slavery becomes evident. In slavery, naming does not immediately equate with marriage, and Dana seems to be unaware of the extent that consensual and nonconsensual miscegenation were quite pervasive in colonial times as well as during the enslavement period. Despite her own amorous relationship with a white man, Dana seems to be awestruck that one of her Black female relatives could have a relationship with a white man or that this relationship was coercive. Dana's questions also raise the question: Did Dana's uncle and aunt know that Rufus Weylin was a white slave master and how he came to father Alice's children? Dana's lack of specific knowledge of how Rufus connects to her family is part of the silence associated with trauma. As Judith Lewis Herman reminds us, there is a dialectical aspect of trauma that causes the fragmentation of memories associated with traumatic events. Butler suggests the importance of the family story as a historical compass and its ability to keep family members anchored. Butler conveys that those who are unaware of their family's story are subject to illusion, confusion, collusion, and self-deception in terms of race. Through another series of silent contemplations, Dana, still somewhat confused, comes to understand her present situation here in slavery's past:

> I looked at the boy who would be Hagar's father. There was nothing to him that reminded me of any of my relatives. Looking at him confused me. But he had to be the one. There had to be some kind of reason for the link he and I seemed to have. Not that I really thought a blood relationship could explain the way I had been twice drawn to him. It wouldn't. But then, neither would anything else. What we had was something new, something that didn't even have a name. Some matching strangeness in us that may or may not have come from our being related. Still, now I had a special reason for being glad I had been able to save him. And all . . . after all what would have happened to me, to my mother's family, if I hadn't saved him? (29)

Ensuring her survival in the present and her family's legacy connects Dana to keeping Rufus alive and harmless. Butler gives us one of the most disturbing and paradoxical paradigms of the slave system: a modern-day Black female married to a white male must go back to the past to make sure the legacy of sexual violence comes to fruition so that her maternal family will exist, and so that she can have the opportunity to marry a white male, an individual who initially has some romantic perspective of life during the 19th century. Simply put, Dana must make sure that Alice Greenwood, her female ancestor, is raped by a brutal white slave master.

During the second journey to save Rufus, Dana experiences firsthand the racial and sexual violence of slavery. Terrified and in a strange place, and desperate to find Alice's mother, Dana discovers the Greenwood cabin, but eight white men on horseback are looking for slaves without passes. When Dana arrives at the cabin, white men are there as well and they give Dana her first experience of slavery's violence. After breaking down the cabin door and throwing a man, a woman, and a little girl outside, the terrorizing violence begins when they discover that the Black man has no pass. Hidden in the bushes, Dana watches the horrible whipping:

> The man was forced to hug the tree, and his hands were tied to prevent him from letting go. The man was naked, apparently dragged from bed. I looked at

the woman who still stood back beside the cabin and saw that she had managed to wrap herself in something. A blanket, perhaps. As I noticed it one of the whites tore it from her. She said something in a voice so soft that all I caught was her tone of protest. . . . By now, the man had been securely tied to the tree. One of the whites went to his horse to get what proved to be a whip. . . . I could literally smell his sweat, hear every ragged breath, every cry, every cut of the whip. I could see his body jerking, convulsing, straining against the rope as his screaming went on and on. My stomach heaved, and I had to force myself to stay where I was and keep quiet. Why didn't they stop! (36)

Whipping of a Black male slave represents emasculation and a symbolic rape of the individual. As an extension of the white man's phallus, the cowhide whip penetrates Black flesh. Here, Dana, as a traumatized voyeur, views a whipping that has a sexual component. Similar to Richard Wright's poem "Between the World and Me," the Black man and the tree become one as both victims are assaulted. Also, in Douglass' narrative he relates watching his Aunt Hester being sadistically whipped by her white master; Douglass' account of Captain Anthony whipping his Aunt Hester conveys the synthesis of physical and sexual violence:

Before he commenced whipping Aunt Hester, he took her into the kitchen, and stripped her from neck to waist, leaving her neck, shoulders, and back, entirely naked. He then told her to cross her hands, calling her at the same time a d——d b——h. After crossing her hands, he tied them with a strong rope, and led her to a stool under a large hook in the joist, put in for the purpose. He made her get upon the stool, and tied her hands to the hook. She now stood fair for his infernal purpose. Her arms were stretched up at their full length, so that she stood upon the ends of her toes. He then said to her, "Now, you d——d b——h, I'll learn you to disobey my orders!" and after rolling up his sleeves, he commenced to lay on the heavy cowskin, and soon the warm, red blood was (amid heart-rending shrieks from her, and horrid oaths from him) dripping to the floor. I was so terrified and horror-stricken at the sight, that I hid myself in a closet, and dared not venture out till long after the bloody transaction was over. I expected it would be my turn next. It was all new to me. I had never seen any thing like it before.[4]

For Douglass, this represents a primal scene that formulates a triangle of sexual desire, especially when Douglass expects that he will encounter the same fate. Like Aunt Hester, Dana's account of the Black man being viciously whipped and raped of his dignity (Butler's discourse suggests that the man and woman might have been having sexual relations when the white men broke the door down), along with the Black women's clothing ripped off, reveals the duality of this sexual violence. Alice's mother is further humiliated when one of the whites arrogantly states: "What do you think you've got that we haven't seen before?"

Other white men chime in with their "raucous laughter" and "obscenities, more laughter" (36). These statements insinuate that the rape of Black women or other sexual violations against them were common occurrences with these white men. Dana provides Kevin with a description of these men: "Patrollers made sure that slaves were where they were supposed to be at night, and they punished those who weren't. They chased down runaways—for a fee. And sometimes they just raised hell, had a little fun terrorizing people who weren't allowed to fight back" (45–46).[5] Here, among other sadistic acts, "fun" means whipping slaves and raping slaves. As a slave patrol, these white men were routinely in contact with Black slaves who were attempting to escape or visit other plantations with or without passes. This contact, with its enormous sense of power, could lead to these white males raping or sexually attacking Black females. Whipping Black males and sexually assaulting Black females were as common as day following night. Both the man and the woman are punched in the face during this assault. For Dana, this physical violence has a surreal component that makes her recall aspects of her modern-day life in suburban Los Angeles:

> I had seen people beaten on television and in the movies. I had seen the too-red blood substitute streaked across their backs and heard their well-rehearsed screams. But I hadn't lain nearby and smelled their sweat or heard them pleading and praying, shamed before their families and themselves. I was probably less prepared for the reality than the child crying not far from me. In fact, she and I were reacting very much alike. My face too wet with tears. And my mind was darting from one thought to another, trying to tune out the whipping. (36)

While the white men are half-dragging the Black man behind them, one remains to question the woman and ends his interrogation by punching her in the face. Although it is unstated, this Black man and woman's decision to establish some sexual autonomy outside of the plantation represents an affront to white-male supremacy. Since Alice's mother is free, her children are also free; this represents an unprofitable aspect for the system of slavery. Beyond a clear understanding of the violently sadistic nature of these patrols, it is here that Dana encounters this little girl; the girl's name is Alice. It is also at the Greenwood cabin that Dana experiences her first physical encounter with a white slave catcher. Once outside to retrieve a blanket, Dana encounters the white man who punched Alice's mother. Dana questions him and he slaps her in the face while holding her with his other hand. Immediately he views Dana as property to be sold and consumed: "Her runaway sister. I wonder what you're worth" (41). Digging her hands into his arm and ripping his flesh from elbow to wrist, Dana and this white man begin to fight. At some point, the white man announces his sexual intentions: "I guess you do as well as your sister," he states. "I came back for her, but you're just like her" (42). His desire represents a triple punishment: the Black woman is to be punished because he did not like her previous response and the Black man is punished by having his woman raped after he had sexual relations with her. Of course, Alice would be punished by viewing or hearing her mother being beaten and raped; the mother with her daughter present would have to make a hard decision about acquiescing or resisting. Indeed, this white man's desire is to replace the Black phallus with the white phallus. Not surprisingly, this white man came back to rape Alice's mother and perhaps rape Alice as well, but now he intends to rape Dana. If he does not intend to rape the little girl, the question arises concerning the girl watching her mother being raped and hearing her screams. Early, Alice's mother and her daughter refuse to watch the Black man being whipped, but they hear his screams and his pleas for them to stop. While the trauma to the mother and daughter is not visual, the trauma resides at the auditory level; nightmares can still ensue. Turning his sadistic attention to the Black woman whom he believes is Alice's mother's sister, he rips Dana's blouse open and tears loose her bra. The exposure of Dana's breasts perhaps excited him in the same manner that whipping the naked Black man excited him. It is also interesting to note that this white man returns alone; it appears that he did not want to share the raping of Alice's mother with the other white males. We wonder if the smell of the whipped Black-man flesh has excited this man, or perhaps it was the smell of sexual relations between the Black man and the woman that has excited his desire. As noted in my analysis of Wright's poem, sexual relations at lynchings were not uncommon, and the smell of burning Black flesh also created an appetite for those who watched or participated. With her modern-day sensibilities and self-respect, Dana decides to fight and grabs a heavy stick and brings it down on the white man's head; he falls on top of her, unconscious. Shortly afterward, a bruised Dana loses consciousness and returns to the present, but the dead or badly beaten white man in front of Alice's mother's cabin will bring some violent retribution. Butler's synthesizing of the past with the present is evident in Dana's thinking that the patroller is calling her name, until she realizes that it is Kevin who is calling her. Dana notes: "Kevin lay half on top of me, holding me, smearing himself with my blood and his own. I could see where I had scratched his face—so near the eye" (43–44). Despite the obvious violent sexual aspects to this description, Butler suggests that Dana is beginning to lose her sense of time and place. Amazingly, Kevin informs Dana that the hours that she spent in the South (Maryland, somewhere on the Eastern Shore), and 3,000 miles away in the past, only convert to three minutes in the present. Kevin also fervently asks Dana if the white patroller raped her. Kevin's question reveals that he is not naïve to the sexual violence that many Black women experienced during enslavement. Kevin realizes that sexual violence will mainly occur by the hands of other white males like him; this allows us to speculate as to whether any of Kevin's male ancestors were involved in the rape of Black women during slavery. Attempting to address Kevin's fears, Dana tells him: "Oh, they won't kill me. Not unless I'm silly enough to resist the other things they'd rather do—like raping me, throwing me into jail as a runaway, and then selling me to the highest bidder when they see that my owner isn't coming to claim" (48). Dana's response reflects the fundamental paradox of her existence in the past, in that she is alone and she has no master. Not having a white slave master makes Dana especially vulnerable to sexual violence and being sold by white-male slave traders. Ironically, Dana's status could lead to more sexual violence than a slave who had a master would suffer, because the slave who was owned would have the master's protection. However, this protection means that the Black female was his property and her body was his to use and consume in whatever manner he decided. Being free meant you were vulnerable to white males and their sexual desires. Dana and Kevin's conversation, upon Dana's return from her second trip, highlights the complex reality of Dana going back to the past with her knowledge of the present. In response to Kevin's fears about Dana committing suicide, she states:

> Oh but I'm talking about suicide, Kevin—suicide or worse. For instance, I would have used your knife against that patroller last night if I'd had it. I would have killed him. That would have ended the immediate danger to me and I probably wouldn't have come home. But if that patroller's friends had caught me, they would probably have killed me. And if they hadn't caught me, they would probably have gone after Alice's mother. They . . . they may have anyway. So either I would have died, or I would have caused another innocent person to die. (51)

Here Dana reflects on the very dangerous reality of her existence in the past; every action that she engages in affects her and the other Black people, especially her ancestors. Nevertheless, the brief bond formed between Dana and Alice will represent the base of a miscegenous triangle of sexual desire where Rufus is at the apex.

As readers we are forced to contemplate Dana's relationship with Kevin as well as the miscegenous relationships between white slave masters and Black females. Butler suggests that slavery brings to mind questions of present-day racial symbolism and the substance of racial relationships between Blacks and whites. The "something new" that has no name represents the surreal miscegenous surrogate connection that foreshadows incestuous miscegenation, the strange blood connection. In a society so firmly structured by racial division, Dana and Kevin's child (if they would have one) would represent "something new," a child that is based on a phenotype that can be considered neither Black nor white, yet both. Another "something new" is Butler's reconfiguration of the "Middle Passage"; this period of slavery was ripe with the sexual violence of white males against Black females. However, Dana is not transported back to the past to change the past but to ensure her present safety and comfort with Kevin. More important, Dana needs to learn firsthand the physical, social, economic, and psychological impact and consequences of nonconsensual miscegenation, rape. Black women on the slave plantations had little safety or comfort with their white slave masters; they had to be constantly on guard because, generally, Black males could

not protect them and they could not protect themselves without violent retribution in the form of whippings and beatings. Ironically, many white women on
the plantations made matters worse by taking out their psychological frustrations, about their husbands' sexual indiscretions with the Black females on the
female slaves; they would beat them for being raped. White women were generally powerless individuals (white slaves), but they had little compassion for the
plight of Black women. For example, Tom Weylin's wife, Margaret, is irate that
Dana sleeps in Kevin's room in the Weylin household but is silent about her
husband's sexual indiscretions with his Black female slaves. On one occasion
after she views Dana coming out of Kevin's room, Margaret screams at Dana:
"You filthy black whore!" And then she states: "This is a Christian house!" At
some point, Kevin notices: "Hell, I saw three little kids playing in the dirt back
there who look more like Weylin than Rufus does. Margaret's had a lot of practice at not noticing" (85). Dana also confirms the rampant miscegenation on
Weylin's plantation and the consequences:

> I knew which children he meant. They had different mothers, but there was a
> definite family resemblance between them. I'd seen Margaret Weylin slap one of
> them hard across the face. The child had done nothing more than toddle into
> her path. If she was willing to punish a child for her husband's sins, would she be
> any less willing to punish me if me if she knew that I was where she wanted to
> be with Kevin? I tried not to think about it. (85)

Here we see that Black women slaves and their children would be victims
of physical violence by the wife of the white slave master. In Harriet Jacobs'
slave narrative, Jacobs focuses on the role of the white wife on the slave plantation. Slave masters who have sexual relations with their Black female slaves
create a climate of fear and jealousy. On this point, Jacobs states: "Southern
women often marry a man knowing that he is the father of many little slaves.
They do not trouble themselves about it. They regard such children as property,
as marketable as the pigs on the plantation and it is seldom that they do not
make them aware of this by passing them into the slave trader's hands as soon
as possible, and thus getting them out of their sight" (33). We also see that Tom
Weylin has established a pattern of sexual behavior for his son Rufus to emu-
late. Tom Weylin consumes Black female genitalia, so his son will also consume
Black female genitalia. Logically, it stands to reason that violence against these
children would escalate or that Margaret would use her influence to have them
sold, because they would be a daily reminder of her husband's desire for Black
female genitalia.

Dana Franklin's third trip to the Weylin plantation to save Rufus occurs
when he falls from a tree while playing with the family slave, Nigel, and breaks
his leg. This journey is significant because Kevin joins her, although Dana
attempts to push him away. Fortunately, Dana and Kevin did some research at

the library for forgeable "free papers" and packed a satchel of essentials before Dana's sickening dizziness occurs. It should be noted that, with the experience of Kevin being transported back to the past, Dana realizes the danger that it holds for everyone around her:

> I was still afraid to leave the house, walking or driving. Driving, I could easily kill myself, and the car could kill other people if Rufus called me from it at the wrong time. Walking, I could get dizzy and fall while crossing the street. Or I could fall on the sidewalk and attract attention. Someone could come to help me—a cop, anyone. Then I could be guilty of taking someone else back with me and stranding them. (116)

On this trip Butler synthesizes the past and the present by having Kevin assume the role of a white slave master (with Dana his slave), and by illustrating the symbolic miscegenation between Rufus and Dana.[6] Additionally, the symbolic miscegenation between Rufus and Dana signifies the ensuing nonconsensual miscegenation between Rufus and Alice. Paradoxically, Kevin's presence in the past would protect Dana from sexual violence because she would be his property. Being a free Black woman during this time was an extremely precarious status— the expectations of whites were that most Black people were enslaved in service to whites. Rufus, who is able to see Dana in the present, is rightly puzzled by Kevin and Dana's relationship when they confide in him that they are from the future. Rufus arrogantly and contemptuously states: "Niggers can't marry white people!" (60). The paradox of Rufus' crude statement of miscegenation is that white people are not forbidden to rape or molest "niggers." Anti-miscegenation laws are quite common during these times, but they did little or nothing to prevent Black female slaves from being raped by their white slave masters. Dana's response to Rufus is designed to educate on race and language: "Where we come from," she states, "it's vulgar and insulting for whites to call blacks niggers. Also, where we come from, whites and blacks can marry" (61). Knowing that Rufus will have a relationship with her ancestor Alice, Dana is attempting to make Rufus more sensitive to how he thinks about and treats Black people when he becomes the slave master of the Weylin plantation. Indeed, Dana acknowledges the paradoxical role she plays with Rufus and her psychological intent:

> The boy was literally growing up as I watched—growing up because I watched and because I helped to keep him safe. I was the worst possible guardian for him—a black to watch over him in a society that considered blacks subhuman, a woman to watch over him in a society that considered women perennial children. I would have all I could do to look after myself. But I would help him as best I could. And I would try to keep friendship with him, maybe plant a few ideas in his mind that would help both me and the people who would be his slaves in the years to come. I might even be making things easier for Alice. (68)

The double inferiority represents a fundamental reality for a Black female slave, and Dana's status is compounded by her need to somehow make Alice's future sexual life with Rufus easier. Paradox is also fundamental to Butler's narrative structure as Dana highlights the paradox of Black people's relationships with white people. White people desire for Black people to take care of their children, yet believe that their slaves are inferior to them. Obviously, this does not say much for white people's concern for their own children. Moreover, the other profound paradox that is restated is that Dana must plan to help Rufus rape her ancestor so that Dana will exist in the future. Put in different terms: Dana must facilitate the miscegenous consumption of her maternal ancestor, Alice, so that she can enjoy her modern-day miscegenous relationship with Kevin, who plays the role of her slave master while they are in slavery's past. For a Black female to help a racist white-male slave master consume another Black female's genitalia, so that a white male in the future can consume her genitalia, represents a profound paradoxical paradigm of possession and protection. Beyond Dana's intentions, she also registers apprehension concerning the effect slavery will have on her husband, Kevin. In a society where white-male supremacy is the law of the land and where Black females should submit to the law, Dana wonders if Kevin would change:

> But he'd be in another kind of danger. A place like this would endanger him in a way I didn't want to talk to him about. If he was stranded here for years, some part of this place would rub off on him. No large part, I knew. But if he survived here, it would be because he managed to tolerate the life here. He wouldn't have to take part in it, but he would have to keep quiet about it. Free speech and press hadn't done too well in the antebellum South. Kevin wouldn't do too well either. The place, the time would either kill him outright or mark him somehow. I didn't like either possibility. (78)

Implicit in Dana's apprehensions about Kevin is the culture of rampant sexual violence against Black female slaves; Kevin would be expected to go along with or support this culture unless he moved to the North. The problem with this is that Dana needs to be close to Rufus in order to protect him from himself, but without Kevin close by Dana would be unprotected from any sexual violence by white males on the Weylin plantation. Dana feels that miscegenation between white males and Black females could possibly mark Kevin. Perhaps it is here that Dana is beginning to speculate that her relationship with Kevin may be the reason why she is summoned to the past. Another aspect of Kevin joining Dana on this journey is the effect it has on their relationship. The normal sexual relationship that they had in the present becomes problematic while they are on the Weylin plantation. Leaving Kevin's room one morning, Dana reflects on Margaret's hypocrisy: "I knew then that if Margaret got me kicked out, it wouldn't be for doing a thing as normal as sleeping with my master. And somehow, that disturbed me. I felt almost as if I was doing something shameful, happily whoring for my supposed owner. I went away feeling uncomfortable, vaguely ashamed" (97). Again, Butler gives us another paradox of her theme of miscegenation as sexual consumption. The present (legal) miscegenation becomes shameful sexual relations in the past; this is significant because Dana gains a better understanding of the psychological aspects that confront Black female slaves who are victims of Tom Weylin's abuse.

Butler constantly juxtaposes the miscegenation between white slave masters and Black female slaves with sadistic racial violence. Similar to many slave narratives, the rape of Black females goes hand in hand with the sadistic whipping of Black males. Both forms of violence are meant to control those Black individuals who are the direct victims of the violence as well as those who become aware of the rape or view the whipping. Dana relates being called to view a whipping of a Black male who committed the crime of answering back Tom Weylin:

> Weylin ordered the man stripped naked and tied to the trunk of a dead tree. As this was being done—by other slaves—Weylin stood whirling his whip and biting his thin lips. Suddenly, he brought the whip down across the slave's back. The slave's body jerked and strained against its ropes. I watched the whip for a moment wondering whether it was like the one Weylin used on Rufus years before. If it was, I understood completely why Margaret Weylin had taken the boy and fled. The whip was heavy and at least six feet long, and I wouldn't have used it on anything living. It drew blood and screams at every blow. I watched and listened and longed to be away. But Weylin was making an example of the man. He had ordered all of us to watch the beating—all the slaves. . . . The whipping served its purpose as far as I was concerned. It scared me, made me wonder how long it would be before I made a mistake that would give someone reason to whip me. Or had I already made that mistake? (92)

Here there is obviously a sexual element to this public spectacle of torture, represented by having the Black male slave being naked and having the other slaves watch. Weylin's whip functions as an extension of his phallus, which he uses to have sexual relations with the three different Black slave women who bear his light-skinned children whom his wife, Margaret, despises. The blood erupting from the Black man's back during the whipping becomes analogous to the eruptions of semen from Weylin's penis. If the three Black female slaves were raped, then the Black victims screamed during both types of physical brutality. Nevertheless, in both cases there is a white man's penetration of black flesh, and Weylin satisfies his sadistic sexual desires. Psychological and physical scars will remain with these Black individuals years after these physical assaults, and the onlookers will experience psychological trauma that will affect generations. As the novel states: "Slavery was a long slow process of dulling" (183). Dana has her own trauma to pass on to future generations when Tom Weylin discovers that she has been teaching Nigel how to read. The whipping that he gives Dana is analogous to a rape scene. Like a hot iron searing into her black flesh, Dana relates the trauma of tasting the true barbarity of slavery for the first time:

> I screamed, convulsed. Weylin struck again and again, until I couldn't have gotten up at gunpoint. I kept trying to crawl away from the blows, but I didn't have the strength or the coordination to get far. I may have been still screaming or just whimpering. I couldn't tell. All I was really aware of was the pain. I thought Weylin meant to kill me. I thought I would die on the ground there with a mouth full of dirt and blood and a white man cursing and lecturing as he beat me. By then, I almost wanted to die. Anything to stop the pain. (107)

Before Kevin reaches Dana, she repeatedly vomits and passes out. Her worst fears of a whipping have come true, as Butler's description suggests a sexually sadistic component. Even so, Dana returns to the present to heal. Tom Weylin's beating of Dana Franklin is significant in two aspects. First, the beating reveals that teaching slaves to read represents a serious crime because it would give them some subjectivity that could lead to their desire to successfully escape. Second, Tom Weylin takes it upon himself to beat a female slave whom he does not own and the whipping is particularly vicious. Paradoxically, Dana returns to California and Kevin remains in the past, but Kevin will have a difficult time explaining her disappearance. Similar to many of her science-fiction novels, Butler connects the past to the present in Dana's description of her whipping: "My blouse was stuck to my back. It was cut to pieces, really, but the pieces were stuck to me. My back was cut up pretty badly too from what I could feel. I had seen old photographs of the backs of people who had been slaves. I could remember the scars, thick and ugly. Kevin had always told me how smooth my skin was . . ." (113). Although this atrocious whipping is a direct result of Dana teaching a slave to read, the larger issue is Dana learning about her family and how it connects to her present life. Like Sethe in Toni Morrison's *Beloved,* who has a tree growing on her back, Dana's scars will be a constant reminder of the past in the present. However, this experience has a disorienting effect on Dana: "My memory of a field hand being whipped suddenly seemed to have no place here with me at home. . . . I'd gone away for nearly two months and came back yesterday—the same day I left home. Nothing was real" (115, 116). "Home" becomes another paradox in the novel as Dana struggles with the Weylin plantation being her home in the past and the disruption of her home life in Los Angeles makes her psychologically homeless. In both places, Dana makes life-altering decisions. Just as Dana has made certain choices in her present life, she also made certain choices as a slave on the Weylin plantation; both have consequences.

Miscegenation as sexual consumption reaches a fever pitch in Dana's fourth journey to the Weylin plantation, but she discovers that Kevin has gone North. Here Dana is snatched back to the past because Rufus is being killed in a bloody fight with a Black male slave, Isaac Jackson, after Rufus attempts to rape a free Black woman, Isaac's wife, Alice Jackson. Alice is the little girl whom Dana met at the Greenwood cabin. Hence, saving Rufus becomes even more critical for Dana:

> Then it occurred to me that he might be doing just that—killing the only person who might be able to help me find Kevin. Killing my ancestor. What happened here seemed obvious. The girl, her torn dress. If everything was as it seemed, Rufus had earned his beating and more. Maybe he had grown up to be even worse than I had feared. But no matter what he was, I needed him alive—for Kevin's sake and for my own. (118)

Dana begins to reason with Isaac in an attempt to save Rufus; she asks him: "What will they do to you if you kill him?" This question causes Isaac to release Rufus, but he is quite suspicious of Dana and her intentions, because the reality is: "A slave had no rights and certainly no excuse for striking a white man" (121). Isaac and Alice eventually leave Dana with the unconscious Rufus, but before they leave, Alice tell Dana that Rufus: "Got to where he wanted to be more friendly than I did. . . . He tried to get Judge Holman to sell Isaac South to keep me from marrying him" (120). Like Old Man Corregidora, Rufus manipulates in order to keep Alice for himself. Later, Rufus' sexual obsession with Alice becomes clear when he states, "We grew up. She got so she'd rather have a buck nigger than me!" (123). Rufus' use of the word "buck" explicates the latent sexual desire he has for this Black woman; this word conveys the sexual breeding on the plantation, where Black males and females were forced to have sexual relations in order to increase the slave population on the plantation. And Dana's sarcastic response points to the incredulous possibility for a Black woman: "How dare she choose her own husband. She must have thought she was a free woman or something" (123). Yet Alice is free, just like her mother; but for Rufus, all Black people are slaves, and in his mind, inferior, especially a Black woman for whom he has strong sexual desires. For Rufus, his whiteness and maleness trump everyone who is the Other. Butler increases the complexity of the miscegenation when Dana begins to understand that this is not simply sexual violence: "I was beginning to realize that he loved the woman—to her misfortune. There was no shame in raping a black woman, but there could be shame in loving one" (124). For a white man, declaring his love for a Black woman is viewed as a sign of weakness, but raping a Black woman is viewed as an act of masculinity. As Frederick Douglass makes clear in his brilliant narrative, the slave system destroys both the slave and the master because the slave is meant to believe in his or her inferiority, and the slave master is deluded in his or her superiority. Also, in Harriet Jacobs' *Incidents in the Life of a Slave Girl*, Jacobs relates a gruesome and bloody whipping of a Black male slave that reinforces and reinscribes elements of consumption and the supremacy of the white slave master:

When I had been in the family a few weeks, one of the plantation slaves was brought to town, by order of the master. It was near night when he arrived and Dr. Flint ordered him to be taken to the work house, and tied up to the joist, so that his feet would not escape the ground. In that situation he was to wait till the doctor had taken his tea. I shall never forget that night. Never before, in my life, had I heard hundred of blows fall, in succession on a human being. His piteous groans, and his "O pray don't massa" rang in my ears for months afterwards. There were many conjectures as to the cause of this terrible punishment. Some said master accused him of stealing corn, others said the slave quarreled with his wife, in presence of the overseer, and had accused his master of being the father of her child. They were both black, and the child was very fair. I went in the work house next morning and saw the cowhide still wet with blood and the boards all covered with gore. (15)

It is unlikely the slave's consumption of corn would cause this type of punishment; the more likely issue is the quarrel over the father of her child. And as Jacobs relates, it was a crime for a slave to tell who was the father of her child (15). Here there is no crime for sexual violence, but speaking about the person responsible represents a crime. For Rufus, his infatuation for Alice represents a curse; it foreshadows his sexual interest in Dana. For many whites, consensual miscegenation between a Black woman and a white man represents a transgression, but the same nonconsensual miscegenation represents the Black woman's covetousness for the white man. Even more disturbing is Rufus' rationalization for not using his power to rape Alice: "I didn't want to just drag her off into the bushes. . . . I never wanted it to be like that. But she kept saying no. I could have had her in the bushes years ago if that was all I wanted" (124). Nonconsensual miscegenation with dignity is the paradox Rufus faces in Alice's rejection of his advances.

Isaac and Alice Jackson's four days in freedom represent a tragedy that will ensure that Rufus Weylin will eventually achieve his miscegenous desire. They were captured on the fifth day and eventually Alice is brought to the Weylin plantation "bloody, filthy, and barely alive" (146). Dana becomes responsible for nursing her back to health and in the process Rufus discovers that "they just let the dogs chew on her" (148). For Rufus to have noticed the dogs having chewed on Alice foreshadows his desire to consume her. Like the "hungry yelping of hounds" in Richard Wright's poem, the consumption of the Black body takes on many forms during slavery, especially when it comes to tracking down and punishing runaway slaves. Here the slave catchers could do anything to the slave that they feel is necessary or that they desire, since the slave master is not present. Alice is viciously bitten by dogs and whipped; Isaac is also whipped and has his ears cut off before he is sold to a Mississippi slave trader. When the wounded Alice is placed in Rufus' bed, Dana despondently realizes that Rufus has achieved his objectives:

> I thought of Alice, and then of Rufus, and I realized that Rufus had done exactly what I had said he would do. Gotten possession of the woman without having to bother with her husband. Now, somehow, Alice would have to accept not only the loss of her husband, but her own enslavement. Rufus had caused her trouble, and now he had been rewarded for it. It made no sense. No matter how kindly he treated her now that he had destroyed her, it made no sense. (149)

Once free, Alice becomes a slave (now recovering from the dogs and the whipping) and even worse, she becomes a slave to a white man who is infatuated with her and who is indirectly responsible for the mutilation and elimination of her husband, Isaac. Sarah, a long-time slave on the plantation, sums up the tragic situation: "All because our little jackass here drank too much and decided to rape somebody" (149). No matter how much Rufus would like to romance and rationalize his actions, they come down to rape. Clearly, there is nothing heroic or honorable about Rufus' actions; he becomes characterized as a sadistic individual consumed by his uncontrollable and perhaps demonic lust for Alice. Like most victims of physical and psychological trauma, Alice is reduced to a childlike state: "We had to move Alice from Rufus's bed for his comfort as well as hers, because for a while, Alice was a very young child again, incontinent, barely aware of us unless we hurt her or fed her. And she did have to be fed—spoonful by spoonful" (153). Butler's description is significant because this transformation from an adult to a child reflects Judith Lewis Herman's notion of trauma as dialectical, where the individual may not be able to articulate the horrors of abuse, but the horrors manifest in the body. In Alice's situation, this includes incontinence and the reluctance or inability to speak. One particular wound on Alice's body reinforces the consumption of the Black female's genitals. Dana states: "She put a hand down to her thigh where a dog had literally torn away a mouthful. . . . I looked at the wound. She would have a big ugly scar there for the rest of her life, but the wound still seemed to be healing. . . . It was as though she had just noticed this specific pain in the same way she had just noticed me" (153–154). Alice's recognition of the wound and her recognition of Dana illustrate her coming back to the consciousness of her new position as Rufus' slave, and so to be concubine. With this wound on the thigh, there is the possibility that the dogs could have been allowed to consume Alice's genitals; this desired space becomes a thoroughfare for white slave masters and white slave hunters to invade at will.

As Alice Franklin slowly heals from the assault, Rufus Weylin's desire to have her sexually increases, and Dana Franklin is being forced by Rufus to help accept the reality that Alice will be his sex slave. At the same time Alice is painfully coming to terms with the harsh reality of being a slave. Having committed the serious crime of helping Isaac escape, Alice becomes a slave on the Weylin plantation. By marrying Isaac, Alice acknowledges that she has gone against her mother's advice: "My father was a slave, and they sold him away from her. She said marrying a slave is almost as bad as being a slave" (156). Alice's marital decision is further impacted by Rufus' desire to have her for himself. Talking with Dana reveals the paradox of her journey to the South when Alice asks Dana what it's like to be a slave and Dana states that she does not know what it's like to be a slave. Alice challenges Dana: "How could you not know what it's like to be a slave. You are one" (156). Alice's straightforward statement registers another fundamental paradox of the novel: Dana Franklin is what she is not, a slave. Alice then claims her own status, which contradicts the reality: "But I'm supposed to be free. I was free. Born free!" (157). Later, Alice's vehement anger directed at Dana suggests cultural miscegenation: "Doctor-nigger," she said with contempt. "Think you know so much. Reading-nigger. *White-nigger!*" (160). Along with Alice's understanding of her changed status, she is beginning to remember fragments of the trauma she and Isaac experienced when captured. Alice recalls: "They beat me," she whispered. "I remember. The dogs, the rope. . . . They tied me behind a horse and I had to run, but I couldn't. . . . Then they beat me. . . . But . . . but . . ." (158). Later she remembers about Isaac: "They cut him! They cut off his ears!" A hysterical Alice eventually collapses into Dana's arms as Dana describes the effect and the responsibility associated with this intense emotional release: "She collapsed against me, crying. She would have fallen if I hadn't held her and half-dragged and half-carried her back to the bench. She sat slumped where I put her, crying, praying, cursing. . . . There would be trouble in the house now that Alice had her memory back, and somehow, it had become my job to ease troubles—first Rufus's, now Alice's—as best I could" (158–159). Helping Rufus rape Alice becomes Dana's dreadful responsibility.

Rufus' desire to sexually consume Alice escalates at the same time that Dana's desire to have Kevin return to the Weylin plantation escalates. Dana is anxious over the fact that her letter sent North to Kevin has been unanswered and simultaneously Rufus pressures Dana to talk to Alice about submitting herself to him. Dana explicates this dual desire:

> I caught Rufus alone again the next day—in his room this time where we weren't likely to be interrupted. But he wouldn't listen when I brought up the letter. His mind was on Alice. She was stronger now, and his patience with her was gone. I had thought that eventually, he would just rape her again—and again. In fact, I was surprised that he hadn't already done it. I didn't realize that he was planning to involve me in that rape. He was, and he did. (162)

Rufus' obsession for Alice represents Butler's description of "white men preying upon black women" yet he articulates a sinister father-and-son connection to Rufus' desire. Both father and son have a fetish for Black flesh; indeed, there is something draconian about their desires. Talking to Dana, Rufus relates: "'She'll never get away from me again. Never!' He drew a deep breath, let it out slowly. 'You know, Daddy wants me to send her to the fields and take you. . . . He thinks all I want is a woman. Any woman. So you, then. He says you'd be less likely to give me trouble'" (163). Here, Butler makes the paradox of Rufus' desire even more complex. First, Tom Weylin encourages his son to rape Dana instead of waiting for Alice to heal. Second, there is no sense of respecting another white man's property (they both know that Dana belongs to Kevin Franklin) because he has gone North. Third, like Old Man Corregidora, Tom Weylin's view on Black female slaves is exceptionally crude; he essentially views them as things to be fucked and discarded. Obviously, this revelation shocks Dana, who seeks to be reunited with her husband, Kevin. Even Rufus, who knows that Kevin and Dana are married, seems to acknowledge the reality: "You want Kevin the way I want Alice" (163). However, there is a momentous and fundamental difference: he has no plans to marry Alice, and Dana's relationship with Kevin is consensual. Rufus is also in denial of his role in having Alice and Isaac tortured, whipped, and mutilated. Simply put, Rufus wants Alice's genitals and Kevin wants his wife, Dana. Dana's lack of sympathy for Rufus' desire enrages him: "'You think you're white!' he muttered. 'You don't know your place any better than a wild animal'" (164). Not surprisingly, Alice also becomes enraged at Dana. When Dana confides in her about not hearing from Kevin, Alice states: "You ought to be ashamed of yourself, whining and crying after some poor white trash of a man, black as you are. You always try to act so white. White nigger, turning against your own people!" (165). Dana's speech, mannerisms, and behavior provoke this response. At this point, Alice does not realize the full and personal extent of her words, but she will soon discover their importance. Nonetheless, Dana becomes caught in the middle of doing something that is detestable but that she must do for her own existence. Dana painfully relates Alice's attacks and the paradox of healing Alice and helping Rufus hurt Alice:

> I never really got used to her sudden switches, her attacks, but I put up with them. I had taken her through all the other stages of healing, and somehow, I couldn't abandon her now. Most of the time, I couldn't become angry. She was like Rufus. When she hurt, she struck out to hurt others. But she had been hurting less as the days passed, and striking out less. She was healing emotionally as well as physically. I had helped her to heal. Now I had Rufus tear her wounds open again. (165)

Working with the element of the surreal, Butler has clearly given us one of the most complex, engaging, and paradoxical scenarios in African American literature, as Dana Franklin lives and acts out a complex version of W.E.B. Du Bois' theory of double consciousness. Equally significant is the complex construction of the African American family based on the widespread miscegenation, both consensual and nonconsensual, during the enslavement period. Eventually Dana tells Alice of Rufus' intentions and tells her: "Well, it looks as though you have three choices. You can go to him as he orders; you can refuse, be whipped, and then have him take you by force; or you can run away again" (167). After some moments of silence and asking Dana what she should do, Alice launches into an angry tirade that denounces Dana and Rufus. Alice declares: "'I ought to take a knife in there with me and cut his damn throat.' She glared at me. 'Now go tell him that! Tell him I'm talking 'bout killing him!'" Dana responds: "Tell him yourself." Then Alice states: "Do your job! Go tell him! That's what you for—to help white folks keep niggers down. That's why he sent you to me. They be calling you mammy in a few years. You be running the whole house when the old man dies" (167). Clearly, Alice's threat to kill Rufus with a knife represents a danger to Dana, and her other sarcastic remarks convey that Dana represents a handkerchief-wearing Aunt Jemima house-nigger and a traitor to the Black race. Dana's whole existence on the Weylin plantation centers on protecting Rufus, but as Alice surely knows, Dana's role on the plantation is not simply as she states, especially considering her helping her to heal and the whipping that she received when she was helping Nigel to read. Alice's remarks are clearly related to the trauma of hurt and loss along with the ensuing trauma of being forced to have sexual relations with the white slave master who is responsible for her husband being mutilated and sold away to Mississippi. Alice Greenwood's situation is analogous to Harriet Jacobs' psychological torment by Dr. Flint. Jacobs relates the loss of her innocence:

> My master began to whisper foul words in my ear. Young as I was I could not remain ignorant of their import. I tried to treat them with indifference or contempt. . . . He tried his utmost to corrupt the pure principles my grandmother had instilled. He peopled my young mind with unclean images, such as only a vile monster could think of. I turned from him with disgust and hatred. But he was my master. I was compelled to live under the same roof with him—where I saw a man forty years my senior daily violating the most sacred commandments of nature. He told me I was his property; that I must be subject to his will in all things. My soul revolted against the mean tyranny. . . . No matter whether the slave girl be black as ebony or as fair as her mistress. In either case, there is no shadow of law to protect her from insult, from violence, or even from death, all these are inflicted by fiends who bear the shape of men. (27)

In both cases, the psychological violence lays the foundation for the physical violence. Unlike Rufus, Alice does have a complete understanding of the complexity of Dana's situation, and especially how it relates to Rufus' survival and Dana's existence. With little or no healthy physical or psychological alternatives, Alice goes to Rufus: "She went to him. She adjusted, became a quieter more subdued person. She didn't kill him, but she seemed to die a little" (169). Killing Rufus would destroy any possibility of Dana returning to her present relationship with Kevin, and at the same time Alice is being destroyed by her illicit relationship with Rufus. With his objective achieved, Rufus becomes more jovial and begins to drink more heavily. One morning Dana notices its effect on his victim: "Alice came downstairs with her whole face swollen and bruised" (169). As a slave woman married to this relationship of forced adultery, Alice ensures Dana's existence in the present world because she gives birth to Hagar, a maternal ancestor. Ironically, both Alice and Dana were free, but now they are slaves with husbands who have been displaced, Isaac by being sold to Mississippi and Kevin by leaving because Tom Weylin was whipping his wife for teaching reading.

With Rufus having achieved his miscegenous desires by Alice's unenthusiastic and reluctant submission, Dana's attempt to reunite with her white husband, Kevin, results in conflict with her white slave masters, Rufus and Tom Weylin. When Dana discovers that her letters ("their seals broken") to Kevin have not been sent by Rufus, she decides to run away from the Weylin plantation. Rufus' profound betrayal hurts Dana and yet suggests some subliminal miscegenous desire for her. Rufus' deceptive actions concerning the undelivered letters reinforce the aforementioned construct of a triangle of miscegenous desire, but Dana has her own miscegenous plans. She carefully plans her escape but acknowledges her concerns associated with the consumption of the Black body: "I wasn't really afraid. Dogs with white men frightened me, or dogs in packs—Sarah had told me of runaways who had been torn to pieces by the packs of dogs used to hunt them. But one lone dog didn't seem to be much of a threat" (172). The dogs and the white men recall the consumption that Alice and Isaac experienced when they briefly escaped; the gaping wound on Alice's thigh and the loss of Isaac's ears represent acts of miscegenous consumption, one by the dogs and the other by the white men. Douglass relates another lynching where a lame young woman was whipped "with a heavy cowskin upon her naked shoulders, causing the warm red blood to drip" (44), and this violence is framed around the issue of consumption: "Master would keep this lacerated young woman tied up in this horrid situation four or five hours at a time. I have know him to tie her up early in the morning and whip her before breakfast; leave her, go to his store, return at dinner, and whip her again, cutting her in the places already made raw with his cruel lash" (44). This cruel treatment is compounded by the fact that this woman was badly burned in a fire to the extent that her hands were useless. During the enslavement period, both dogs and white males have been trained or socialized to consume Black flesh. When a lone dog runs across a field and lunges at Dana, she clubs him and he goes whimpering away. Not a whole day goes by before Rufus and Tom Weylin begin searching for her on horseback (Dana realizes that someone has betrayed her) and they find her hiding in some thick bushes. They drive their horses into the bushes, forcing Dana out into the open and then Dana affirms that Tom Weylin "strode over and kicked me in the face" (174). This represents the first of the physical violence that Dana will receive for running away as Rufus half-drags her while perched on his horse. The kick causes Dana to lose consciousness, but unfortunately, because a severe cowhide whipping is coming, she remains in the past. Two lost teeth, a bleeding mouth, and a sore jaw greet

Dana when she regains consciousness. Like the whipping of Aunt Hester in Fred-erick Douglass' slave narrative, Dana relates:

> They took me to the barn and tied my hands and raised whatever they had tied them to high over my head. When I was barely able to touch the floor with my toes, Weylin ripped my clothes off and began to beat me. He beat me until I swung back and forth by my wrists, half-crazy with pain, unable to find my foot-ing, unable to stand the pressure of hanging, unable get away from the steady blows slashing blows. . . . He beat me until I tried to make myself believe he was going to kill me. I said it aloud, screamed it, and the blows seemed to emphasize my words. He would kill me. Surely, he would kill me if I didn't get away, save myself, *go home!* (176)

With Dana being naked (ripping the clothes begins the stripping of her dignity), the sadistic sexual aspect of Rufus' whipping becomes evident. Having her arms tied and placed over her head positions Dana in an extremely vulnerable position; Rufus has total access to her body as he consumes her both with his gaze and with the cowhide whip as an extension of his phallus. Unlike Aunt Hester's whipping, where the slave master curses her, we do not know what Rufus states while he is pleasuring himself by beating a Black woman who repeatedly saved his life. Dis-cussing the loss of her teeth, Rufus says: "Well, if you don't laugh big nobody'll notice. They weren't the teeth right in front" (175). Rufus' father, pouring verbal abuse into Dana's physical wounds, humiliates her by saying: "Educated nigger don't mean smart nigger do it?" Amazingly, Dana does not return to the present; however, there is a sense that the longer Dana remains in the South, the more violence she must sustain before she can return to the present. Another profound paradox is that it is Rufus who whips her, the individual who summons her to the past when he is in mortal danger. Drawing on history, Dana acknowledges her limitations and the paradox of her whipping when she states:

> Nothing in my education or knowledge of the future had helped me to escape. Yet in a few years an illiterate runaway named Harriet Tubman would make nineteen trips into this country and lead three hundred fugitives to freedom. What had I done wrong? Why was I still slave to a man who had repaid me for saving his life by nearly killing me. [sic] Why had I taken yet another beating. [sic] And why . . . why was I so frightened now—frightened sick at the thought that sooner or later, I would have to run again? (177)

Beyond the basic desire for survival, Dana seems committed to return to the pres-ent and her life with her white husband, Kevin. Killing Rufus could negate this because the relative whom he must father does not yet exist. Equally significant is the fact that the beating represents the price Dana must pay because her rela-tionship with Kevin represents a crime here in the past. Another aspect of Rufus' violent actions is that they could send her into the present, but they could also delay or prevent Dana from returning to the present, and Dana's intense desire to kill Rufus or his father seems to foreshadow some malevolent violence on her part. Perhaps Rufus beats Dana so his father would not render a worse beating, as he did when he caught her teaching Nigel to read. Still, the critical question here is: How does this vicious whipping, which Dana experiences from Rufus, affect her ability to be transported in the present? This question is germane because when Tom Weylin whipped Dana, she was transported to the present in California.

Paradoxically, Rufus' cruelty in this miscegenous beating is juxtaposed with his genuine concern for Dana's care after this sadistic flesh-ripping whipping. Rufus carries Dana into Carrie's and Nigel's cabin and directs Alice and Carrie to wash and care for her. Rufus demands that everything used on Dana be clean; this represents his concern for the possibility of infection. By making sure that Dana survives, Rufus unknowingly ensures his own existence. Because of the emotional connection created by Dana saving Rufus' life, perhaps there is also some guilt being expressed by Rufus in his guidance on Dana's care. Family concern and reciprocity are sincerely expressed to Dana by Alice: "'Just rest' she said, 'Carrie and me'll take care of you as good as you took care of me'" (177). The concern and compassion that enslaved Black individuals showed for each other was expansive in that those individuals who were victims of miscegenation were generally not excluded or seen as traitors. Most Black individuals understood that the power relations on the slave plantations forced them into situations that they had little power to resist. That Dana did not return to the present after this brutal whipping raises the concern of the possibility of her permanency on the Weylin plantation. Consequently, Dana Franklin begins to contemplate whether she has the psychological courage and physical stamina to run away again. Dana also learns that another slave woman named Liza, the sewing woman, had gone to Rufus and informed him that Dana had run away. Liza had informed on Dana in order to get back at Alice, whom she hated. Dana receives another surprise when she discusses the unsent letters with Rufus. Rufus' response: "I wanted to keep you here. . . . Kevin hates this place. He would have taken you up North" (180) reveals his deep-seated miscegenous desire for Dana, regardless of her relationship with her husband. Rufus desires to replace Kevin's phallus with his phallus. Dana begins to understand that Rufus loves her, but not in the same way that he loves Alice. She states: "He loved me. . . . He didn't seem to want to sleep with me. But he wanted me around—someone to talk to, someone who would listen to him and care what he said, care about him" (180). The critical word is "seem" and because Rufus has Alice as his sexual slave, he appears to be satisfied, but this could change. Dana knows Rufus cannot be trusted. At this point, Dana thinks deeply about this triangle of miscegenous desire and the possible ramifications:

> I stared out the window guiltily, feeling that I should have been more like Alice. She forgave him nothing, forgot nothing, hated him as deeply as she loved

Isaac. I didn't blame her. But what good did her hating do? She couldn't bring herself to run away again or to kill him and face her own death. She couldn't do anything at all except make herself more miserable. She said, "My stomach just turns every time he puts his hands on me!" But she endured. Eventually, she would bear him at least one child. And as much as I cared for him, I would not have done that. I couldn't have. Twice, he had made me lose control enough to try to kill him. I could get that angry with him, even though I knew the consequences of killing him. He could drive me to a kind of unthinking fury. Somehow, I couldn't take from him the kind of abuse I took from others. If he ever raped me, it wasn't likely that either of us would survive. (180)

Dana's self-reflective discourse raises a number of issues with regard to Rufus' miscegenous desires. The emotional bond between Dana and Rufus has made her experience guilt, even while she desires to be more like Alice, but she does not understand Alice's deep-seated hatred. Alice's disgust for Rufus is connected to the loss of Isaac, who is gone forever. Even though she knows the future, she contemplates the unpredictable reality of slavery. Anything can happen to Dana, especially the violence, because she is a slave. Sexual violence is always a possibility for a Black female slave, and this reality does not escape Dana's understanding of her precarious situation. Dana's comment on having a child with Rufus reflects the unstable nature of being in the South, despite her knowledge of what is supposed to happen. Having a child with Rufus would make it impossible for Dana to exist in her present life in California. Not thinking that she could be viciously whipped on two occasions, Dana is aware that anything can happen. Psychologically, Dana's discourse reflects the complexity of slavery and Dana's life in the present. Accordingly, saving a person's life and then being maliciously whipped and deceived by this individual are difficult actions to accept, but Dana stills reveals that she cares for Rufus. As exemplified by Martin's question in *Corregidora*, it appears that desire and antipathy during slavery went both ways with masters and slaves.[7] With thoughts of being reunited with her husband, Kevin (Dana becomes aware that Rufus' father sent a letter North to Kevin), Dana draws the line of physical abuse at rape.

Kevin Franklin's return to the Weylin plantation and Dana's final two journeys back to the antebellum South represent another miscegenous triangle of desire with Kevin, Rufus, and Dana, and the enduring psychological and physical tragedy/trauma that often comes with miscegenous sexual violence. While working in the field one day, Dana views a stranger riding a horse coming up to the Weylin house; the stranger turns out to be Kevin Franklin. With Rufus and Tom Weylin away from the plantation, Dana and Kevin decide to leave. Kevin is initially reluctant after he discovers that Dana has been whipped, but after some quick goodbyes to Alice, they mount Kevin's horse and proceed down the road. Here they meet Rufus, who with his long slender Kentucky rifle aimed at Kevin, declares to Dana that: "You're not leaving . . . Dana you, you're not leaving me!" (187). Here Rufus is hysterical with a violent rage that articulates his miscegenous desire for Dana, which is analogous to his desire for Alice. When he threatens to kill Kevin, Dana clearly understands his bizarre actions: "He [Kevin] didn't understand the kind of relationship Rufus and I had, how dependent we were on each other. Rufus understood though" (187). Despite Dana's understanding of Rufus' psychological state, she is adamant about never returning to the Weylin plantation. "I already know all I ever want to find out about being a slave," Dana states. "I'd rather be shot than go back in there" (187). Dana's valiant statement reflects the African American saying: "I rather be buried in my grave than be a slave." The miscegenous analogy between Rufus and Dana and Rufus and Alice becomes apparent when Dana understands the displacement and transference that is occurring in Rufus' psyche: "I was Alice all over again rejecting him" (188). In Rufus' head, Dana and Kevin become Alice and Isaac running away from the plantation. When Dana senses that Rufus will shoot, she dives past the mare's head and falls on the ground; Kevin falls on Dana's back and they return to the present.

After a five-year absence, Dana and Kevin return to the present bringing with them pain, relief, and frustration of a past laden with trauma. Both Dana and Kevin have physical and psychological wounds from the past. Kevin has a scar on his forehead and Dana's back is whip-scared, but they decide to have sexual relations. Dana relates: "He was so careful, so fearful of hurting me. He did hurt me, of course. I had known he would, but it didn't matter. We were safe. He was home. I'd brought him back. That was enough" (190). Dana's hurt represents the wounds inflicted by Rufus and the physical pain encountered in making love to Kevin, a sexual synthesis of the past and the present. In a sense, Dana is having relations with Kevin and Rufus because the hurt involves both of them. Indeed the synthesis becomes more profound when Dana, discussing Kevin, states: "And I heard him cursing. He had a slight accent, I realized. Nothing really noticeable, but he did sound a little like Rufus and Tom Weylin. Just a little" (190). Just as the doctor asks Ursa Corregidora, "Is Mr. Corregidora with you," here we have two white slave masters with Dana as she makes love to her white husband. Both Tom Weylin and Rufus Weylin have penetrated Dana with their cowhide whips, creating the wounds that Kevin embraces when he makes love to Dana. While Tom's and Rufus' penetrations of Dana's flesh are symbolic, both of these white slave masters have a history of miscegenation, sexual penetrations of Black female slaves. Tom has penetrated Tess and numerous other slaves, and Rufus has penetrated Alice. Hence, Butler uses the whipping during slavery to juxtapose it with the miscegenous sexual violence that many Black female slaves experience. Phallic transference synthesizes the past and present, along with the symbolic incestuous miscegenation between Dana and Rufus, her white ancestor. Paradoxically, Rufus suffers from a slave-dependency syndrome where he finds it difficult to function without the psychological support from Dana and the sexual relations he has with Alice. Rufus's white-male subjectivity

becomes defined by his relationships to these two Black women and the elimination (symbolic castration) of Alice's husband, Isaac. Butler provides another
racial synthesis when: "The news [on the radio] switched to a story about South
Africa—blacks rioting there and dying wholesale in battles with police over
the policies of the white-supremacist government" (196). Apartheid in South
Africa and slavery in the United States are very similar in the level and extent
of the violence and humiliation that Black people experienced, but the miscegenation in America represents a distinction in the social interaction between
Black and whites. However, in Southern Africa and in America the control of
the land and Black people's labor were similar. As Dana contemplates: "South
African whites had always struck me as people who would have been happier
living in the nineteenth century, or the eighteenth. In fact, they were living
in the past as far as their race relations went. They lived in ease and comfort
supported by huge numbers of blacks whom they kept in poverty and held in
contempt. Tom Weylin would have felt right at home" (196). Laws under apartheid prohibited most social contact between races, authorized separate public
facilities, and denied nonwhites any representation in the national government.
Based on the large number of Africans in Southern Africa compared to those in
the South, there was less sexual violence in Southern Africa compared to the
sexual violence in America. Fewer Black people to control equates with more
terrorizing sexual violence. Only hours pass before Dana is snatched back to
the past to save a drunken Rufus from drowning "in a puddle so deep the water
almost covered his head. Face down" (198). Again Dana saves Rufus' life so that
he can father her ancestor.

Butler's section called the "Storm" represents not only the dreary and rainy
weather conditions but a drastic escalation in the level of psychological and
physical violence on the Weylin plantation. After Nigel carries Rufus into the
house, Dana and Tom engage in verbal conflict. Tom asks Dana about a scar
on her face and Dana responds that it is a result of him kicking her in the face
six years ago. During their conversation about Kevin's return to the present,
Dana expresses her indignation and Tom threatens her with a "good whipping."
Dana's response reveals the anger and frustration over the whippings by Rufus
and Tom, along with the other abuses: "I said nothing. I realized then, though,
that if he ever hit me again, I would break his scrawny neck. I would not endure
it again" (200). Dana's insubordinate response is similar to Douglass' in his
physical encounter with the slave master and "nigger breaker," Covey. When
Covey attempts to whip Douglass, Douglass fights back and begins to choke
the slave master. At this point, Douglass has a profound psychological change
when he declares that he may be a slave in fact, but that he will never again
be a slave in his mind. When he states: "You have seen how a man was made
a slave; you shall see how a slave was made a man" (50). Here in this powerful
chiasmus, Douglass discovers his male subjectivity as he chokes his slave master. Like Douglass, now Dana represents the "bad nigger" and the "crazy nigger."

In this short period of time, Dana has been traumatized by the violence that she has experienced as well as the violence she has seen or heard about. Tom tells Dana: "You damned black bitch" (201) and orders her, "Go to Rufus. Take care of him. If anything happens to him. I'll flay you alive!" (202). Tom's malevolent threat causes Dana to consider the legacy of physical violence: "My aunt used to say things like that to me when I was little and did something to annoy her—'Girl, I'm going to skin you alive!' And she'd get my uncle's belt and use it on me. But it never occurred to me that anyone could make such a threat and mean it literally as Weylin meant it now" (202). Dana's linguistic analysis suggests the extent to which some Black parents threaten and whip their children is part of the inheritance of slavery's violent legacy. Sexual violence within the Black community and incest within some Black families may represent aspects of slavery's legacy. The post-traumatic slave syndrome articulates the theory that there are certain behavior characteristics that Black people have carried over from the days of slavery. Butler makes the prolific argument that slavery's past resides in many aspects of the present, especially in terms of intra-racial and interracial conflicts.

Rufus' relationship with Dana reveals the enduring sexual trauma that Alice experiences. Once Dana returns after her brief absence in the present, which equals six years of absence in the past, she discovers from Nigel that Alice has lost two babies with Rufus and that the one she has left is sickly. Loss of children during the enslavement period represents another of the traumas that many Black people faced. Deaths of children by illness and neglect were common and the loss of children occurred when children were sold; these children became deaths in their parents' minds. Discussing his children, Nigel states: "It's good to have children. . . . . Good to have sons. But it's so hard to see them be slaves" (210). Alice's children became sick with a fever and Rufus allowed the doctor to bleed them and purge them; nevertheless, they still died. Alice blames Rufus for their deaths. Alice's attitude becomes reflected in Rufus, who blames Dana when his father dies. Immediately after Tom Weylin's funeral, a spiteful Rufus sends Dana to labor in the fields to chop corn. After chopping the first stalk, the overseer, Fowler, slashes Dana on the back. Dana relates: "I screamed, stumbled, and spun around to face him, still holding my knife. Unimpressed, he hit me across the breasts" (212). Here again the violence of slavery has sadistic sexual overtones, as Dana's breasts become a target in this assault. Following a previous pattern, Dana contemplates resistance and its possible effects:

> He was a big man. . . . I was afraid that even if I managed to hurt him, I wouldn't hurt him enough to keep him from killing me. Maybe I should make him try to kill me. Maybe it would get me out of this Godawful place where people punished you for helping them. Maybe it would get me home. But in how many pieces? Fowler would take the knife away from me and give it back edge first. (212)

Another critical issue, raised here in Butler's description of the overseer whipping Dana, is that both Blacks and whites were used on the plantation to discipline Black slaves. Regardless of race, these individuals had to be men of impressive stature and great physical strength, a constant reminder of the force with which the driver's whip could strike the bare backs of misbehaving field hands. As William L. Van Deburg points out, Black overseers sometimes had special rights and yet they experienced the same realities as other slaves:

> Although accounts exist that tell of various sexual "privileges" being granted to members of the slave elite, drivers who were assigned to stand duty or were allowed to have more than one wife cannot be said to typify the foreman class. Wide-ranging sexual freedom on the plantation was not reserved exclusively for black field labor supervisors, nor was such activity always authorized by the planter. . . . As with other black families during the era of slavery, driver families lived under a constant threat of temporary or permanent separation occasioned by forces over which they had little control. (16–17)

Dana's assistance in trying to save Rufus' life is rewarded with being sent to the fields and being whipped. Tom has instructed Fowler to be harsh with Dana and lashes her again when he believes that she is moving too slow. He tells Dana: "Move! You're not in the cookhouse getting fat and lazy now. Move!" (213). The results of Fowler's actions leave Dana terrified: "He did that all day. Coming up suddenly, shouting at me, ordering me to go faster no matter how fast I went, cursing me, threatening me. He didn't hit me that often, but he kept me on edge because I never knew when a blow would fall. It got so just the sound of his coming terrified me. I caught myself cringing, jumping at the sound of his voice" (213). Dana attempts to make the adjustment from working in the house to working in the fields, but the brutal Fowler is relentless in his verbal abuses and physical attacks and at some point Dana passes out.

Still on the Weylin plantation, Dana awakes and confuses Rufus with Kevin, but the reconciliation that they have is short-lived as the terror continues. Dana's confusion of Rufus with Kevin is indicative of the synthesis of the past and present as well as the synthesis of Butler's theme of miscegenation as sexual consumption. Rufus desires for Dana to remain in the past and Kevin desires for Dana to return to the present. Having formed relationships with other slaves on the plantation, Dana is also affected by the trauma that other slaves experience. Tom Weylin's former concubine, Tess, a tall, strongly built, handsome woman, is sold, and Dana speculates on the reason: "I'd seen her only two or three times this trip. She was still working in the fields, still serving the overseer at night. She'd had no children, and that may have been why she was being sold. Or maybe this was something Margaret Weylin had arranged. She might be that vindictive if she knew of her husband's temporary interest in Tess" (222). Like Alice, Tess represents another example of miscegenation as sexual consumption.

With the slave master Tom Weylin dead, Tess becomes vulnerable despite her having sexual relations with the overseer. Also, having not produced any children, Tess becomes a liability. Deeply saddened by Tess being sold, Dana speaks to her, but Tess never looks up and never responds. Later, when challenged by Dana, Rufus reveals that his father had arranged for the sale before he died. That Tess does not respond speaks to the fact that she has been sexually exploited by Tom Weylin and then passed on to the overseer, and now she is being sold and placed on the slave coffle. Butler describes the coffle that Tess joins: "A white man went by on horseback leading two dozen black men chained two by two. Chained. They wore handcuffs and iron collars with chains connecting the collars to a central chain that ran between the two lines. Behind the men walked several women roped together neck to neck. A coffle—slaves for sale" (221). Like human garbage, Tess is used and discarded, a commodity of miscegenous consumption. Incidents like this human tragedy make Dana feel like a traitor and she experiences guilt for repeatedly saving Rufus' life. "I guess I can see why there are those who think I'm more white than black" (224). Dana states this when she understands that Rufus has little compassion or decency. Butler illustrates the difference between the overseer and the slave master: "But then slavery of any kind fostered strange relationships. Only the overseer drew simple, unconflicting emotions of hatred and fear when he appeared briefly. But then, it was part of the overseer's job to be hated and feared while the master kept his hands clean" (230). Like a puppet on a string, the overseer administers the violence to Dana while the slave master, Rufus, can act like a savior when Dana suffers from the overseer's whippings. Rufus has also become like his father, emotionally detached from his children, until Dana suggests that he take an interest in his son: "He had spent his life watching his father ignore, even sell the children he had with black women. Apparently, it had never occurred to Rufus to break that tradition. Until now" (231). Like Douglass' narrative, where he discusses his disconnection from his Black slave mother and his white slave-master father, the theme of natal alienation becomes evident in slave masters having no relationships with their children from Black women.

Alice's illicit relationship with Rufus continues to be a source of tension for both Alice and Dana. While Rufus shows attention to their son, Joe, Alice has little trust for Rufus in terms of him selling their children. Rufus requests that Alice should like him, but Alice wants him to legally free their children. Pregnant with Rufus' child, Alice confides in Dana her desire to escape the plantation because of her apprehension of her children being sold. Alice's desire presents difficulties for Dana, but Dana understands: "I didn't like it. Didn't like the idea of her trying to run with a baby and a small child, didn't like the idea of her trying to run at all. But she was right. In her place, I would have tried. I would have tried sooner and gotten killed sooner, but I would have done it alone" (233). Knowing what happened to her and Isaac, Alice's desire represents a phenomenon of extraordinary risks to herself and her children, but the possible loss of her children propels this desire. Alice gives birth and the girl is given the name Hagar. Although Rufus hates this name, Dana states: "I thought it was the most beautiful name I had ever heard. I felt almost free, half-free if such a thing was possible, half-way home" (234). Hagar's birth ensures Dana's existence, but danger still remains. "The danger to my family was past, yes Hagar had been born. But the danger to me personally . . . the danger to me personally still walked and talked and sometimes sat with Alice in her cabin in the evening as she nursed Hagar" (234). Dana is still a slave and she cannot trust Rufus; Alice defiantly reminds Dana of this as she plans to escape. In order to ensure her existence, Dana must ensure that Hagar is not placed in danger; this seems to be Dana's hesitation in helping Alice escape. At some point, Alice derides and threatens Dana: "I got to go before I turn into what you are! . . . You'll care. And you'll help me. Else, you'd have to see yourself for the *white nigger* you are, and you couldn't stand that" (235; emphasis added). Alice's reference to Dana as a white nigger suggests biological miscegenation, but her reference is to Dana's psychological relationship with Rufus, which is not the traditional master and slave relationship that Gayl Jones illustrates in *Corregidora*. Here, Alice seems to take out her frustrations at Rufus on Dana. Dana endures these personal attacks because, as she states: "I got the feeling that Alice was keeping him happy—and maybe finally enjoying herself a little in the process. I guessed from what she had told me that this was what was frightening her so, driving her away from the plantation, causing her to lash out at me. She was trying to deal with guilt of her own" (237). Alice and Dana become locked inside the paradox of Rufus' desire for both of them. Missy Dehn Kubitschek writes, "To a certain extent, each woman feels the other's choices as a critique of her own; each sees, in the distorting mirror of the other, her own, potential face" (39). Alice and Dana become dependent on each other because they feed Rufus' physical and psychological needs. Even here, in the horrors of slavery, some of the needs and desires of both masters and slaves are being satisfied.

When another Black male slave named Sam comes to Dana with the desire for her to teach his brother and sister to read, this causes conflict with Dana and Rufus, creating a dual tragedy. Dana and Sam also engage in an innocent conversation about life on the Weylin plantation, and about three days later Sam is placed in a slave coffle and led away in chains. Dana's pleas to Rufus to let Sam stay are ignored. Viewing Dana as being responsible for her brother being sold, Sam's sister, Sally, bellows at Dana: "'You whore,' she screamed. She had not been permitted to approach the coffle, but she approached me. 'You no-'count nigger whore, why couldn't you leave my brother alone!'" (238). By virtue of her relationship with Rufus, Dana is viewed as a whore by this Black slave woman. Because Dana works in the house, there is the thought that she must be having sexual relations with Rufus. This was true in many cases of Black female slaves working in the house, but this was not the situation with Dana. Ironically, this Black woman slave blames another Black woman slave when both are powerless.

Like his father, Tom, Rufus represents a whoremonger who has physically forced himself on Alice and psychologically manipulates Dana. Again, Dana's teaching a slave to read causes another tragedy. Like Old Man Corregidora in Gayl Jones' novel, who does not want any Black man "fucking" his Black women slaves, Rufus becomes jealous because Sam talks with Dana. Again, he views Sam and Dana in the same manner that he viewed Isaac and Alice. Not having a white wife or any other white woman, Rufus places all of his emotional attention on his Black female slaves, Alice and Dana. Dana continues to plead with Rufus: "Please, Rufe. If you do this, you'll destroy what you mean to preserve" (239). When Rufus hits Dana and drives her away, she gets a warm basin of water, washes her knife in antiseptic, and in the warm water cuts her wrists. This tragic attempt at suicide returns her to the present and to her life with Kevin. Back home, Kevin bandages Dana's wrists and they spend fifteen days together before her last journey to Rufus and the Weylin plantation.

In Dana Franklin's final journey to save Rufus Weylin's life, Octavia Butler illustrates a Shakespearian-like tragedy of miscegenation as sexual consumption. On July 4th, Dana feels dizzy again and returns, only to discover that Rufus is not in any physical danger, but that another tragedy has taken place. Rufus leads Dana to the barn; Alice has committed suicide:

> I stared at her not believing, not wanting to believe. . . . I touched her and her flesh was cold and hard. The dead gray face was ugly in death as it had never been in life. The mouth was open and staring. Her head was bare and her hair loose and short like mine. . . . Her dress was dark red and her apron clean and white. She wore shoes that Rufus had made specifically for her, not the rough heavy shoes or boots other slaves wore. It was as though she had dressed up and combed her hair and then. . . . (248)

After cutting her down, Dana removes the rope from her neck, holds her, and cries for a long time. For many Black slaves, death by their own hands represents their desire to take control of their lives and end the daily torment of physical and psychological violence. For Black slave mothers, the selling of their children represents one of the cruelest aspects of slavery. Rufus never responds to Dana's questions about why she killed herself or the location of her children, Joe and Hagar. Dana learns from the long-time cook, Sarah, that Rufus sold her children: "'He did it,' she hissed. 'Even if he didn't put the rope on her, he drove her to it. He sold her babies!'" (249). The significance of the date, July 4th, connects to Frederick Douglass' speech on the Fourth of July, 1852, denouncing this nation's celebration as a sham:

> What, the American slave, is your 4th of July? I answer: a day that reveals to him [and her], more than all other days in the year, the gross injustice and cruelty to which he [and she] is the constant victim. To him, your celebration is

a sham, your boasted liberty, an unholy license, your national greatness, swelling vanity, your sounds of rejoicing are empty, all heartless; your denunciation of tyrants, brass fronted impudence, your shouts of liberty and equality, hollow mockery; your prayers and hymns, your sermons and thanksgivings, with all your religious parade and solemnity, are hypocrisy—a thin veil to cover crimes which would disgrace a nation of savages. There is not a nation on the earth guilty of practices more shocking and bloody than are the people of the United States, at this very hour. ("Oration, Delivered in Corinthian Hall" 94–95) [8]

Having caused Alice's death, Rufus flees to the library with a gun, where Dana finds him. She now knows that the reason she has been brought back to the plantation is because Rufus plans to commit suicide. Alice had run away and before she was captured, Rufus sent the children to Baltimore to be with his mother's sister. Alice believed that they had been sold. In the library, Dana tells him what he does not want to hear: "You killed her. Just as though you had put that gun to her head and fired" (251). Rufus' guilt causes him to legally free his children, but his desire for Dana becomes clearer when he acknowledges to Dana that he sold Sam because he believed that he wanted Dana. Rufus also acknowledges his obsession for Alice: "But if I lived, I would have her. And, by God, I had to have her" (257). Then he makes a remarkable statement about Alice and Dana: "You were one woman. . . . You and her. One woman. Two halves of a whole" (257). Rufus' relationships with these two Black female slaves, Alice and Dana, represent miscegenation as consumption, one sexually and the other emotionally. With Alice dead, Rufus can finally reveal to Dana his deep-seated sexual desire for these Black female slaves. At some point, Dana realizes that Rufus wants her sexually: "He was not hurting me, would not hurt me if I remained as I was. He was not his father, old and ugly, brutal and disgusting. He smelled of soap, as though he recently bathed—for me? The red hair was neatly combed and a little damp. I would never be to him what Tess had been to his father—a thing passed around like the whiskey jug at a husking. He wouldn't do that to me or sell me or. . . ." (260). When it's clear that Rufus intends to rape Dana, she defends herself by stabbing him, but his actions of placing her in danger send her to the present. The tension caused by Rufus's life being in danger and Dana's life being in danger cause the conflict between the past and the present. With Dana's life at risk, she becomes transported to the present, but with Rufus still clutching her arm in the past, Dana's left arm is ripped off. With only a stump remaining, Dana's left arm becomes the sacrifice; it is as if the past requires a blood, bone, and flesh offering for some of her present indiscretions. Beyond the loss of the arm, the scar on her head, the numerous whippings that Dana has experienced, slavery and its violence will always haunt her. *Kindred* suggests that the sexual sins of the past affect the sexual present. Kevin being arrested by the police for suspicion of domestic violence represents another twist of fate, since he is innocent of hurting Dana, but white slave masters were almost never held accountable for their malicious crimes of sexual violence against Black females. Dana's excruciating pain is part of the process of revelation.

Beyond the trepidation, terror, and pain of enslavement, Black people have reconstructed their lives in complex and paradoxical ways, ways that challenge the legacy of white-male supremacy and some ways reinforce and reinscribe white-male supremacy. Dana Franklin has learned a powerful lesson about her multiracial family's past, with regard to the sexual violence that her maternal ancestors experienced by white slave masters. Dana's consensual sexual and legal relationship with Kevin signifies on the nonconsensual sexual violence (extralegal) that her Black female ancestors experienced, and the loss of her left arm will always remind her of slavery's violent miscegenous past, the terror of rape and its dehumanizing effect on the psyche. Dana and Kevin have experienced profound personal and historical lessons that may strengthen their relationship or tear them apart. Indeed, in the first few pages of the novel, Dana, beyond the loss of her appendage, states: "And I lost about a year of my life and much of the comfort and security I had not valued until it was gone" (9). Equally significant, Dana claims responsibility for the loss of her arm; she informs Kevin that she told the police (a neighbor calls the police upon hearing Dana's screams) that "[I]t was an accident. My fault" (10). Dana's acceptance of blame raises some questions. For what specific part of this surreal incident is she claiming to be at fault? Is her ignorance about her family's history and the history of slavery her fault? In light of her family's history of racialized sexual violence, is the loss of her arm the price Dana must pay for having a miscegenous marriage with Kevin? Are Dana's Black female ancestors affronted and sending her a message? Would Dana's Black ancestors, who had to bow so that their future generations could stand, be proud of her? Would the spirits of Harriet Jacobs, Lucy Terry, Harriet Tubman, Sojourner Truth, Ellen Craft, Ida B. Wells, Mary McCloud Bethune, and other courageous Black women who fought against white-male supremacy and its violence against Black women, be pleased with Dana Franklin before her return to the past? Did they struggle so that Dana Franklin could be naïve about Black people's history during slavery and also marry a white man who is also ignorant about the impact of slavery in America? Perhaps Butler uses the surreal to contemplate the spiritual realm of existence in time and space. With the foundation for *Kindred* being slavery's past, Amos Wilson establishes the importance of knowing history:

> When we become socially amnesiac we forget our location in time and space, because history is about locating one's self in time and space. History is a grid, a set of coordinates that permit the individual to locate himself [or herself] in reference to other points in the world. . . . When one is shorn of one's past and does not see the direction of one's future and is very uncertain of one's present, then one cannot tell from whence one comes and where one is going, where one is—and suffer as a result. (41)

Butler suggests that Dana, in her present life with Kevin, is lost in time and space and has become socially amnesiac, especially about sexual violence. Going back in time forces Dana to become more grounded in her family's history as well as the history of Black people and their relationships with white slave owners during the 19th century. Although the experience was traumatic, Dana has been reborn by the past. Connecting the present to the past, Yanick St. Jean and Joe R. Feagin maintain: "These women can set themselves in opposition to the white memory and white oppression because of their knowledge of the past and of false white assumptions, knowledge communicated over generations of black families. Although there is often a cost for challenges to white actions and memories, these black women still take countering actions, survive, and even thrive" (214). Considering Kevin's warning to Dana that, "You're gambling. Hell, you're gambling against history" (95), Ashraf H.A. Rushdy notes: "By becoming an agent capable of transforming history, Dana becomes to the same degree subject to history—one who is liable to be transformed by seemingly dead historical forces. When she gambles against history, in other words, she can also lose to history" (145). Friend or fiend, Dana Franklin becomes locked into the realities of her family's history.

What remains unclear in the novel is how Kevin viewed Dana, within the context of American slavery, before she is repeatedly transported back to the past. Despite white America's grand celebration of its Bicentennial, there still exists little recognition and no compensation for Black people's unpaid labor, much less any understanding of the enduring trauma. Paradoxically, a famous slaveholder and pedophile (his sexually exploitative relationship with the young slave Sally Hemings suggests this characterization), Thomas Jefferson articulated his apprehensions and the consequences (as a prophet Jeremiah) of America's enslavement of Black people:

> Indeed I tremble for my country when I reflect that God is just: that his jus-
> tice cannot sleep for ever: that considering numbers, nature and natural means
> only, a revolution of the wheel of fortune, an exchange of situation, is among
> possible events: that it may become probable by supernatural interference! The
> Almighty has no attribute which can take side with us in such a contest.—But
> it is impossible to be temperate and to pursue this subject through the various
> considerations of policy, of morals, of history natural and civil. . . . The spirit
> of the master is abating, that of the slave rising from the dust, his condition mol-
> lifying, the way I hope preparing, under the auspices of heaven, for a total eman-
> cipation, and that this is disposed, in order of events, to be with the consent of
> the masters, rather than by their extirpation. (163)

Despite his seemingly heartfelt concerns about the horrors of slavery, Jefferson never freed his own slaves. This speaks to Dana's insistence that Rufus free the two children he had with Alice; this illustrates some sense of redemption on his part, but obviously his attempt to rape Dana reveals the fundamental evil that slavery creates. Regardless of the future of their miscegenous marital relation-ship, Dana Franklin can never, ever, be naïve about her family's tragic past of racialized sexual violence or about the collective past of Black people's experi-ence under slavery.

chapter 6

White Police Penetrating, Probing, and Playing in the Black Man's Ass

The Sadistic Sodomizing of Abner Louima

The notion of the "Black male predator" is so historically rooted in the American consciousness that we have come to accept the brutalization and murder of citizens by the police as an acceptable method of law enforcement. . . . This attitude, ingrained since slavery, is nurtured and manipulated by the police, who are quick to release the prior-arrest or medical records of their victims, as if getting a speeding ticket, or jumping a subway turnstile, or being a graffiti artist, or smoking marijuana, or being mentally ill, or serving time in prison for any reason whatsoever, somehow justified being killed by the police.

Jill Nelson, *Police Brutality: An Anthology*

Why are all these people angrily waving toilet plungers in the air? Why are there hordes of police officers with riot helmets standing here in front of the precinct with faces fixed like stone? Why do so many Black parents in New York City have more solicitude for their sons and nephews? The degenerately sadistic rape and torture of a 32-year-old Black man and Haitian immigrant named Abner Louima, with a dirty broomstick,[1] by two white New York City police officers in

Brooklyn's 70th Precinct bathroom, raises some profoundly problematic issues, which graphically speak to the quintessentially violent characteristics of white-supremacist culture in America. This villainous racial and sexual assault began on a hot and steamy August 9, 1997, when Abner Louima had a physical confrontation with police officers outside of the Club Rendezvous nightclub in Flatbush, Brooklyn. Later, at the 70th Precinct on Lawrence Avenue in the borough's Kensington section, Police Officer Justin A. Volpe forced a broomstick five to six inches into Abner Louima's rectum while another officer, Charles Schwarz, held him down. Then, according to Louima, Volpe attempted to humiliate him by forcing the excrement-stained stick into Louima's tear-stained face while bellowing racist statements. Other officers were to be charged, including officers who allowed the crime to continue.

This repulsive incident recalls the brutal sexual torture and rape that Black people encountered while enslaved by white people. Moreover, the homosocial, homoerotic, and miscegenous aspects of this torturous rape suggest a question of transgression accompanied by deep sexual and racial desire. Indeed, evidence seems to point to the fact that 27-year-old Justin Volpe appears heterosexually and homoerotically attracted to the race he desires and despises. Like some horrific account from a slave narrative, this incident reflects the synthesis of psychological and physical violence. Accordingly, in my mind, historical and psychological aspects are at the heart of this execrable transgression, where miscegenation as sexual consumption connects to homoerotic desire.

This American narrative of the interracial coupling and torturing of Abner Louima draws our gaze below the waist. Sensational in its impact, the torture illustrates what the Black psychiatrist Frantz Fanon describes as "an irrational longing for unusual eras of sexual license, of orgiastic scenes, of unpunished rapes, of unrepressed incest" (165). And, as Fanon argues, too often within white-supremacist discourse, the Black male becomes defined relative to his genitalia and imagined sexual transgressions. Thus, my argument here is that what Police Officer Justin Volpe did to Abner Louima was perhaps subliminally what he wanted to do without any artificial means and what he wanted to have done to himself. However, unable to realize his libidinous desire because another white police officer was present during the sodomy, Volpe turned Louima into a modern-day version of "strange fruit."

Let us go back to the genesis of the situation. At the Club Rendezvous, a fight between two women broke out on the street, and Justin Volpe was punched in the face and knocked flat in front of other officers. Although he was wrong, Volpe somehow believed that Abner Louima was the individual who hit him, so Volpe arrested Louima. A Black man wearing a vest sucker-punched Volpe, and Louima, because he was wearing a vest, was misidentified. Before arriving at the Brooklyn police precinct, Louima was repeatedly beaten by Justin Volpe and allegedly two other police officers, Thomas Bruder and Thomas Wiese. In court testimony, Louima stated: "I was sitting in the back of the police car when one of the officers hit me on the left side of my face." Then he recalled, "One of them said to me, 'Stupid nigger, I'm going to teach you how to respect cops.' He hit me again and then another police officer started to beat me." Louima also stated that he was driven to the corner of Glenwood and Bedford; here he was beaten again, in the legs too. While at the 70th Precinct, a bruised and disoriented Louima was booked, taken into the bathroom, and stripped from the waist down. Then, while handcuffed, Volpe began the unauthorized and premeditated use of the dirty broomstick. After being kicked and hit in the genitals with the broomstick, Louima's rectum, bladder, and colon were violently ruptured by Volpe while Schwarz held him down as they screamed racial epithets. According to some reports, twenty police officers were on duty and present at the stationhouse at the time of the assault. Like Kitty Genovese, whose agonized screams for assistance were ignored by her neighbors while she was murdered, Louima cried out in agony, but not one of the police officers in the precinct responded to his pleas for assistance. After several hours of hemorrhaging nearly to death in a jail cell, another Black prisoner convinced some police officers to get medical treatment for Louima. About an hour and a half later, EMS technicians arrived at the police station and examined Louima. Several more hours lapsed before a traumatized and humiliated Louima, in critical condition, was taken to Coney Island Hospital, escorted by white police officers. A hole had been torn in Louima's colon, his bladder had been punctured, and he was bleeding internally. The first police officers to show up at the hospital on Saturday told the nurses they found Louima half-naked and bleeding and they said he was a homosexual.

While at the hospital, Abner Louima was kept handcuffed; he claimed Volpe threatened him and his family with death if they said anything about his being raped and tortured, charges Volpe vociferously denied before his trial. There at the hospital, a nurse of Caribbean descent, Magalie Laurent, persisted in demanding answers about Louima's unusual injuries, and refused to be a part of the white police officers' attempt to "cover their asses." She played a critical role in comforting Louima and exposing this sexual assault by calling the New York Police Department's Internal Affairs Bureau at the consistent urging of another concerned Black nurse who treated Abner Louima in the emergency room. IAB did not respond to this complaint and did not assign the case a number. Laurent then began calling Louima's family and told them: "He didn't injure himself that way. They did this to him." The doctor on the case, who gave his name only as Levin, stated that Louima suffered a "blunt-force trauma to the anus" and that "his injuries were consistent" with his frightening tale of medieval torture. Also, there was an unidentified individual who called *Daily News* columnist Mike McAlary. After investigating, McAlary wrote, "This is a story to stop the city." The Louima case finally broke wide open and for his reporting McAlary was awarded the prestigious Pulitzer Prize.

Many people in New York City were outraged. A crowd estimated by police at 7,000, and by organizers at 15,000, marched on City Hall; many of these individuals were waving toilet plungers in the air as they marched and denounced the police officers involved in this act of police brutality and other incidents of misconduct. Protestors especially targeted New York City Mayor Rudy Giuliani, because it was believed that he created a climate that caused this assault to occur. From the early stages in his term, Mayor Giuliani was viewed as an ardent supporter of the police department; this support placed him at odds with most of the Black people in New York City. In his book *A Lawyer's Life* (2002), Johnnie Cochran states:

> I had seen too much police abuse to be shocked. But even I had never seen anything quite as depraved as this act. This was truly barbaric. Volpe has said it, he had it right, he had tried to break a man sexually. . . . I also recognized that like the Simpson case this one was going to make or break reputations and careers. It was the kind of case that potentially could rip apart the city. As I was learning, the people of color in New York did not trust Giuliani and they were watching him closely to see if he supported the torturers or the victim. (145)

Over a span of 64 grueling days, Louima's internal injuries resulted in three major operations and tremendous distress to his family and friends. While at the hospital, a plastic tube ran from Louima's ruptured bladder into a plastic bag. His urine was red. For many days, he had to wear a colostomy bag because of the soft tissue injuries he sustained. It is still unknown if Louima will regain normal bowel function. When the news of Louima's torture broke, many people, and especially Black people around the world, were enraged and appalled by these white police officers' depraved indifference to human life. Families across America, suffering the long-term effects of barbaric police brutality, were especially horrified as they were forced to revisit their tragedies of loved ones beaten or killed by police officers. Of critical concern was that this assault occurred not in some dark, desolate field or alley but in a New York City government building designed to "serve and protect" all citizens. On the contrary, however, with white rage careening out of control, Volpe, absent of any moral imperative, committed this assault in the precinct bathroom and held court there *because* he believed that his behavior would be protected, an assumption borne out by the fact that only four white police officers were tried for a crime that occurred when about 20 police officers were in the precinct at the time of the attack. These invisible spectators would vicariously experience the torture when Volpe later boasted to his colleagues about "breaking a man." More importantly, Volpe and Schwarz's pathological behavior suggests a pattern of violence and torture of prisoners that was routinely tolerated by police officers at this Brooklyn house of horrors and similar police precincts. "This is not a corruption case," said Brain Figeroux, a former assistant district attorney and one of Louima's lawyers. "This is a torture case. Cops are going to jail." Louima's wife, Micheline, the mother of their son, Abner Jr., said: "He has never been in trouble in his life. The cops are going to try and say this was some sort of homosexual thing. How much will they take from him?" Writer and lesbian activist Barbara Smith acknowledges her trauma and contextualizes the sheer horror of Abner Louima's heartbreaking torment within the Black experience:

> For nights after learning what happened to Abner Louima, it was difficult for me to sleep. Every time I awoke I thought about him and felt the horror again. Day or night, I was near tears whenever I focused upon what he and his family were going through. The despair and fury I felt were nothing new. Since childhood I have been forced to live this nightmare again and again. In 1955, although I was too little to know what it meant, I learned fourteen-year-old Emmett Till's name when he was lynched in Mississippi for whistling at a white woman. In 1957, when I was ten, I watched nine Black students attempt to enter Little Rock High School while a mob of screaming white adults attacked them verbally and physically. (192)

Emmett Till, who suffered a gunshot in the temple, was castrated and had his eyeballs gouged out before he was thrown in the Tallahatchie River with the 125-pound blower motor from a cotton-gin fan tied to his neck with barbed wire. Till and the nine Black students attempting to enter Little Rock High School are similar to Abner Louima because of their transgressions against the relentless authority of America's white culture and its racially hegemonic institutions. Louima suggests the broader implications of his assault. He states: "I believe there are other victims who are either ashamed to come out or did not know how to speak out for themselves." Elaine Scarry's analysis of the relationship between language and acts of torture posits that "torture is such an extreme event that it seems inappropriate to generalize from it to anything else or from anything else to it. Its immorality is so absolute and the pain it brings so real that there is a reluctance to place it in conversation by the side of other subjects" (60). Although fully horrific, Abner Louima's experience highlights the construction of racial difference as a threat to white masculinity, to which ritualistic violence has been an extreme response.

Historically, the raping and sexual torture-mutilation of Black men is not a new phenomenon. White individuals in positions of power have systematically attacked the sexuality of African Americans for purposes of subjugation and control. While in the slave castles on the west coast of Africa, on the slave ships during the Middle Passage, and on the slave plantations of the Caribbean and the Americas, Black men, women, and children were routinely subjected to sexual violence by their white masters and overseers. In fact, during the notorious Middle Passage between Africa and the New World, some Black men, women, and children were allowed mobility on board ships so that white sailors could have unlimited sexual access to them. America's system of enslavement with its philosophy of white domination and Black subordination was intended to dehumanize Black people, and in this process, in the psyches of some whites, Black people became simply Black bodies to be physically and sexually exploited. During slavery, Black men, women and children were forced to stand naked on the slave auction blocks while they were penetrated, probed, and played with by prurient white males seeking to exploit Black bodies. Discussing the utterly horrific plight of Black people during their enslavement and the degendering of Black bodies, Hortense J. Spillers states:

> First of all, their New-World, diasporic plight marked a theft of the body—a willful and violent (and unimaginable from this distance) severing of the captive body from its motive will, its active desire under these conditions, we lose at least gender difference in the outcome, and the female body and the male body become a territory of cultural and political maneuver, not at all gender-related, gender-specific. But this body, at least from the point of view of the captive community, focuses a private and particular space, at which point of convergence biological, sexual, social, cultural, linguistic, ritualistic and psychological forces join. ("Mama's Baby, Papa's Maybe" 67)

In America, white masculinity has often been culturally and psychologically defined as the beating, lynch-burning, castrating, and overall killing of Black men, and by the sexual conquest (rape) of Black women. The lynching of Black men by white men suggests that white men fear Black men; however, the rape of Black women by white men suggests that white men do not fear Black women. Since 1859, approximately 5,000 Black individuals have been lynched in America for alleged or real acts against white supremacy. Accordingly, Justin Volpe had a fiancée, an attractive dark-skinned African American woman named Susan Lawson, his live-in lover who worked as a clerk in Volpe's precinct. Defending her white lover, Lawson stated: "Justin wouldn't do this to our life. If it happened, he didn't do it." Later, she revealed doubt when she speculated on the fruits of miscegenation: "But I know he is not an evil person. His life with me would have to be a lie. We are planning on getting married and having children. If Justin Volpe did this, he did it to me and his children." This last statement suggests that by raping a Black man, Volpe, by logical extension, rapes her, a Black woman, and abuses his own Black children. More importantly, through his transgression of emasculation and castration, Volpe briefly makes a Black man, Louima, into his Black "woman." Although Louima's genitals were left intact after this savage assault, he may never think about his Black body, his sexuality, and his masculinity the same way. Thus, America's white-supremacist culture sucks up the shadows of Black men, leaving them invisible to the dominant society and often to themselves. As Zora Neale Hurston notes, some Black people become "slave ships in shoes."

It is a known fact that many white slave masters would routinely rape Black women and years later rape their own daughters from these forced miscegenous relationships. Susan Lawson's relationship with Justin Volpe embodies a little-discussed wound in the heart of many whites: the Black woman lover.

Ever since Black people were enslaved, white males have used their power over Black women, and whites have generally frowned upon these sexual relations. Within white-supremacist discourse, Black women often become a synthesis of race, pleasure, and service. Although Lawson was there when the trial opened and had been in the courtroom during the trial and heard the testimony for the first few days, she soon disappeared. This embrace-and-avoidance strategy seemed orchestrated to distance Volpe and Lawson with regard to the public, but highlighted the remote possibility that Volpe has no racial animus. Interestingly, Police Officer Thomas Wiese also has had a long-term relationship with a Black woman and has a child from this relationship. With white women still standing on the pedestal of purity, white men are permitted to roam sexually with the dark exotic Other. But unlike white women who have Black lovers and who bear the burden of keeping white civilization "pure," white men who have Black lovers too often retain their true-white manhood or favorite-son status. Despite numerous anti-miscegenation laws, these miscegenous relationships also speak to the fundamental amalgamation between Blacks and whites since the founding of this country.

In some ways, Volpe and Lawson's miscegenous relationship echoes the relationship between the white-supremacist Thomas Jefferson and the enslaved Sally Hemings. Despite being an advocate for freedom, justice, and the pursuit of happiness, Jefferson was a slave owner who had his enslaved Blacks whipped. Although Jefferson states in *Notes on the State of Virginia* (1787) that Black people are "inferior to the whites in the endowments both of body and mind" (143), he allegedly had many children with this Black woman; obviously Jefferson's head and heart were in conflict. As Stanley Crouch argues, miscegenation is "not a one-sided or simple story. Sometimes it is a story of love, sometimes it is a story of power, sometimes it is a story of both. And there are even those stories that are about no more than who happened to be there when the big net of spring fever fell from the sky" (39). Susan Lawson's clerical position in the precinct and her devotion to a lawless Justin Volpe suggest the possibility of a story of both power and love. By embracing the white phallus, some Black women and men think that they obtain access to white power and white privilege; too often this embrace suggests racial transcendence where blackness becomes marginalized. Extending the argument of whiteness as property, George Lipsitz analyzes the materiality of whiteness:

> Whiteness has a cash value: it accounts for advantages that come to individuals through profits made from housing secured in discriminatory markets, through the unequal education allocated to children of different races through insider networks that channel employment opportunities to the relatives and friends of those who have profited most from present and past racial discrimination, and especially through intergenerational transfers of inherited wealth that pass on the spoils of discrimination to succeeding generations. (vii)

Despite her embrace of white privilege signified by the white phallus, Susan Lawson appears to have been naive or just plain insipid in believing that racist white men are not interested in having sexual relationships with Black women or Black men. In a white-supremacist culture, interracial relationships and marriages do not always exclude some white people from racist thoughts and behavior. Indeed, some racist white people find some Black individuals acceptable (commonly known as token Blacks or honorary whites), while they regard the masses of Black people as innately inferior and socially pathological. As James Baldwin argues: "Blacks are often confronted, in American life, with such devastating examples of the white descent from dignity; devastating not only because of the enormity of white pretensions, but because this swift and graceless descent would seem to indicate that white people have no principles whatever" (*The Devil Finds Work* 7). In essence, in a society where many white men feel threatened by a rising Black population and increasing Caribbean and African immigration, they desire to recapture and reassert their power and their sexual dominance over Black men and women. These whites, with their unlimited capacity for cruelty, fervently long for the past where all Black bodies, whether enslaved or free, had to submit to their will or, if they resisted, be beaten, tortured, mutilated, and killed. As Ann duCille points out: "White men's sexual desire for and exploitation of black women is historically manifest; their erotic desire for black men, however, is equally well covered up—so much so, in fact, that it most often masquerades as both hyper-heterosexuality and rabid racism" (*The Unbearable Darkness of Being* 306). America's white-supremacist culture of racial violence had the effect of terrorizing many Black communities; however, like the numerous protests and marches for Abner Louima, with people waving toilet plungers, resistance to white-supremacist violence by Black people has been steadfast and psychologically beneficial. Led and organized by Rev. Al Sharpton, the protests and marches, with many people waving Volpe's instrument of torture and humiliation, helped to unite New Yorkers and especially African Americans and Blacks from the Caribbean and Africa; in fact, this repulsive debasement helped to lessen the intra-racial conflict in the Black community.

The work of community activist and scholar Bobby E. Wright helps to place Abner Louima's unbelievable moment of torture and ethnic cleansing into a psychological context. Wright places the experience of Black people within the metaphor of a bullfight and describes the "moment of truth" when, after being brutalized while making innumerable charges, the bull really sees the matador. For the bull however, this "moment of truth" comes too late. Wright advocates that Black people should really see white supremacy, a narcissistic ideology, as the matador who holds the banner that represents genocide. Even more helpful, analyzing the psychopath, Wright makes four points that suggest Volpe's matadorish behavior. First, the psychopath simply ignores the concept of right and wrong; this behavior represents a lack of ethical and moral development. Second, the psychopath appears to be very honest and humane but really has no concern or commitment except to his or her own selfish interest. This individual shows great indignation and anger when his or her integrity is questioned. Third, the psychopath is usually sexually inadequate, with a limited capacity to form close interpersonal relationships. On this point, Wright argues that historically, some white psychopaths attempted to achieve sexual gratification by such methods as raping Black women and castrating Black men. Fourth, psychopaths have an inability to accept blame or to learn from previous experience and therefore reject constituted authority and discipline (1–10). This then is the psychopathic personality and these characteristics strongly suggest the psychological motivations behind Volpe's dastardly deed and his subsequent denials of tormenting Louima with his swordlike broomstick. Simply put, like the Haitian SD, a special torture unit of the Tonton Macoutes under the cruel Jean-Claude Duvalier dictatorship, Police Officer Justin Volpe, in the traditional role of a swashbuckling matador, brutally gores Abner Louima in the rectum. However, turning Wright's argument on its head, perhaps Volpe represents a raging white bull that runs the streets of New York City, goring innocent Black individuals.

From the most recent nationwide narratives of violence and torture directed at Black men by white police, we can connect Abner Louima's experience to the senseless murder of West African immigrant Amadou Diallo by four white NYPD police officers (who fired 41 shots at him), the brutal beating of motorist Rodney King in Los Angeles, and the court testimony of Los Angeles ex–police officer Mark Fuhrman, who in an interview with a white-woman filmmaker said that he and other white police officers routinely tortured Black and Hispanic suspects in their custody. In one particular incident, Fuhrman revealed that the walls in an apartment were covered with blood after he and other police officers had beaten and tortured suspects. Also, in court testimony, Fuhrman stated that he was not a racist and that he had never used the word "nigger." In fact, the depreciative word "nigger" seems a most appropriate description for Volpe and Fuhrman, along with their sadistic partners in crime. As one of William Faulkner's characters aptly points out: "Nigger is not a person so much as a form of behavior." Not surprisingly, most white people believed that Fuhrman was telling the truth whereas most Black people knew that he was lying through his teeth. When Fuhrman was exposed by tape recordings in court testimony, many whites believed that he was an aberration. Like Volpe's orgy of brutality, Fuhrman's defense against charges of racism and racial violence was that he once dated a Black woman. Police have a virtual license to kill, and Black males are the primary target. The denial of police violence directed at Black people represents a critical component of white-supremacist culture: America's long history of Black men and boys being tortured and castrated and Black women and girls being tortured and raped by white males.

More specifically, in April 1994 there were stunning charges of police brutality that graphically foreshadowed Volpe's attack on Louima. Earl Caldwell, formerly a reporter for the *Daily News*, related that six Black men came forward to report that on separate occasions a Latino police officer abducted them, took them to an isolated place and raped and sodomized them, and then threatened to kill them if they said anything. Attorney Adam Thompson, who represented five of the men, identified the police officer as Reggie Rivera of the 101st Precinct in Queens. Yet unlike the Louima incident, there were witnesses who saw Officer Rivera with his pants down and his half-naked victim handcuffed inside a van with his pants and underwear down. Those witnesses were threatened by the officer (Caldwell 12). Using the terminology of war, many Black people view arrogant white police officers as an occupying force in their communities. A common aspect of many civil wars and military occupations is the rape of civilians; evidence graphically shows that men, women, and children are raped, tortured, and killed as if they are enemy territory and the spoils of war.

Beyond the racial aspects of this inhumane transgression, sexual desire is a possibility in Volpe's assault of Louima; essentially, Volpe's behavior suggests his desire for a more penetrating, probing, and playful Black sexual experience. Indeed, some racist individuals might consider Volpe to be a "nigger lover." It can be argued that anyone who is obsessively, deathly afraid of, or hateful toward another individual has an intimate investment in the individual feared or hated. With the attractive dark-skinned Susan Lawson as his lover, it is likely Volpe was acting out a repressed desire for anal intercourse, and rationalized that desire by the anger he felt for the dark-skinned Louima. The individual who is sexually obsessed fixes his gaze on the object of desire as a way of realizing his or her desire. Equally important, sexual obsession is a hidden form of narcissism. In taking Louima into the bathroom, Volpe indicates he had some narcissistic intentions of performing an intimate and illicit action that required privacy. Here some critical questions come to mind: Did Volpe know that there was a stick in the bathroom before he brought Louima in the bathroom? Did Volpe pull down Louima's pants and underwear before he found the stick or did he discover the broomstick first? If Volpe pulled down Louima's clothing first and there was no stick, what was he going to do to his victim? Did Volpe become tumescent while he was penetrating and probing Louima's rectum? Did the other white police officer in the bathroom encourage Volpe to "break" Louima as they screamed racial remarks? Did thoughts of Susan Lawson come to Justin Volpe's mind when he was penetrating Abner Louima's anus? Considering the nature of sadism, did Volpe become more forceful in his rectal thrusts as he heard Louima's tormented screams and pleads? In terms of transference and projection, did Louima become Susan with a penis? Lastly, whose semen was found in the precinct bathroom and when did this eruption occur?

In "Waiting for Justice," Rance E. Huff postulates on Volpe's sexual desire: "It is not too far a stretch to imagine that when Volpe had Louima bent over in front of him that steamy August night, the sight of Abner's dark, chocolate buttocks probably caused a rush of sexual adrenaline in him and he lost control of himself" (1). Maybe this "rush of sexual adrenaline" was the same feeling that

Volpe experienced many times with Susan, but the pure anger manifested in a violent sexual performance. Perhaps Volpe internalized the dominant-white discourse of the Black woman as a Jezebel/whore and viewed Susan as sexually uninhibited and aggressive. Equally important, this was a time for Volpe to examine a Black man's genitals and paradoxically to explore his homosocial and homoerotic desires in a psychologically and physically safe location but in a sadistic manner. As Ann duCille argues in "The Unbearable Darkness of Being: 'Fresh' Thoughts on Race, Sex, and the Simpsons": "Such racial hatred veils a triply transgressive desire that crosses the boundaries of gender, race, and sexuality. In a Lacanian analysis, the tyranny born of the white man's unrequitable desire for the black phallus might be known as the Out-Law of the Father. . . . White homophilia can only countenance itself by feminizing the black male it desires" (307). Through displacement, Volpe attempts to "castrate" Louima through a sadistic act of sodomy, a heuristic tool of lynch law. Here I use the word "castrate" to convey the physical and psychological destruction of an individual. As duCille explicates: "This displacement represents the ultimate intentional 'phallusy': white men project their own latent desire for the black male penis onto white women and punish black men for a desire that is finally their own: to fuck a black man, to fuck like a black man, to fuck a white woman with a black penis" (306). For Volpe, this displacement of desire also suggests an attempt to "fuck" a Black woman (Susan Lawson) with a Black penis. Also, as Sigmund Freud argues, displacement occurs when something in a dream stands for something quite different in the waking world, even its opposite, as when an enemy represents a lover whom the sleeper does not entirely trust. Like the thousands of Black men lynched, castrated, and burned all across America who were victims of white males' displaced desire, Abner Louima's rectum became the site of a barbaric ritual of human sacrifice to the demonic power-laden philosophy of white racial superiority and Black inferiority. Moreover, like the Roman gladiators who fought to the death to please their bloodthirsty emperors and spectators, Louima's anus became the bloody and muddy sacrifice to New York City's throne of white male police privilege and power. In New York, Black male bodies are often ordered by white police to "assume the position"; they are frisked, patted down, probed, and spread. Of course, this represents the position for anal intercourse. Ironically, even Mayor Rudolph Giuliani, who some say orchestrated a police state, conveyed the horror of this incident: "I thought the actions here were horrendous and perverse and sick, and I think every police officer felt that way. I don't think police officers in any way identified with the kind of conduct that was involved here. I think they found it reprehensible and perverse, and some kind of display of a violent sickness." Mayor Giuliani's use of the words "violent sickness" appropriately defines the philosophy of worldwide white supremacy that seems to operate within the New York City's Police Department. Bob Herbert's essay "A Cop's View" relates an incident that conveys the police's pervasive abuse of power. "In one of the [drug] raids an innocent man was dragged handcuffed and naked from his apartment and put through several hours of grotesque humiliation before being released. It turned out the police had raided the wrong apartment" (17). We can only contemplate the humiliation and psychological trauma this innocent individual endured and perhaps still endures.

In New York City, most white people have difficulty believing that police brutality against Black people is an aberration, on the other hand, most Black people, Latinos, Asians, and a small amount of white people view police misconduct as a pervasive problem. In her poem "Rape," Adrienne Rich sagaciously captures the inherent power and violence associated with the police: "There is a cop who is both prowler and father: he comes from your block, grew up with your brothers, had certain ideas./ You hardly know him in his boots and silver badge/ on horseback, one hand touching his gun./ You hardly know him but you have to get to know him:/ he has access to machinery that could kill you" (206). The machinery in the poem refers to the physical, psychological, and legal components used to give the white police officers an almost godlike status within the Black communities they occupy. Rich's description of the rape in the poem and the psychological aftermath echoes the humiliation, intimidation, and rape of victims like Louima who are often "raped" again by the legal process. "And so, when the time comes, you have to turn to him,/ the maniac's sperm still greasing your thighs,/ your mind whirling like crazy. You have to confess to him,/ you are guilty of the crime of having been forced" (206). Interestingly, the film *In Too Deep* (1999), directed by Michael Ryner, captures a scene that signifies on Louima's assault. Here the merciless and narcissistic Black drug-dealing character named "God," brilliantly played by the rapper LL Cool J, tortures a naked and bound, disloyal Black subordinate by sodomizing him with a pool stick. Connecting sexuality to violence, God sadistically screams: "Love it. Love it!" as he viciously rams the stick up Frisco's rectum. Later, imitating the act of fellatio, God tortures a drug-addicted Black female by forcing an automatic pistol in her bloody mouth and ordering her to suck on it like a crack pipe. Although Louima's assault was horrific, it reinforces the tragic fact that, worldwide, women are too often the victims of sexualized violence. For example, in Bosnia an anonymous 16-year-old Muslim girl poignantly and painfully describes her traumatic rape:

> One of the soldiers, around thirty years old, ordered me into the house. He told me to undress. I was terribly afraid. I took off my clothes, feeling that I was falling apart. The feeling seemed under my skin. I was dying. My entire being was murdered. I closed my eyes. He did it to me. I cried. I twisted my body convulsively. I bled. I had been a virgin. He went out and invited two other soldiers to come in. I cried. Two others repeated what the first had done to me. I didn't even know when they had left. I stayed there lying on the floor alone in a pool of blood. My mother found me. I couldn't imagine anything worse. I had been raped, destroyed, and terribly hurt. But for my mother this was the greatest sorrow of our lives. We both cried and screamed. She dressed me.

In America a woman is raped every six minutes, and every twelve minutes a woman is beaten. Additionally, 2,000–4,000 women are beaten to death annually, and 73 percent of women above the age of 12 will be victimized sometime in their lifetimes. Sixty-one percent of all rape victims are less than 18 years old. Once they encounter the legal system, rape victims, regardless of gender, are often victimized again by a process that often objectifies them. Although the physical rape of Black males by police officers might appear to be rare, Black men get the proverbial shaft when they are symbolically castrated by systematic white-supremacist practices that deny them the ability to take care of themselves and their families.

Also, within a literary context, James Baldwin's "Going to Meet the Man" (1965) illustrates the sexual violence that Black men have experienced in American society. In this short story, a white Southern deputy sheriff has trouble becoming tumescent with his white wife, Grace. Only when the sheriff remembers his father and mother taking him to a grassy clearing where he witnesses a sexualized lynch-burning of a nameless African American man does his sexual desire for his wife escalate. With graphic detail of the homosocial and homoerotic aspects for the Black male body Baldwin describes the absolute horror and diabolical desire of white racial violence:

> The man with the knife took the nigger's privates in his hand, one hand, still smiling, as though he were weighing them. In the cradle of the one white hand the nigger's privates seemed as remote as meat being weighed in the scales; but seemed heavier, too, much heavier, and Jesse felt his scrotum tighten, and huge, huge, much bigger than his father's flaccid hairless, the largest thing he had ever seen till then, and the blackest. The white hand stretched them, cradled them, caressed them. Then the dying man's eyes looked straight into Jesse's eyes—it could not have been as long as a second, but it seemed, longer than a year. Then Jesse screamed, and the crowd screamed as the knife flashed, first up then down, cutting the dreadful thing away, and the blood came rushing down. The crowd rushed forward, tearing at the body with their hands, with knives, with rocks, with stones howling and cursing. Jesse's head, of its own weight, fell downward toward his father's head. Someone stepped forward and drenched the body with kerosene. Where the man had been, a great sheet of flame appeared. Jesse's father lowered him to the ground. (247–48)

This passage, with its sexualized nuances, captures the complex desire of sadistic white people to embrace, but still destroy, the Black body, and especially the Black phallus. Reinforcing the issue of consumption, Jesse's father states: "I reckon we better get over there and get some that food before it's all gone" (249). Yet there is some ambiguity here because Baldwin does not make any direct reference to food before the father's statement. The direct context to his statement involves the African American male body. "The head was caved in, one eye was torn out, one ear was hanging. . . . He lay spread-eagled with what had been a wound between what had been his legs" (248). After recalling this castration-lynching that reduces the African American man to "a black charred object on the black ground" (248), instead of being repelled by the horror of this fiendish castration, these whites rush forward to tear Black flesh. With the image of the big Black phallus in his psyche, the story concludes with displacement: the white sheriff softly stroking his wife and whispering "Come on sugar, I'm going to do you like a nigger, just like a nigger, come on, sugar, and love me just like you'd love a nigger" (249). More often than not, white people who attended the lynch-burnings would fight in order to take home the fingers, toes, ears, and penises of Black men who were lynched-burned. Unlike the scavengers for flesh, the young Jesse has taken home memories. As a grown man, Jesse displaces and projects himself into the body of the African American man and his use of the word "nigger" has a decimating effect on the Black body where the African American man becomes nameless and reduced to a "thing" for consumption and elimination. Taking Jesse's discourse a bit further, there is the symbolic posses-sion of the "nigger" phallus, used to sexually satisfy his wife. Jesse by his own definition, becomes the nigger with the "dreadful thing" as he views his white wife loving a "nigger" in a manner that would be different than a white man like himself. Jesse's white phallus becomes useless as the nigger's phallus becomes his sexual instrument. While Jesse is sexually empowered by his possession of the nigger's phallus, his wife becomes sexually liberated. For Baldwin lynching is figured as a psychosocial ritual of enjoyment and displacement in this pro-cess of phallic inversion. Here a triangle of sexual desire becomes complicated as Jesse becomes a white man with a nigger's phallus, who has sexual relations with his white wife, miscegenation by displacement. Lastly, the fact Jesse represents legal authority reinforces the intersection between white supremacist organiza-tions and those charged with upholding the law. Like Wright, Baldwin, although much less subtle, captures that consumptive sexual desire; the subjectivity. Better still, there is a psychological consumption that empowers these sadistic whites and reduces the African American male body to a commodity. In Wright's poem and Baldwin's short story, the Black male body loses sense of human identifica-tion as the two crowds become hysterical in their desires to murder. Consider-ing the significant number of African American individuals that were killed, in a perverse sense, lynching as a social ritual of redemption becomes not only acceptable but also natural. This ritual of castration and consumption relates to a recent decapitation. In June 1998, the murder of James Byrd Jr. in Jasper, Texas, by three white supremacists, resulted in his body parts being spread over a wide area when Byrd Jr. was chained to the back of a truck and dragged until he was dismembered.

Aside from slavery, lynching represents the most horrific evidence of Ameri-ca's white-supremacist culture. Between 1882 and 1930 more than 3,386 known Black (mostly male) lynchings occurred. Furthermore, between 1920 and 1932, white police officers were responsible for more than half of all of the murders of Black citizens. Historical accounts reveal that white police officers assisted and were present at lynchings of Black people (Russell, *The Color of Crime* 35). In his rather private "lynching-castration" ritual, Justin Volpe played out the traditional Hegelian master and slave dialectic. Here, Black people from Africa were first brought to the Caribbean for seasoning, a dehumanizing process designed to brutally break, beat, and psychologically manipulate African people into serving the socioeconomic and sexual interest of white people, so that they would never come together to work in their own self-interest. In this regard, Susan Lawson appears to be a victim of the modern-day seasoning process, where Black people are psychologically manipulated to glorify whiteness and embrace the white phallus at the expense of their own psyches.

Within the context of American history, Justin Volpe's behavior exposes white America's relentless systems and practices of physical, psychological, legal, medical, scientific, environmental, educational, and economic violence directed at poor whites, and most especially Native Americans, Latinos, Asians, and Blacks. From its founding to the present day, violence is a quintessentially American phenomenon. For example, in Walter White's critical study of lynching in America, *Rope and Faggot*, a witness recounts the lynch-burning of a pregnant Black woman who openly protested her husband's lynching:

> Securely they bound her ankles together and by them, hanged her to a tree. Gasoline and motor oil were thrown upon her dangling clothes, a match wrapped her in sudden flames. . . . The clothes burned from her toasted body, in which, unfortunately, life still lingered. A man stepped towards the woman and with his knife, ripped open the abdomen in a crude Cesarean operation. Out tumbled the prematurely born child. Two feeble cries it gave—and received for answer the heel of a stalwart man, as life was ground out of the tiny form. ("Violence Is American" 84)

It should be noted that the sodomy of Abner Louima illustrates that this incident is also about power. Within an international context, this torture in the bathroom recalls Joan Dassin's discussion of the torture of Apio Costa. Dassin relates that: "on a certain occasion, police authorities inserted into his anus an object that looked like a bottle washer; that on another occasion, these same authorities made the defendant stand on tops of cans, in which position he would be burnt with cigarettes and hit with closed fists" (22). It appears that the male's anus is a prime target when police torture male individuals. Because Louima resisted arrest outside the Brooklyn nightclub and is said to have hit Volpe, it was rumored that Volpe said that he had to break a man down. Indeed, Volpe did just that by rupturing Louima's internal organs. The mechanisms of torture, the lacerations, tears, openings, ruptures, and punctures of the body, create a distance between the cultural community and the culture of the state represented by judges and police officers. Of course, it was the Internal Affairs Bureau of the New York City Police Department that had to investigate this nefarious incident and the damning evidence given by Police Officer Eric Turetzky. In court testimony, this officer reported that he saw Volpe, moments after the assault, swinging a broken broomstick as if it were a sword. Another officer, Sergeant Kenneth Wernick, a fourteen-year veteran, testified that Volpe told him: "I took a man down. I took a stick and put it five to six inches up his ass." Waving the stick like someone waving his phallus, Volpe's orgasmic-cathartic experience of invading and conquering Louima's rectum characterizes the narcissistic aspects of worldwide white supremacy. In fact, considering the cases of Charles Stuart in Boston and Susan Smith in South Carolina, who both falsely accused Black men of committing crimes against their white families, Black people seem to be always available to the sexual fantasies and hoaxes of some white people.

In New York, police work is often about the power that reinforces the Black and white bi-polar relationship, and when Volpe used the wooden stick to anally rape his victim, he asserted his white-male power and privilege. "They said, 'Take this, nigger,'" Louima said, "'and stuck the stick in my rear end.'" Furthermore, when Volpe forced the excrement-covered stick into Louima's face, he vicariously asserted his desire to receive fellatio by a Black man, but humiliation was Volpe's central objective. Also, this aspect of the abuse synthesizes language and torture, as Volpe attempts to silence Louima. Here, Justin Volpe acted out a disturbing scene in Richard Wright's *Native Son* (1940), where an enraged Bigger Thomas terrorizes and humiliates another Black individual by forcing him to lick the gleaming blade of a knife:

> Gus looked round the room without moving his head, just rolling his eyes in a mute appeal for help. But no one moved. Bigger's left fist was slowly lifting to strike. Gus's lips moved toward the knife; he stuck out his tongue and touched the blade. Gus's lips quivered and tears streamed down his cheeks. (481)

Richard Wright is not alone in exploring the "rape" of Black men by other men. For example, Toni Morrison's *Beloved* (1987) relates an incident on a Black chain gang in Alfred, Georgia. Here, during slavery, with the threat of death, Black men are being forced to perform fellatio on their white overseers:

> Chain-up completed, they knelt down. . . . Kneeling in the mist they waited for the whim of a guard, or two, or three. Or maybe all of them wanted it. Wanted it from one prisoner in particular or none—or all. . . . Occasionally a kneeling man chose gunshot in his head as the price, maybe, of taking a bit of foreskin with him to Jesus. Paul D did not know that then. He was looking at his palsied hands smelling the guard, listening to his soft grunts so like the doves . . . (108–109)

Hovering over Louima with the stick in his face, Volpe's sublimation of his homosocial and homoerotic desire occurred because there was another white-male officer present. Simply stated, like his black nightstick, the broomstick that Volpe used to inhumanely penetrate, probe, and play in Louima's rectum was an extension of the white phallus. Also, Bigger Thomas' analysis of worldwide white supremacy gives weight to Louima's experience. Like the case with the deeply pathological Jeffrey Dahmer, who sexually terrorized, killed, and consumed parts of more than a dozen men, especially Black males, we can only wonder what would have happened if Volpe was alone with his Black victim. Obviously, in America's patriarchal society, violently sodomizing a man with a foreign object is perhaps one of the most humiliating, physical, and psychologically harmful acts for a married heterosexual man with children to endure. Obviously, Louima experienced an incredible amount of shame when this private act became a public spectacle. Furthermore, this sexual assault suggests, to use Bobby E. Wright's term, an act of "menticide," which he defines as the "deliberate and systematic destruction of a group's minds with the ultimate objective being the extirpation of the group," and a desire to murder the spirit and soul of an individual. We can only wonder what long-term effect this horrific incident will have on Abner Louima, his wife, Micheline, his two children, his extended family, and most especially on the psyche of the Black community worldwide. Of critical interest are: Does this incident reinforce the real sense of powerlessness and "social death" that too many Black men feel? How does this incident affect the subjectivity of many Black women who feel unprotected and alone? How do Black parents explain Justin Volpe's truly depraved act of indifference to themselves and especially to their male children? Lastly, does this incident reinforce white-supremacist culture in that most whites, especially white males, believe that this incident could never happen to them?

Since the founding of this country, the projection of the white phallus and white penal law into the internal (anal) affairs of Black male individuals has remained an enduring problem. It is important to remember that, too often, American laws are constructed to serve the political and socioeconomic interests of wealthy white males. Yet, as Baldwin points out, regardless of class, many white people are socialized with a specious sense of superiority:

> White children, in the main, and whether they are rich or poor, grow up with a grasp of reality so feeble that they can very accurately be described as deluded—about themselves and the world they live in. . . . The reason for this, at bottom, is that the doctrine of white supremacy, which still controls most white people, is itself a stupendous delusion: but to be born black in America is an immediate, a mortal challenge. (*No Name in the Street* 128–129)

Volpe's psychopathic behavior and desire to experience phallic satisfaction, backed by white legal authority, was a performance of tremendous psychological and physical violence, and also produced economic violence, in that Louima was the sole provider for his family, working, ironically, as a security guard even though he has a degree in electrical engineering. Equally ironic, Abner Louima's employment status illustrates how America's white society exploits Black males and females, especially immigrants, as low-paid security guards to protect white people, white property, and white privilege.

Without a doubt, we can say that many power-crazed, racist, and sexually perverted white male police officers in New York City fervently believe that regardless of their nationality, Black people "ain't shit." In the rape of Abner Louima in the bathroom of the Brooklyn police station, bloody shit came out on the broomstick used by Volpe to sodomize Louima. Then, once the racial incident was exposed to the public, shit hit the proverbial fan. In court testimony, a witness, 19-year-old Connelle Lugg, who was in the holding cell on the night of the crime, states that when Volpe pushed a moaning Louima into the cell, Louima's pants and underwear were at his knees and that they were covered with feces. Discussing the case, Johnnie Cochran states: "This wasn't simply a case of a cop beating up on an innocent person, it was much more perverse than that. This was a sexual assault on a man. These police officers had to be sick to do something like that, but they also had to feel empowered by the system that they felt confident they could do whatever they wanted and get away with it, that nobody was going to stop them" (146). It is interesting to note that Volpe, discussing police work in urban America, stated, "It is a dirty job but somebody has to do it." This quote accurately sums up Volpe's defiling bathroom behavior and subsequent boasting to his white-male colleagues in the precinct.

During the trial, Justin Volpe's lawyer, Marvyn M. Kornberg, claimed that his client was innocent and implied that Abner Louima had been involved in a consensual homosexual (anal) encounter at Club Rendezvous. He stated that Louima's injuries are "consistent with those of consensually placing an object into the rectum." This white Policeman Benevolent Association lawyer is absolutely correct with regard to the homosocial and homoerotic aspects of Louima's sexual trauma; however, although the confrontation began outside of the Club Rendezvous, the brutal homosocial encounter was not consensual, and it was initiated and driven to conclusion by his truly sadistic and sexually degenerate client, Justin Volpe. Kornberg's malicious statement on behalf of his client attempts to connect Louima to the dominant discourse of Haitian people being diseased and infected with AIDS. During jury selections, Robert Volpe, Justin Volpe's father, consistently maintained that his son was innocent, and with resonation to the discourse of Clarence Thomas' defense, told reporters that his son was the victim of a "modern-day lynching." No one believed Kornberg's absurd allegation. Four other police officers testified that they had seen Volpe carrying a plunger and leading Louima into the men's room. After three weeks of testimony, when it had become obvious that Justin Volpe was going to be convicted, he pleaded guilty. On Tuesday morning, May 24, Justin Volpe, standing before Judge Eugene

Nickerson, entered a plea of guilty and tearfully confessed to striking a hand-cuffed Louima several times and to violently sodomizing Abner Louima. In this personal tragedy and public spectacle, he stated: "While in the bathroom, in the presence of another officer, I sodomized Mr. Louima with a stick up his rectum." With no apologies to Louima or Louima's family, Volpe further states that "I was in shock at the time, your honor" and "I was mad at the time." Here under the mask of racial animosity, Volpe acknowledges Louima's masculinity and his per-verted interracial act that can be viewed as homosocial desire. No debonair mas-culinity here; faced with devastating and damning testimony from other police officers, Volpe, who showed Louima no mercy, threw himself on the mercy of the court. Volpe was ordered to pay a $525.00 fine and $277, 495.00 in restitution to Abner Louima. Recalling the aftermath of the verdict, where the jury consisted of six African Americans, five whites, and one Latino, Johnnie Cochran states:

> After these police officers were found guilty in the criminal cases, the city knew it couldn't win a civil action. They knew that we were well prepared to fight the case in court. The only real question was the terms of the settlement. What is the price of Abner Louima's physical and psychological damages, as well as that to his reputation? I wanted the city to make him whole again, to make him like he was before that night in August. But that was a miracle that no one could accomplish, so I wanted them to pay for it. (162)

In a later civil suit, Abner Louima was awarded nearly nine million dollars; the city offered him $7.125 million and the New York City Police Benevolent Asso-ciation agreed to pay an additional $1.625 million for a total of $8.75 million. This was by far the most ever paid to a victim of police abuse in New York City. Louima's attorney fees came to about $2.9 million.

More than in any other trial in America's long history of violence, this epi-sode of torture and this trial exposed the fundamentally violent character of American society. Ironically, in an interview after his son's confession, Volpe's father claimed that what has happened to his son is "nothing less than an Amer-ican tragedy." With America too often being defined with regard to whiteness, this statement suggests that any time white-male privilege and white author-ity come under attack by Black people, a tragedy ensues. Perhaps, in Robert Volpe's understanding, whiteness should always trump blackness. More impor-tantly, his statement suggests the denial of America's tragic history, where white supremacy continues to cause disease to the American body politic. A few days later, Charles Schwarz was convicted of violating Abner Louima's human rights and was convicted of sexual assault; he was sentenced to fifteen years for hold-ing down Louima during the brutal assault; Schwarz was ordered to pay Louima $277,495.00. Officers Thomas Bruder and Thomas Wiese were charged with obstruction of justice for allegedly covering up the crime. Years later, a federal appeals court overturned Schwarz's conviction and released him from jail, where he had served only three years of his sentence. However, Thomas Bruder, Thomas Wiese, and Michael Bellomo (who is a police sergeant accused of attempting to cover up the assault) were acquitted of all charges. They cannot be put on trial again. Justin Volpe, with his villainous cruelty that wears the mask of mercy, faces thirty years in prison without the possibility of parole. When these police officers are sentenced, many Black people vigorously believe that Volpe and Schwarz, along with Officers Rolando Aleman and Francisco Rosario, who were recently indicted and accused of repeatedly lying to FBI agents when questioned about the torture of Abner Louima, should feel the full force of penal law. Ironically, the sodomy of this Black man exposes these white police officers to similar violent sexual experiences if they are incarcerated in a prison predominated with acrimonious Black and Latino male inmates who might have experienced white male police brutality.[2]

From the tragedy of Scottsboro Boys case and the vicious murder of Emmett Till, to the heinous torture of Abner Louima, Black men seriously at odds with white legal authority have always been on the hot seat, and their sexuality has been the battleground for stereotypical discourse. White America attempts to make Black men semblances of compliance and castrated shadow men, who would always bend and break in the presence of white supremacy. While at the hospital, Louima expressed his thoughts on being an immigrant: "Haitians have to come to the United States to really appreciate their country. When you come here you have to endure humiliation and other indignities, like people calling you all kinds of racist names. In Haiti, with all of the troubles, you are respected as a human being." Louima's discourse speaks to a fundamental aspect of America, where enslaved Africans were not viewed with the same humanity as were whites. This racist view from the past remains in present-day society, especially in a culture where Black males are too often viewed as dangerous. When racist and crude, medieval-like individuals like Justin Volpe engage in criminally depraved acts of inhumanity and humiliation against Black individuals such as Abner Louima, they negate their own humanity and place themselves in a position inferior to animals, which only kill in order to survive. Jill Nelson makes the point that police brutality affects the very fabric of American society:

> Meanwhile, White Americans too often remain surprised, at best insisting that what happened to Abner Louima and Amadou Diallo is exceptional. Most Whites believe that Louima and Diallo are exceptions—good Blacks—and that there is in the police department no systematic problem, just a few rotten apples who need to be thrown out. All Americans pay an enormous price as a result of these divergent and extreme attitudes. Police misconduct toward people of color is a cornerstone of the perpetuation of racism and white privilege. Fear, indifference, paranoia, passivity, rage, alienation, and violence are a few of the by-products of living in a society in which we are victims of, or silent partners in, abusive, brutal, and racist behavior by the police. Such behavior rends the

fabric of democracy, not only for the immediate victims of police violence and their families, but for all of our neighborhoods, towns, and cities and for the whole nation. (15)

Furthermore, with the illusion of power, these white male police officers make a Faustian covenant with the demonic philosophy of worldwide white supremacy, and thereby lose their souls. However, for many Black men living and struggling in America's white-supremacist culture, violently racist and xenophobic white male police officers, who obstruct the law by prevaricating, will remain a persistent and permanent pain in the Black man's ass.

conclusion

For much of the last century the burden of being Black in America was the burden of a systematic denial of human and constitutional rights and equal economic opportunity. It was also a century in which much of what America sold to the world as uniquely American in character—music, dance, fashion, humor, spirituality, grassroots politics, slang, literature and sports—was uniquely African American in origin, conception, and inspiration.

Greg Tate, *Everything but the Burden, What White People Are Taking from Black Culture*

The African American experience encompasses capture, enslavement, torture, emancipation, racism, segregation, and redemption, and these historical aspects and their legacies continue to inform the reality of life for most Black people in America. There is little to suggest that white supremacy will not be a permanent aspect of American life and culture. Keeping in mind the four African American literary texts and the brutal sodomizing and torture of Abner Louima addressed in the previous chapters, an examination of America's white-supremacist culture reveals that miscegenation as sexual consumption represents a fundamental aspect of the commodification of the Black body. White racism and sexism, inherent in white supremacy, are ultimately responsible for the ways in which Black individuals and situations involving them are defined. The fact of slavery refuses to disappear, along with the deeply embedded philosophies, personal attitudes, and public-policy assumptions that supported it for so long. Slavery in America has been fundamentally about consumption of Black people's bodies, labor, and reproduction.[1]

In many cases, whites' consumption of blackness leads to an internalization of inferiority, where some Black individuals seek to consume other Black individuals or offer themselves up for consumption. Popular culture is replete with examples of whiteness consuming blackness. For illustration, consider the exposure of popular-music singer Janet Jackson's right breast and star-adorned nipple by Justin Timberlake at the Super Bowl 38. The half-time show on February 1, 2004, produced by MTV, was a continuation of the ongoing paradigm of the miscegenous sexual consumption of the Black woman in a white-supremacist patriarchal society. An estimated 140 million people were watching the show when, at the end, pop star Timberlake popped off part of Jackson's corset, exposing her pugnacious breast.[2] Jackson's baring a star-jeweled nipple at the football show was a chance for modern-day whites and others to embrace the sexuality of female blackness. Janet's nipple was, for a few quick seconds, available to the gaze and for subliminal sucking to all who wanted to consume more than just the sexualized image reinforced by her singing and sexually suggestive gyrations. Within a historical context, Janet Jackson's actions enhance the portrayal of Black women as lascivious by nature, an enduring stereotype signified by the name Jezebel. Current popular singers Lil' Kim, Foxy Brown, Ashanti, Ciara, and Beyonce Knowles are some of the most notorious examples of Black female individuals who are portrayed as hypersexual "bad Black girls" who use their sexuality to get paid. Black female bodies, especially their buttocks, become reduced, to use the common musical vernacular, to "juicy bootylicious" commodities. In Destiny's Child's song "Bootylicious," the constant question is "Is my body too bootylicious for you, babe?" In the video, the Black female's "booty" becomes equated with jelly as the Black female dancers shake their bodies in a spasmodic frenzy of sexual desire. More lyrics include: "Move your booty up and down. Make it touch the ground." Like a modern-day minstrel performance, Black bodies provide entertainment for whites and others at the psychological expense of the Black performer and Black women in general.[3] Many music videos aired on cable televisions such as Black Entertainment Television (BET) and MTV show Black females in manners that sexually objectify them. For example, in one outrageous music video entitled "Sugar" by Trick Daddy and Lil' Kim, Black females are juxtaposed with candy; they both become consumable commodities. With scanty clothes and a discourse that defines them in only sexual terms, Black females are degraded and become eye candy for consumption. Furthermore, they reinforce and reinscribe the racist discourse of the Black female as a wanton and lascivious individual.[4] Accordingly, these bodaciously staged incidents also reveal the sexually precarious status of many Black women in this society. While there are numerous examples of images that counter the sexual exploitation, they do not receive the widespread exposure. For example, in a music video, popular Black female singer India Aire states: "My mama says a lady is not what she wears but what she knows." Thus, the aspects that become lost are Black women's beauty, strength, pride, and sexual autonomy, which resonate in Black female artists such as Alicia Keys, India Aire, Mary J. Blige, Faith Evans, Erykah Badu, and Jill Scott.

Historically, Black women and their breasts and other parts of their bodies have always been available for consumption by whites, especially white males; many white males, during the horrific period of Black people's enslavement and now, believe that Black women's bodies should always be available for their sexual desires.

During white America's enslavement of Black people, untold numbers of white children have sucked the mammary glands of lactating Black women, who often could not nurse their own enslaved children. Indeed, Black bodies and, more specifically, Black female breasts, have been sucked and milked dry by the avarice and greed of white males in their journey to amassing tremendous wealth. We recall in Toni Morrison's *Beloved* (1987) the scene where the white slave master's two sons attack Sethe in the barn and violently suck on her lactating breasts as her husband, Halle, looks on from the loft in a flummoxed and emasculated state of bewilderment. Sethe tells Paul D: "After I left you, those boys came in there and took my milk. That's what they came in there for. Held me down and took it" (16). Paul later confirms the traumatic effect of seeing Sethe raped of her breast milk: "The day I came here. You said they stole your milk. I never knew what it was that messed him up. That was it, I guess. All I knew was that something broke him. Not a one of them years of Saturdays, Sundays, and nighttime extra work never touched him. But whatever he saw go on in that barn broke him like a twig" (68). Here the symbolic rape of the Black woman and the castration or emasculation of the Black man become synthesized. The sexualized Black woman has been a fundamental aspect of white-male supremacy. Janet Jackson on stage was symbolic of the naked Black woman on the auction block; here, white-male slaveholders had total access to their bodies. They examined their teeth, their breasts, and their sexual organs for the purposes of the reproduction of slave capital (breeding) and for their own sadistic sexual desires. The clear difference here is that the more experienced performer, Janet Jackson, if this incident was staged, was in a position of power with the white male acting as an agent in this primetime sexualized performance. Perhaps we can view Justin Timberlake as a benign male whore, who was used by the manipulative Black female pimp for her economic subjectivity. Perhaps Janet Jackson had the white singers Madonna and Britney Spears in mind in this seemingly orchestrated sexual performance. Janet Jackson becomes Black pussy on stage as the Internet feeds on this sexualized spectacle, with one individual creating a recipe for Janet Jackson Breast Cupcakes. As a commodity in the mammoth music industry, where fame comes and goes, Janet Jackson is in a constant state of selling and reselling herself (her body) by any means necessary; a pound of pussy for sale. Calling attention to the body in a manner that invites the gaze—to mishandle Black female bodies—does not subvert sexist/racist representations. Indeed, a new Janet Jackson album was to be released soon after this incident, making this a publicity stunt. Despite an initial denial, Jackson eventually admitted that it ("a wardrobe malfunction") was indeed a publicity stunt to garner more exposure. Like many other performers, Janet Jackson makes her body expendable. Discussing the Black body as an expendable commodity, bell hooks argues:

> Bombarded with images representing black female bodies as expendable, black women have either passively absorbed this thinking or vehemently resisted it. Popular culture provides countless examples of black female appropriation and exploitation of "negative stereotypes" to either assert control over the representation or at least reap the benefits of it. Since black female sexuality has been represented in racist/sexist iconography as more free and liberated, many black women singers, irrespective of the quality of their voices, have cultivated an image which suggests they are sexually available and licentious. Undesirable in the conventional sense, which defines beauty and sexuality as desirable only to the extent that it is idealized and unattainable, the black female body gains attention only when it is synonymous with accessibility, availability, when it is sexually deviant. (*Black Looks* 65–66)

Janet Jackson's actions fall into the assertive paradigm of hooks' analysis, making her body available and deviant at the same time. Thus, even though Justin had the handheld microphone, Janet, with her microphone on her headset, was the phallic female and Justin was her young male bitch, role reversal with Black female consumption.

Yet at the symbolic level, the rape of Black women by white males was in the minds of many Black people as the song being sung by Timberlake announced that Janet would be naked at the end of the song, "Rock Your Body." The lyrics state: "Let's do something, let's make a bet, 'cause I gotta have you naked by the end of this song." A naked Black woman on stage fulfills the lusty desires of a repressed white-American alter ego. Janet Jackson's hypervisibility speaks to what bell hooks names the "commodification of Otherness." Ann duCille notes:

> Mass culture, as hooks argues, produces, promotes, and perpetuates the commodification of Otherness through the exploitation of the black female body. In the 1990's, however, the principal sites of exploitation are not simply the cabaret, the speakeasy, the music video, the glamour magazine; they are also the academy, the publishing industry, the intellectual community. ("The Occult of True Black Womanhood" 592)

Accordingly, Black individuals in the entertainment field as well as many other arenas requiring exposure remain symbols of sexuality, immorality, and violence. In her defense, Jackson stated that the incident "was a malfunction of the wardrobe; it was not intentional. . . . He was supposed to pull away the bustier and leave the red-lace bra." This statement is hard to believe since a star-shaped ring covered the areola of the right breast. If the red bra was to be there, why was the jewelry on Janet Jackson's nipple? Madonna's appearance on Jean Paul Gaultier's runway in a dress with her breasts exposed, Lil' Kim's appearance in a purple outfit with one breast exposed, and Diana Ross fondling her breast on stage—all come to mind. Halle Berry's performance as Leticia Musgrove in *Monster's Ball* also comes to mind as the most graphic example of the sexual consumption of the Black female body by the white male who facilitates the killing of a Black woman's husband. The media's repeated showing of the incident gave white America an ongoing chance to have a sublimated sexual experience with a very attractive Black woman. Moreover, Janet Jackson, reflective of her third CD, *Control* (1986), reverses the paradigm of the sexual consumption of the Black female body for economic gain. During slavery, slaves were not supposed to have pleasurable feelings on their own; their bodies were not supposed to be like that, but they were to have as many children as they could reproduce to please whoever owned them. However, they were not supposed to have sexual pleasure deep down. Here, a Black woman allows a white man to snatch her clothing off (a symbolic rape scene based on Janet's seemingly shocked expression) in a possible attempt to increase her fading CD sales and concert appearances. Interestingly, similar to the revealing picture with her on the cover of *Rolling Stone* magazine (her ex-husband of 11 years was holding her naked breasts), Janet Jackson's next album reveals her naked with her hands covering her breasts. Paradoxically, at the same time that Janet Jackson is being sexually exposed as eye candy, her older brother, Michael Jackson, is being accused of numerous acts of criminal sexual conduct with underage boys at his Neverland Valley Ranch, with its 16 amusement-park rides and a Michael Jackson museum. In early March 2005, Michael Jackson's trial started and the prosecutor, District Attorney Thomas Sneddon, remained bent on painting Jackson as a repeat perpetrator of unlawful and "strange sexual behavior." On the other hand, Jackson's defense team, headed by attorney Thomas Mesereau Jr., claimed that the charges were false and that the defendants were seeking to exploit Jackson for monetary gain.[5] Michael and Janet may have a sexual preference for young white males. Nevertheless, on June 13, 2005, in a Santa Monica, California, courtroom, 46-year-old Michael Jackson was found not guilty on all ten charges ranging from child molestation to conspiracy. Most of the other members of the Jackson family were in the courtroom when the verdict was read; Janet Jackson waited outside the courtroom because the Jackson family was only allowed a certain number of seats. Discussing the trial and verdict in his article "Unsafe at Any Age," Andrew Vachss argues:

> Let us not pretend that the fanatical interest in the Michael Jackson case signals a new wave of concern about child protection throughout the world. Sure producers are emptying their Rolodexes, and professional pontifications are clogging the airwaves. Yes, the "false allegations" crowd is already crowing that this

case proves the validity of their contention that most such prosecutions are a witch hunt. At the same time, the contingent that claims that children never lie about sexual abuse is bemoaning how power and privilege overrule justice. But not one single word of any of this represents change. The only thing altered by the Michael Jackson verdict is that now we won't have to listen to the prison rape "jokes" that would inevitably have followed a conviction. (A23)

Reports convey that most African Americans support the verdict and that most whites oppose the verdict; race continues to divide. Jackson's ambiguous racial identity, strange behavior, and his incredible musical skill place him in schism of support and suspicion. However, Janet Jackson's "wardrobe malfunction" and Michael Jackson's trial relate the stereotypical discourse of the Black women as promiscuous and the Black man as sexually out of control. Simply put, the Black woman is reduced to a licentious slut and the Black man is reduced to an oversexed buck. With Michael Jackson, Kobe Bryant, R Kelly, and Bill Cosby involved in sex-related trials and sex-related lawsuits, the image of the Black man as a feral buck dominates the white media. With regard to the halftime show, the suggestion of sexual violence against Black women by whites is hard to miss, especially since white-male subjectivity has too often been constructed on the rape of Black women and girls and the killing of Black men and boys. Hence, to be a nigger in America means to be unloved, unprotected, unwanted, and subjected to random violence, especially sexual violence at the hands of white males. The murder and castration of Emmett Till was a prime example of sexual violence directed at a young Black boy. Yet Till represents just one of the thousands of Black males who became casualties in white males' desire to protect the white woman from all threats real or imaginary. In this case, it was a simple case of disrespect on the part of the young Black male.

Pedophilia is also an issue, metaphorically, in this primetime exposure. Janet Jackson is perhaps 15 years older than Justin Timberlake. On the other hand, Michael Jackson (now 47 years old) is being accused of numerous charges of inappropriate sexual conduct with young boys. Hence, this raises the question of Janet's showing her breast to take some of the white media's attention away from her beloved brother. We know that Janet did accompany her brother at the arraignment and appeared at the trial and verdict. Did a symbolic act of pedophilia attempt to mask numerous acts of pedophilia? If Michael Jackson and Justin Timberlake were on stage, would Michael Jackson want Justin Timberlake to grab Michael's crotch? Do Janet and Michael have preferences for young boys based on some shared sexual trauma during their childhoods? Is there some incestuous pedophilia being suggested by the media in Michael Jackson's relationship with his children and with a white woman, Debbie Rowe, with whom he no longer has a relationship? Historically, white males have sought out young Black girls and boys for slaves so that they could have sexual relations with them. In terms of incest, many white slave masters would have sexual relations with a Black female and later have sexual relations with the child from this sexual relationship. Incestuous miscegenation would be the term for white males who engaged in this immoral sexual conduct. The honorable Thomas Jefferson is a prime example of a pedophile in his illicit miscegenous relationship with the Black slave Sally Hemings. Perhaps the reason so many white males in the media are so fixated on Michael Jackson's alleged inappropriate sexual conduct is because it reminds them of the behavior of their white-male ancestors. Indeed, recent figures of sexual abuse by members of the Roman Catholic clergy show that some 4,450 priests have been accused of sexually abusing minors since 1950. Sexual assault by white males represents a fundamental aspect of American society. However, the myth of the Black male as a rapist of white females remains a larger fundamental stereotype. The most spectacular example of this began on March 25, 1931, when a fight broke out between a group of white youths and a group of Black youths on a freight train traveling through northern Alabama. Both groups were stealing a ride and the white group received the worst of the fight and complained to the nearest stationmaster. Nine Black males and two white females were rounded up and someone said something about rape. The Black males were arrested and taken to Scottsboro, the Jackson County seat. Twelve days later the Black males were put on trial for rape, and in four days four separate juries convicted eight of them and sentenced them to death. Although it was eventually discovered that these white girls were not raped, these Black males spent no fewer than six and as many as nineteen years in jail.

The infamous "Central Park Jogger" rape case in New York City represents another case of the issue of miscegenation as sexual consumption, where a number of young Black and Puerto Rican males between the ages of 14 and 17 were wrongly convicted of the repeated rape and severe beating of a white female jogger. On Wednesday, April 1989, the rape and beating of a highly educated, white 28-year-old Salomon Brothers stockbroker shocked the country and made the term "wilding" a popular phrase. Real-estate mogul Donald Trump played a critical role in this case by calling for the restoration of the death penalty and by running $85,000 worth of advertisements in the *New York Times*, *The Daily News*, and *New York Newsday*. According to Trump, New York City families of all races and classes had lost the freedom to walk in the park, visit the playground, ride bicycles at dawn, or sit on their stoops because "roving bands of wild criminals roam our neighborhoods, dispensing their own vicious brand of twisted hatred on whomever they encounter." As Valerie Smith point outs, the language polarized racial groups: "The inflammatory rhetoric of the journalistic accounts of the Central Park rape reveals the context within which the narrative was constructed. In and of itself the crime was certainly heinous. Yet the media coverage intensified and polarized responses in New York City and around the country, for it made the story of sexual victimization inseparable from the rhetoric of racism" (11).[6] Thirteen years later, in 2002, the five young Black and Latino youths who were arrested and convicted in this high-profile case were found to have been wrongly accused. Robert Morgenthau, Manhattan's district attorney, asked the judge to vacate convictions of the five youths accused of the crime. Morgenthau's office revisited the case in May 2002, when Matias Reyes admitted to the crime after being convicted of another rape. Reyes says he was the sole perpetrator in the Central Park attack, and DNA testing confirmed his connection to the sexual assault. The semen evidence recovered from the victim could not be traced to the DNA of any of the five Black males who were originally convicted in the case. The victim, who was in a coma and close to death when found, was unable to recall any details of the attack. The five youths ranged in age from 14 to 16 at the time of the attack and were convicted by two separate juries based on their own "confessions," which conflicted greatly in important details such as the weapon, descriptions of the victim's clothing, and her injuries.[7] Trickery and coercion by New York City police officers were critical because the young males may have believed they were making statements as witnesses, but their testimonies implicated them as accomplices. In 2003, all of the teenagers originally convicted of the crime were exonerated, after some, unfortunately, had served lengthy jail terms. It seems that no action will be taken against the mainly white detectives and prosecutors who handled the case that won the convictions. Discussing the intersection of race, gender, and Black masculinity, Patricia Hill Collins points out that: "African American men live with the ideological legacy that constructs Black-male heterosexuality through images of wild beasts, criminals and rapists" (*Black Sexual Politics* 102). This remains true despite the voluminous evidence to the contrary; especially when there are Black males in the hip-hop industry who promote a violent sexual image that becomes embraced by white-male executives in the music industry. Simply put, the image of the Black male as a violent sexual buck sells music, newspapers, magazines, and receives significant coverage on white-controlled television.

Many white males seem to be particularly interested in the sexual conduct of Black individuals. During the 1991 Senate Judiciary Hearing (heavily televised), Clarence Thomas responded to the charge of sexual harassment by referring to the Senate Hearing as a lynching. During Thomas' confirmation for the Supreme Court, law professor Anita Faye Hill, using graphic language, testified that Clarence Thomas, her former boss, engaged in sexual misconduct when she worked with him at the Equal Employment Opportunity Commission in the 1980s. Hill stated that Thomas, who was chairman of the EEOC and not married at the time, made numerous references to his genitals and discussed pornographic material with her. Also, Hill claims that Thomas attempted to date her and constantly made her uncomfortable with his sexual innuendos. More specifically, Hill's testimony reveals the nature of Thomas' sexual misconduct:

> After a brief discussion of work, he would turn the conversation to discussions of sexual matters. His conversations were very vivid. He spoke about acts that he had seen in pornographic films involving such matters as women having

sex with animals and films showing group sex or rape scenes. He talked about pornographic materials depicting individuals with large penises or large breasts involved in various sex acts. (Miller 92)

Hill states that that she found Thomas' conversation offensive, disgusting, and degrading. In a speech to the all-white male senators at the hearing, Thomas, in response to these charges, stated that he did not engage in any sexual harassment and that he believed that this hearing was a travesty of justice. Thomas states:

> I would like to start by saying unequivocally, uncategorically, that I deny each and every single allegation against me today that suggested in any way that I had conversations of a sexual nature or about pornographic material with Anita Hill, that I ever attempted to date her, that I ever had any personal sexual interest in her, or that I in any way ever harassed her. A second and I think more impor-tant point, I think that this today is a travesty. I think that this is disgusting. I think that this hearing should never occur in America. This is a case in which this sleaze, this dirt, was searched for by staffers of members of this committee, was then leaked to the media, and this committee and this body validated it and displayed it at prime time over our entire nation. How would any member on this committee, any person in this room, or any person in this country, like sleaze said about him or her in this fashion? Or this dirt dredged up and this gos-sip and these lies displayed in this manner? How would any person like it? The Supreme Court is not worth it. No job is worth it. I'm not here for that. I'm here for my name, my family, my life and my integrity. I think something is dreadfully wrong with this country when any person, any person in this free country would be subjected to this. This is not a closed room. There was an FBI investiga-tion. This is not an opportunity to talk about difficult matters privately or in a closed environment. This is a circus. This is a national disgrace. And from my standpoint as a black American, as far as I'm concerned, it is a high-tech lynch-ing for uppity blacks who in any way deign to think for themselves to do for themselves, to have different ideas, and it is a message that unless you kowtow to an old order, this is what will happen to you. You will be lynched, destroyed, caricatured, by a committee of the U.S. Senate rather than hung from a tree. (Phelps and Winternitz 332)

A close examination of this speech suggests some understated contradictions. While Thomas claims that he did not engage in any sexual misconduct, he states that these things should have been discussed in private behind closed doors. Indeed, Thomas' angry reference to the hearing as a "circus" and a "high-tech lynching" was reversing the present paradigm of a Black woman accusing a Black man of sexual harassment, and changing it into a paradigm of a white woman accusing a Black man of rape. By bringing up lynching, Thomas is signifying on miscegenation between Black males and white females. This controversy allowed

Thomas to discuss the historical aspects of Black-male subjectivity under Jin Crow. Thomas reveals:

> Throughout the history of this country and certainly throughout my life, language about the sexual prowess of black men, language about the sex organs of black men and the sizes, et cetera, that kind of language has been used about black men as long as I've been on the face of this earth, and these are charges that are impossible to wash off, and these are the kind of stereotypes that I have in my tenure in government and conduct of my affairs . . . attempted to move away from and to convince people that we should conduct ourselves in a way that defies these stereotypes. But when you play into a stereotype, its as though you're skiing downhill, there's no way to stop it, and this plays into the most bigoted racist stereotypes that any black man will face. (Phelps 339)

Definitions of Black men have always centered on their sexuality and, as pointed out in Wright's poem, miscegenation was a critical reason for the lynching of Black males. Not one of these white-male senators commented or challenged Thomas on these explosive remarks. In a symbolic manner, his hyperbolic discourse placed his Black phallus (manhood) on the table and asked the white-male group of senators to embrace his phallus and disregard what he depicted as an outrageous claim by a Black women that she had been sexually harassed. There is also the possibility that the some of the white senators viewed Thomas' phallus as white. Nevertheless, Thomas' dialectical discourse transformed a Black woman, Anita Faye Hill, into a symbolic white woman, charging a symbolically white male, Thomas, with a symbolic rape. Thomas' marriage to a white woman, Virginia Thomas, along with his ultraconservative views, makes him an honorary white man.[8] Sitting behind and to the right of Clarence during the hearing, Virginia had a strange expression as she watched Clarence deliver his lynching discourse. This hearing received national and international attention because of the confluence of the explosive issues of sexuality, race, gender, and class; Thomas was only the second Black man in the history of America to be nominated to the Supreme Court. Even here though, with a male and a Black female, the issue of miscegenation as sexual consumption becomes symbolically evident. Historically, Black women in America have experienced very little justice, especially when it comes to legal matters of sexual violence involving white men. This aspect combined with the enormous number of Black males lynched tells a narrative of Black people's bodies always being placed and positioned in some sexual context.

Three years after the Clarence Thomas judiciary hearing in 1994, O.J. Simpson was arrested for the murder of his estranged white wife, Nicole Brown Simpson, and a friend of hers named Ron Goldman. In January 1995, this trial began and it also received significant national and international attention. Again we have the issue of miscegenation as sexual consumption because the thinking of the prosecutors was that Simpson was jealous of his white wife and became so enraged that he killed her and her white-male friend. Indeed, as the trial began, Ron Goldman became invisible as the crime was reduced to O.J. Simpson allegedly killing Nicole Simpson; this erasure reinforces and reinscribes miscegenation between Black males and white females. For a Black man to have a sexual relationship with a white woman and to murder that white woman encompasses the major racial and sexual taboos in America illustrated in the film *Birth of a Nation*. Despite the time period, these racial and sexual taboos remain true. Without a doubt, as illustrated in Richard Wright's poem "Between the World and Me," a Black man living in the Jim Crow period who was accused of these sexual crimes would be immediately castrated, lynched, and burned alive. Most whites believed that Simpson was guilty and most Blacks believed that he was innocent. Although O.J. Simpson, with the excellent legal expertise and planning of the African American lawyer Johnnie Cochran, along with Peter Neufeld and Barry Scheck, was found to be innocent of the two capital murders, the trial and verdict exposed the deep-seated racial divide in America. Despite his wealth and his ambivalence to his Black identity, Simpson was eventually viewed by most whites as a dangerous and brutal black buck who violated the white body politic symbolized by his blond-haired, white wife. The mutilation and murder of Nicole Brown Simpson was a symbolic rape. On this point, Ann duCille states: "In reality, though, the historically volatile racial dynamics of this particular case—white female and male victims and a black male celebrity assailant—gave cinemascopic dimension to a horror story, the movie version of which might be titled *The Rebirth of a Nation*, in dubious tribute to D.W. Griffith's 1915 film" (*Skin Trade* 144). In the minds of most whites and some Blacks, the possible theory of this Black man raping this white woman is not an absurd issue if we consider the documented incidents of Simpson physically abusing his wife, Nicole Simpson. The vicious nature of the murders (Nicole Simpson's throat was cut to the point of her decapitation) was also a critical factor in this issue of miscegenation as rape.

For many people around the world, especially African Americans, Abner Louima's miscegenous rape and torture were made more understandable when the news of the horrible abuses in Guantanamo Bay, Cuba, and at Abu Ghraib prison in Iraq were exposed. News reports and graphic pictures documented United States soldiers beating, torturing, and humiliating Afghanistani and Iraqi detainees, males and females. With regard to Guantanamo Bay, the White House, the Pentagon, and the Justice Department had agreed that the prisoners had no rights under federal law or the Geneva Conventions. For African Americans, this decision was cacophonously similar to the 1857 *Dred Scott* decision that stated that African Americans had no right or privileges that the white man was bound to respect. With prisoners having no rights or privileges, it becomes easy for them to be abused, and since these places were not in America, the level of abuse was extraordinarily vicious. Seymour M. Hersh in *Chain of Command:*

The Road from 9/11 to Abu Ghraib (2004), states: "There were continuing protests by human rights groups about prisoner abuse at Guantanamo and at the military's interrogation center at Bagram Air Base in Afghanistan, but in the absence of photographs the complaints got little traction" (18). Soon this would change. Like Angola State Prison in Louisiana, Abu Ghraib, 20 miles west of Baghdad, was one of the world's most notorious prisons, with torture, weekly executions, and vile living conditions. When Abu Ghraib became a U.S. military prison, several thousand individuals, including women and teenagers, were being held there. As Hersch notes, numerous instances of abuse were reported:

> Breaking chemical lights and pouring the phosphoric liquid on detainees; pouring cold water on naked detainees; beating detainees with a broom handle and a chair; threatening male detainees with rape; allowing a military police guard to stitch the wound of a detainee who was injured after being slammed against a wall in his cell; sodomizing a detainee with a chemical light and perhaps a broom stick; and using military working dogs to frighten and intimidate detainees with threats of attack, and in one instance actually biting a detainee. (22)

The use of the broomstick clearly speaks to the torture that Abner Louima experienced in the bathroom of the Brooklyn police station by Police Officer Justin Volpe. Further, with the use of the military police dogs and one dog biting a detainee, the issue of consumption speaks to Richard Wright's poem "Between the World and Me." As with the African American poem discussed, we see the intersection of psychological violence and physical violence with overtones of sadistic sexual abuse. Another horrific element to the torture in Guantanamo Bay is revealed in Jane Mayer's article "The Experiment: Is the Military Devising New Methods of Interrogation at Guantanamo?" in *The New Yorker*. Mayer suggests that Army scientists have developed methods for withstanding abuse and that these methods are being used against the Guantanamo detainees. Mayer relates:

> Documents related to interrogation practices that were released by the Administration last year show that in October 2002, Guantanamo officials asked the Pentagon for permission to use several harsh interrogation techniques on highly resistant detainees, including isolation, sensory deprivation, removal of clothing, hooding, exploitation of the detainee's phobias (such as fear of dogs) to induce stress. And "scenarios designed to convince the detainee that death or severely painful consequences are imminent for him and/or his family." The officials also requested permission to use waterboarding. (68)

Obviously these soldiers learned to do these terrible things in America. Discussing the photographs, Bob Herbert, in his *New York Times* article "Lifting the Censor's Veil on the Shame of Iraq," states:

There are pictures of children who were wounded and barely clinging to life, and some who appeared to be dead. There was a close-up of a soldier who was holding someone's severed leg. There were photos of Iraqis with the deathlike stare of shock, stunned by the fact that something previously unimaginable had just happened to them. There were photos of G.I.'s happily posing with the bodies of dead Iraqis. (35)

Like the aftermath of a lynching, consumption again becomes evident in the sadistic display of body parts and dead bodies. Discussing some other photos from the prison, Herbert states: "In one shot a body bag has been opened to show the gruesome head wound of the corpse. In another, a G.I. is leaning over the top of the body bag with a spoon in his right hand, as if he is about to scoop up a portion of the dead man's wounded flesh" (35). To symbolically consume dead bodies suggests a necrotic element to this bizarre embrace. Like the shame that the New York City Police Department experienced with the Abner Louima case, the United States military experienced a similar shame, but here the shame had a more international effect, especially in Muslim and Arab countries. It should be noted that the pictures of the soldiers reveal that most, if not all, of the soldiers committing the abuses were white-male soldiers; this issue among others highlights the racial tension, especially when the terrorists, insurgents, and citizens are referred to as "sand niggers" by some American soldiers.

Along with the enormous human tragedies (killed and wounded American soldiers and Iraqi people), the economic costs are staggering: the Pentagon says the Iraq war costs us $4.8 billion per month, and the Afghanistan operation costs approximately $700 million per month. To date 2160 American soldiers have died in Iraq and another 236 in Afghanistan, for a total of 2,317. The number of wounded has exceeded 16,000—more than 14,000 in Iraq. While there is no official count of the civilian deaths in this war, surveys place the figure somewhere between 26, 000 and 30,000.

Many individuals consider that this level of violence would only be seen in a Hollywood science-fiction movie. In Thomas Lee's sexually charged science-fiction film *Supernova* (MGM 2000), where human conflict is fundamental to the film and where the past informs the present, there is the illustration of consensual miscegenation that suggests possible harmony between African Americans and Euro-Americans. Miscegenation between Blacks and whites has been foreshadowed by Benjamin Sotomejor (played by Wilson Cruz) by having a subliminal sexual relationship with the shipboard computer called Sweetie. After a game of chess, Sweetie, in saucy language, tells Benjamin that his strategy is "subtle yet forceful and that he can play with her anytime." Also, there is the ongoing sexual activity of Danika Lund (played by Robin Tunney) and Yerzy Penalosa (played by Lou Diamond Phillips), who seek to have a child once they send in their Application for Reproduction Agreement and the Planetary Population Commission approves them. The basic plot involves a small medical crew on a spaceship named the *Trans Solar Nightingale* 229 (a floating hospital and rescue ship) responding to an emergency distress call from Titan 37, a mining colony, and taking aboard what seems to be a human being but turns out to be a type of bomb (a biohazard capable of destruction and rejuvenation). The individual turns out to be a mutant (the alien matter within the individual allows the person to become younger and stronger) that begins to kill crewmembers. A supernova is created by the human conflict, and in five decades it poses a threat and hope for a new future for planet Earth. In the final scene, Dr. Kaela Evers (Angela Bassett is the African American actress), the chief medical officer, and Nick Vanzant (James Spader is the white actor), the co-pilot, are compelled to occupy a single-dimension stabilization unit (a transport module) because a white male named Karl James Larson (played by Peter Facinelli) has destroyed all but one of the modules. In order to do a dimension jump, the crewmembers are required to be naked. The computer announces that in 51 years the supernova could destroy earth or allow humankind to achieve a new level of existence. Once they realize the status of the dimension units, Nick suggests that he stay outside and that Kaela occupy the single unit, but Kaela adamantly responds that they should travel together. Nick states that they "could end up as a genetic experiment gone bad." Kaela refuses to enter the unit alone and tells Nick, "It's your choice—inside or out." Even though he says that it's "crazy," Nick comes inside. Kaela states that before the conflict with Karl started, she thought that all Nick had in mind was having sexual relations with her. Kaela and Nick embrace each other during the journey and arrive intact; the first thing that we observe is that there has been an exchange in the eye colors of Kaela and Nick, each has a blue eye and a brown eye.[9] Also, the computer named "Sweetie" (given a breathy seductive voice by Vanessa Marshall) announces that the body proximity has result in a 2 percent genetic material exchange and that Kaela is pregnant with a female child. With a primary focus on breeding and genetics, the film becomes an exploration of the possibility of racial harmony between Black and whites. However before this final scene, whiteness (more specifically, white males) typically surfaces as an assumed subject, not a nominated object. All of the other four crewmembers are dead, and Kaela and Nick join forces to defeat and destroy the alien-in-human-form. Accordingly, the final scene with its visual and linguistic racial codings, along with the obvious romantic miscegenation intent, places emphasis on the Black woman seeking to join the white man in order to create a new species.

When Kaela asks Nick to come inside the unit, this suggests the double reference of him coming inside of her genitalia, a reversal of the miscegenous relationship that Kaela experienced with Karl. In fact, Nick states that considering all of the human conflict resulting in the deaths of four crewmembers, he is concerned about his sexual performance level. Interestingly, the first interaction between Kaela and Nick occurs when Kaela gives him a physical examination, and later after another discussion about their past lives, Nick attempts to seduce her with some 27-year-old pear brandy with a full pear in the bottle. Their conversation about getting the pear in and out of the bottle signifies on coitus. When Nick asks the question of how the pear got into the bottle, he is contemplating how he will get his phallus into Kaela's vagina. Kaela explains to him the process. Nick's seduction works; they have sexual relations in Nick's zero-gravity tank. Another important issue is that Kaela states that she was in an abusive relationship (her worst nightmare) with Karl and when it was over she could not have children. Troy, as a younger version of Karl and possessed by an alien species, is bent on universal conquest and having Kaela. We later learn that Karl, with the help of the alien being, has taken over the body of his son, Troy. The artifact that Troy has smuggled aboard the ship turns out to be a sex object, only better. In one sense it's just a nugget of pseudoscience, cocooned "isotropic" ninth-dimensional matter that Sweetie explains by flashing a ream of differential equations and apologizing, "I'm afraid human language lacks any vocabulary to describe" the thing. Additionally, it represents a balm for loneliness, absorbing the cravings of addiction and the potential agonies of sexual desire. Yerzy becomes the first victim of the alien matter and abandons Danika for the alien affection. According to Kaela, the alien species that created the alien matter is "Smart as God and a lot less nice." With the film focusing on issues of breeding and genetic superiority, the final scene of concentrated miscegenation ends with Kaela and Nick in a loving embrace as they and their child give hope to the possibility that racial conflict and white supremacy will terminate.

Like Rufus in *Kindred*, Karl is hell-bent on a form of supremacy as he seeks to control Kaela; he arrogantly refers to Dr. Kaela Evers as "his girl." Yet unlike Rufus, Karl has sexual relations with Yerzy's mate, Danika, a white female. Paradoxically, when Karl finally reveals himself to Kaela, he tells her that he did not send the emergency distress call to be rescued personally, but he sent the distress call to rescue Kaela. This white-male arrogance is reflective of Hank Grotowski in his relation with Leticia Musgrove in the film *Monster's Ball*, but Dr. Kaela Evers has a sense of self and subjectivity that Leticia lacks.[10] With no other African American males on the ship, we wonder if he means that he seeks to rescue her from loneliness. When we first encounter Kaela, she has a rigid persona, but the consumption of the pear brandy allows Nick to immediately consume her. Karl further states that he is different and does not want to injure Kaela; he declares that the hurt that he has done to her is in the past. Karl says that he represents the next leap of evolution and wants Kaela to join him; ironically, he utters this while his hand tightens around Kaela's throat as she struggles to free herself. Karl's violent past is present. Indeed, both Karl and Nick refer to the past in their attempts to seduce Kaela. The issue of the past is fundamental to the film as Captain Marley (played by Robert Forster) works on his doctoral dissertation entitled "Cathexis and Catharsis," an exegesis of the ultraviolent 20th-century cartoon "Tom and Jerry." At some point, he reads a portion about narcissistic love and its connection with a deep-rooted "human malevolence."

His exegesis suggests the past abusive relationship that Karl and Kaela shared where Karl's narcissistic behavior resulted in Kaela's abuse. Captain Marley's dissertation reflects his fundamental humanity, as illustrated by the fact that he knowingly has Dr. Kaela Evers take his dimensional stabilization unit because her unit is inoperable; he dies as a result of the dimension jump. Literally the film's most explosive scene occurs when Kaela with the help of Fly Boy (the spaceship's human-sized robot)[11] manipulates the alien matter to explode and says "goodbye, Karl" and gives him the "fuck you" finger before she triggers the explosion that destroys Karl. In the film, there are no African American males present (the possibility of a Black male and a white female remains a dangerous racial mix here in the distant future)[12], and thus Kaela becomes an object of sexual desire by two white males, Karl and Nick (both of these characters were addicted to some mind-altering drug named hazen); this creates a triangle of miscegenous sexual desire. Discussing the psychotropic drug hazen, Dr. Evers states that she does not like what the drug does to the individual who takes it and the way it makes them treat others. Hazen, a drug used to escape reality, becomes analogous to white supremacy, which can be considered an escape from the reality that all human beings regardless of race are fundamentally similar and deserve the same respect. Hence, Karl and Nick are juxtaposed with hazen; this juxtaposition creates their individual juxtapositions with Kaela.

The conflict that develops between Karl and Nick has the character of a chess match, with Kaela representing the Black queen to be possessed and sexually consumed.[13] This sexual desire suggests the mythology associated with African American women. Discussing this myth, Yanick St. Jean and Joe R. Feagin argue: "Some white men, since the beginning of the enslavement of Africans in North America, have had a desire for the black Jezebel, for the mythological 'jungle bunny,' a crude racist term still in use among some white men, particularly those with power. Privilege allows these men to try to actualize the sexual myth" (101). While Nick represents the fully recovered hazen drug addict, Karl has replaced hazen with a more powerful substance, the isotropic ninth-dimensional matter. Karl's previous drug addiction and his current alien addiction cause him to behave in a purely evil manner where individuals on both Titan 37 and *Nightingale 229* have been killed. Like a futuristic slave master, Karl is absolutely vicious in his desire for power and sexual satisfaction. Justin Volpe, Thomas Weylin, Rufus Weylin, Old Man Corregidora, the drunken white man who attempts to rape Laurie Lee Youngblood, the four young white males who attempt to rape Laurie Lee's daughter Jenny, the white sheriff who forces Laurie Lee Youngblood to whip her son Robby, and the horde of sadistic white lynchers in Richard Wright's poem "Between the World and Me"—all can be seen to be intoxicated with the arrogant philosophy of white supremacy; white supremacy represents a disease that is in a constant state of mutation, bringing pain and suffering especially to African American people. The game of chess becomes linked to the ensuing human conflict and racialized sexual desire as Sweetie congratulates Kaela on her new life and welcomes her home. With Kaela's last name being Evers, it is difficult for me not to make the analogy of Dr. Kaela Evers with Medgar Wiley Evers' wife, Myrlie Evers (now Dr. Myrlie Evers-Williams), who represents a woman who attempts to eradicate all aspects of racial, class, and gender hegemony through her Civil Rights and community work.[14] Without a doubt, Nick and Kaela are profoundly changed by this tragedy, but with any trauma there comes the possibility for redemption. In the face of loneliness and a deadly foe, Kaela and Nick have sexual desire for each other, but the film leaves the audience wondering if there will be a long-term loving relationship. The critical question here is: Will Kaela and Nick's consensual sexual consumption lead to an enduring commitment to each other and their child? Structurally, the film has a circular formation when we consider that after she left Karl, Kaela believed she could not have children and now she is expecting a child with Nick. It should be strongly emphasized that this spaceship is a floating hospital and rescue ship designed to heal and be of assistance to all individuals regardless of race, gender, color, or rank. Thus my last point is that a progressive and more compassionate echelon of racial existence in this futuristic world is being implied in *Supernova's* final surreal scene as the spaceship *Nightingale 229* continues to travel through the star-laden universe. This film compels viewers to consider miscegenation in ways that can challenge or reinforce prevailing notions of racial hegemony. As Susan Courtney argues, films like *Supernova* connect the past to the present while considering the future:

> Approaching the question finally in the context of a contemporary culture in which we still struggle to cope with the legacies of slavery and segregation, the ultimate lesson perhaps is that in order to continue to repair the damages implicit in dominant screen fantasies of miscegenation, we need not only to remember the complex social histories they have worked to displace and disavow but also to recognize the consequential positions we can assume in the very processes of consuming, producing, and even renouncing, the fantasies as well as the histories. (294)

In present-day America's white-supremacist culture, when it comes to Black bodies, sexuality sells, and some Black individuals have an opportunity to stand center stage and take part in the eroticized sexual show; many white people and some Black people in America see no difference between the office and the auction block. Perhaps some will say that it is about time that Black individuals get paid for the consumption of their sexuality, but Black people, especially Black females, have a historical context to their sexuality that others do not bring; this context has been one of relentless sexual exploitation during the enslavement period and sexual violence after this period, especially during Jim Crow segregation. Simply put, Black bodies have been a site for consumption by white males in ways that few other people in America have experienced. A most glaring example of white male's desire for the Black body can be found in the revelation that former United States senator and former segregationist Strom Thurmond had a sexual relationship with a Black female who worked as a maid in Thurmond's parents' house as a teenager. Essie Mae Washington-Williams, a 78-year-old mixed-race woman from Los Angeles, went public with her claim that Thurmond was her father and the Thurmond family validated the claim.[15]

The paradox of whites' consumption of Black bodies is that most whites, regardless of their class status, gender, ethnicity, religion, or sexuality, have a Ku Klux Klan mentality when it comes to interracial relationships, especially when it comes to Black males having sexual relationships or marital relationships with white females. Actor and model Taye Diggs, Supreme Court Justice Clarence Thomas, Miami Dolphins star Jason Taylor, golf professional and philanthropist Tiger Woods, musician Seal, and some other high-profile Black men have recently been receiving hate mail that includes threats to castrate, burn, and or shoot them for being married to white women. Interestingly, the target of this vehement hatred is consistently the Black males; it suggests that somehow these famous and affluent Black men forced these white women to do something against their wills. Ironically, most of these Black men have enormous wealth, prestige, power, and security that can protect them from crazed racists (more than likely white males) who would seek to harm them. Consumed with an illogical hatred, these individuals desire to lethally consume these Black men. With these Black men in mind, it is interesting to note that during June 2005, the United States Senate issued a formal apology to lynching victims and their descendants, marking the first time Congress had apologized to African Americans for any reason. As Sheryl Gay Stolberg notes: "The intent was to erase what lawmakers called a stain on the Senate's history: its repeated refusal, throughout the first half of the 20th century, to make lynching a federal crime" (3). However, eight senators and their signatures were missing from a placard expressing support; noticeably absent was Mississippi Senator Trent Lott, who lost his post as Senate majority leader several years ago over racially insensitive remarks concerning Strom Thurmond. Another senator, Lamar Alexander of Tennessee, who did not sign the bill, gave his rationale; Stolberg writes: "Senator Alexander, in a lengthy speech submitted for the Congressional record, argued the best way for the Senate 'to condemn lynching is to get to work' on legislation promoting good schools and better health care for blacks" (3). Perhaps another reason for the reluctance of some white senators is that an apology for the enslavement of African Americans, state-supported Jim Crow segregation, and the enduring policies of white supremacy might have to be addressed.

Most whites have been socialized to support the philosophy and policies of institutionalized white supremacy, and very few go against this socialization, especially since their white privilege affords them certain advantages in employment, housing, and education. As Brian Niro argues, America represents a racial paradox with tragic consequences:

Moreover, there is a fundamental failure within American discourse to maintain the consistency of the register. . . . America represents a location where race remains almost perpetually in motion, and this mobility does not necessarily portent genuine progress. Instead, the American relationship with race is fundamental, but also deeply ambivalent. It embraces the pleasant fiction of the melting-pot beneficence and the violence of racial bigotry in the same breath, and almost always with tragic consequences. (157–158)

The issue of white males having sexual relationships or marital relationships with Black females does not seem to arouse a similar racial anxiety or racial hysterics. Another important point to be made is that most white people are in extreme denial and refuse to confront the white supremacy that lies within them.[16] Accordingly, white-male supremacy and its arrogance have a devastating effect on all Americans and those in other countries as seen in the Enron scandal. Here the absolute arrogance and economic greed of white males resulted in Enron shareholders, Enron employees, and other individuals, especially whites, losing their investments, jobs, savings, houses, marriages, and pensions. This national and international scandal represents a modern-day consumption of countless individuals, American municipalities, and foreign countries at its worst.[17] The white males involved in this scandal—Enron executive officers Andrew Fastow, Jeffrey Skilling, Kenneth Lay, Wesley Colwell, and John Clifford Baxter—were relentless in the pursuit of wealth and power. Skilling's arrogance was profound; he would pronounce: "We were changing the world. We were doing God's work." This type of arrogance has brought danger and loss exemplified by the suicide of John Clifford Baxter with the bullet from a silver .357 Magnum revolver to his right temple. Bethany McLean and Peter Elkind sum up this complex American tragedy:

> In the public eye, Enron's mission was nothing more than the cover story for a massive fraud. But what brought Enron down was something more complex—and more tragic—than simple thievery. The tale of Enron was something of human weakness, of hubris and greed and rampant self-delusion; of ambition run amok; of a grand experiment in the deregulation world; of a business model that didn't work; and of smart people who believed their next gamble would cover their last disaster—and who couldn't admit they were wrong. (xxi)

Corporate wrongdoing and the Black man as a sexual stud and superior impregnator become synthesized in Spike Lee's latest comedic film *She Hate Me* (2004). Discussing the rationale of *She Hate Me*, Spike Lee states that the film is about the ramifications of the choices that people make with regard to sex and money. Indeed, the film begins with money, a portrait of George W. Bush on a three-dollar bill. The message: you cannot spend it; you cannot save it, and you cannot trust it. Here John Henry "Jack" Armstrong (played by Anthony Mackie) is a senior corporate biotech executive (vice president) in a pharmaceutical firm named Progeia, until he is fired when a insider-trading scandal over their latest drug Prexelia for the cure of AIDS is revealed and Jack becomes a whistleblower. When Harvard and Wharton-educated MBA Jack Armstrong is fired, he receives an incredible offer from his ex-fiancée, Fatima Goodrich (Kerry Washington), a high-powered business woman.[18] After a four-year estrangement, Fatima comes to Jack's apartment requesting that he impregnate both her and her current female lover, Alex Guerrero (Dania Ramirez). They are willing to pay Jack the amount of $5,000 each if he will consent to be a sperm donor; also, he must sign a document waiving all of his parental rights. Alex adheres to the notion of "why have sex with a stranger when you can have sex with a friend"; however, the conflict to this sexual desire begins with Jack's initial refusal to be a sexual stud for these lesbian lovers, and once he consents, Fatima desires to have normal sexual relation whereas Alex desires to do artificial insemination, creating conflict between Fatima and Alex. Their reasoning is that most sperm banks are not dependable concerning the genetic quality of the donors[19] and that adoption is expensive and frustrating; Jack represents a perfect candidate because he is educated, charismatic, considerate, kind, and most especially disease-free. When Fatima becomes pregnant on their first attempt, she devises a plan: Jack will sell his sperm to lesbians with Fatima receiving a percentage. Word spreads and soon Jack with his "man milk" is in the baby-making business at $10,000 an encounter. Other lesbians with a similar desire for motherhood and the money begin to seek Jack's services. However, between his dubious fathering activities and the attempts by his former employers—CEO Leland Powell (Woody Harrelson) and Margo Chadwick (Ellen Barkin)—attempting to frame him for Security and Exchange Commission security violations, Jack finds his life, all at once, becoming quite complicated. Desperate for money, Jack (with his swank and artsy apartment and his account frozen) is reduced to a whore, and Fatima becomes his pimp. Some of the women include Oni (played by Ling Bai), Nadiyah (Michole Briana White), Song (Sarita Choudhury), mafia princess Simona (Monica Bellucci), and Stacey (ex-WNBA player Kym Hampton), as well as a selection of "mannish lesbians." Here Jack is symbolically put on the slave auction block as the women demand to see the goods, his penis. Upon viewing Jack's penis (he stands buck naked in front of the women), all of the lesbians agree to the arrangement. Despite Jack's willingness to perform, he has some crude concepts of lesbians. In a conversation with Fatima, he says that: "I know how these lesbians are. They are like vultures, worse than men. As soon as they see someone they want to fuck, they are on your back. They are so persistent." In another scene, when Jack becomes frustrated and wants to stop, Fatima goes through his numerous unpaid bills (car note, health insurance, summer house, and a letter from the IRS), and tells him that he does not have any other economic alternative. Fatima as the "pimp person" adamantly tells Jack to "strip, bitch," and he performs his sexual service for the women already waiting in his living room.

Director and co-writer Lee connects the stereotypical image of the Black male as super stud to the issue of miscegenation as consumption when an Italian woman, Simona, seeks to have Jack impregnate her. The potency of Jack's sperm is evident in that before Simona leaves Jack, she informs him that she has conceived and will have twins. That Jack discovers Simona's father is Don Angelo Bonasera (John Turturro) causes him to wonder if his life is in danger due to him being a Black man having sexual relations with his daughter. Their conversation focuses not on biological miscegenation between Black and whites but on cultural miscegenation—Bonasera's progeny raised on Frank Sinatra embracing Snoop Dogg.[20] Bonasera's forthright acceptance of his daughter's mixed-raced twins surprises Jack and provides one of the less-credulous signs of the believability of lesbians of all races seeking the sexual services of a Black man.

The theme of consumption is layered literally and metaphorically throughout the film. *She Hate Me* opens with Q Tip (Vada Huff) buying four lattes from a breakfast cart in front of the Progeia building and then looking up to the sky. Q Tip removes a cup and gives the remaining cups to Jack, who enters the office of Dr. Herman Schiller (David Bennent). After a brief conversation about marriage and having as many children as one can afford, Jack leaves the doctor to consume his raspberry latte. A few seconds later and down the hall, Jack realizes that something is terribly wrong; he rushes back to discover that the doctor has leaped to his death, landing on the breakfast cart and killing himself and two other individuals. Unknown to Jack at this point in the film, the scientist has learned that the Progeia's much-anticipated drug does not work, though it is scheduled to hit the market (stock and otherwise) within days. Here, Lee gives us a tragic circle of consumption that is both literal and symbolic. Ironically, Q Tip looks up to the upper floors of the building before he enters the company's building. Dr. Schiller's death can be juxtaposed with the hundreds of thousands who are dying from AIDS because the drugs are too costly. Equally important, Dr. Schiller's advice to Jack foreshadows Jack's acceptance of the offer to be a sperm stud. Before the second group of "mannish women" comes to his apartment, we view Jack making a high-powered protein shake in his blender. Between each session with the women, Jack consumes Viagra pills and washes them down with Red Bull beer. Later, Alex tells Jack: "We see you as a dick, balls, and sperm." Essentially, Jack has lost a great deal of his Black male subjectivity (self-respect, dignity, and self-worth) and has been reduced to his genitals. Progeia represents a company involved with the sale and consumption of drugs; Jack's relationship with the lesbians represents sexual consumption and economic consumption. An analysis by bell hooks in *We Real Cool* reveals the paradoxical nature of Black male subjectivity:

> By the end of the seventies the feared yet desired black male body had become as objectified as it was during slavery, only a seemingly positive twist had been added to the racist sexist objectification: the black male body had become the

site for the personification of everyone's desire. In the contemporary social context of hedonistic sexual desire where fantasies of domination and submission are represented as 'cool,' the actual lynching, castration, and cannibalization of the black male body is replaced by symbolic slaughter and consumption. The dreadful black male body is transfigured into the desired body. This shift created an equal opportunity for all on the sexual terrain. (79)

Lee's disturbing cinematic rendition of Black male subjectivity illustrates how desire can be articulated and negotiated within the boundaries of racist sexist archetypes.

Perhaps a similar scenario of the corporate-greed aspects can be said of Tyo, WorldCom, and Adelphia Communications—other companies that went bankrupt due to greed and arrogance. On July 13, 2005, WorldCom's former chairman, Bernie J. Ebbers was sentenced to 25 years in prison for orchestrating a record $11-billion fraud that toppled the telecommunications company he founded. Ebbers was convicted in March 2005 on nine counts of conspiracy, securities fraud, and filing false reports with regulators; his criminal actions wiped out billions of dollars belonging to WorldCom investors, cost thousands of employees their jobs and retirees their pensions. In his book *Democracy Matters: Winning the Fight against Imperialism* (2004), Cornel West views the free-market fundamentalism as a major problem plaguing our democracy. The oligarchs in the economy are demonic in their desire to maximize profits at the expense of the populace. Framing his analysis within the discourse of materialism and consumption, West argues:

In short the dangerous dogma of free-market fundamentalism turns our attention away from schools to prisons, from workers' conditions to profit margins, from health clinics to high-tech facial surgeries, from civic associations to pornographic Internet sites, and from children's care to strip clubs. The fundamentalism of the market puts a premium on the activities of buying and selling, consuming and taking, promoting and advertising, and devalues community, compassionate charity, and improvements of the general quality of life. How ironic that in America we've moved so quickly from Martin Luther King Jr.'s "Let Freedom Ring!" to "Bling! Bling!"—as if freedom were reducible to having material toys, as dictated by free-market fundamentalism. (4–5)

It is not difficult to equate the free-market fundamentalism and arrogance of these white-male business leaders with the arrogance of white slave masters who were relentless in their economic exploitation of Black bodies. Indeed, Black bodies on the slave plantations became the white-male slave masters' Bling! Bling! With the unemployment of adult Black males at more than 25 percent (especially in New York City, Detroit, and Washington, DC), it is not strange to see that the number of Black males in prisons and on probation is steadily increasing.[21] Black males who cannot find work on the streets are forced to labor in the prisons. Indeed the prison industrial complex is one of the largest growth industries in America, where major corporations are using this captive labor forces at wages significantly less than the minimum wage. With a failing education system in most urban cities, it is not surprising that that there is a direct link to failing school districts and inmates in prison.[22] Drawing on Chinua Achebe's famous 1958 novel of internal and external forces that lead to disorder, destruction, and death in an Igbo society, *New York Times* columnist Bob Herbert points out in his book *Promises Betrayed* (2005), the societal effect of this disturbing national problem: "Things fall apart when 25 percent of the male population is jobless. . . . For the most part, jobless men are not viewed as marriageable material by women. And they are hardly role models for young people. . . . This is a tragic situation for the men, their families, and a serious problem for society at large" (16–17). Essentially, this contemporary consumption benefits the white male-dominated society that, since the period of enslavement, has viewed Black males as threat to their power. On the other hand, Black communities continue to be devastated by the loss of significant numbers of Black males, who, if educated and employed, could provide stability to their families and to the society at large because it is significantly less costly to educate individuals than to warehouse them in correctional facilities.[23] With so many Black males in prison, these institutions become places where only the strong survive and where rape is quite common. In many cases, prison is a violent culture of consume or be consumed. Human Rights Watch documents the treatment of male rape victims:

> Prisoners unable to escape a situation of sexual abuse may find themselves becoming another inmate's "property." The word is commonly used in prison to refer to sexually subordinate inmates, and it is no exaggeration. Victims of prison rape, in the most extreme cases, are literally the slaves of their perpetrators. Forced to satisfy another man's sexual appetites whenever he demands, they may also be responsible for washing his clothes, massaging his back, cooking his food, cleaning his cell, and myriad other chores. They are frequently "rented out" for sex, sold, or even auctioned off to other inmates. . . . Their most basic choices, like how to dress and whom to talk to, may be controlled by the person who "owns" them. Their name may be replaced by a female one. Like all forms of slavery, these situations are among the most degrading experiences a person can undergo. (8)

Hence, the consumption of Black bodies in prison occurs on many levels: economically, psychologically, sexually, and physically. White corporations benefit from this Black labor while the society bears the burden of higher taxes and reduced public services such as cuts in library hours and a lack of day-care centers. For these and so many more Black people, they have never realized the American Dream because the nightmare of racial oppression has too often been their reality. Tim Wise suggests how institutionalized racism affects whites and the larger society:

> We've lost something thanks to racism, something necessary for the operation of common sense, something vital to the functioning of our gray matter, something that unless we recapture it will make for some very troubled days and years ahead. Unless we challenge the logic of our political and economic systems— both of which encourage racist mentalities and racially disparate institutions, and pit us against one another in a winner-take-all/loser-takes-nothing grudge match—we'll be unlikely to pull ourselves out of the muck. (150)

Under white supremacy, Black people and Black bodies are especially vulnerable to commodification and consumption, factors that impact on whites. However, complicity and resistance must always be thought of in any discourse around the commodification of Black culture and the exploitation of cultural production. As Henry Giroux maintains:

> The power of complicity and the complicity of power are not exhausted simply by registering how people are positioned and located through the production of particular ideologies structured through particular discourses. . . . It is important to see that an overreliance on ideology critique has limited our ability to understand how people actively participate in the dominant culture through processes of accommodation, negotiation, and even resistance. (194–195)

Like thousands of termites or white ants in the basement of a seemingly beautiful yet divided house, white supremacy is eating away at the foundation of America's body politic and all the inhabitants of the structure will be affected by the immanent collapse. There is little doubt that America's white supremacist culture is destroying America and many parts of the world; the paradox of this destruction is that there are African American and Latino individuals who are assisting the leaders of white supremacy in their destruction. Black and Latinos supporting white supremacy is not a new phenomenon, but it seems especially disturbing in light of the ongoing terrorism that people of color experience. As Paul Robeson Jr. argues in his article: "The Choice Between Two Americas" the poisonous philosophy of white supremacy is profound:

> The Republican Party has become a party with a program of states' rights, unrestrained corporate greed, racism, anti-unionism, imperial war, and domestic fear. This Republican president has lied to the American people about 9/11, the Iraq war, the "war on terror," the domestic economy, and home security. He was utterly incompetent in his response to 9/11, in his prosecution of the Afghanistan and Iraq wars, in his attempts to make America secure, and in his response to the Katrina and Rita disasters. His Republican Party's political gangsters have

brazenly stolen two national elections by 2.3 million (2000) and 3.4 million (in 2004) popular votes. (13)

White supremacy is fundamental to the existence of most white people (benefits accrue in housing, employment, and education) and thus their denial of its existence and their refusal to discuss this poisonous ideology are systematic of the psychological pathology. A glaring example of the pathology is former Education Secretary and Drug Czar William Bennett's recent theoretical remarks on a radio program "Bill Bennett's Morning in America" that crime in America could be reduced if all Black babies in America were aborted. Bennett states: "I do know that it's true that if you wanted to reduce crime, you could—if that were your sole purpose, you could abort every black baby in this country, and your crime rate would go down. This would be an impossible, ridiculous, and morally reprehensible thing to do, but your crime rate would go down. So these far-out, these far-reaching, extensive extrapolations are, I think, tricky." This vile and despicable remark suggests the racist social and political policies that govern America when it comes to African Americans. That Bennett would utter this political theory is "morally reprehensible" and outrageous equivocation is far-reaching since whites commit most of the crimes in America; indeed recent corporate indictments suggest that white males are committing crimes that have a devastating impact on thousands of individuals regardless of race. Bennett's seemingly paradoxical statement is in line with the white supremacist discourse that suggests that Black people are now a dispensable commodity. Moreover Bennett's nauseating yet poignantly deliberate remarks represent a rather statement of the usually coded discourse of white supremacy that Neely Fuller Jr. identifies:

> White supremacists have a code already in place that's why they are smart and successful in what they do. A code just simply means they have a set way of doing everything that they do. Nothing is left to chance. They have a set procedure when they are handling of the non-white people of the world. They have to codify that procedure so that it works for them every time. Nothing is left to trial and error even though they may have done this in the beginning, but over a period of time you iron out your errors and evaluate your strategies. (26)

Many progressive whites are standing side by side with African Americans, Latinos, and Asians, but the vast majority of white people continue to support America's white supremacist culture so poignantly illustrated in African American literature. These four influential African American narratives by Richard Wright, John Oliver Killens, Gayl Jones, and Octavia Butler and the case of white police brutality discussed here reveal that white-supremacist culture and its consuming nature have a negative physical and psychological impact on both Blacks and whites; however, slavery and the ongoing commodification of Black people has produced too many Black individuals who are mainly consumers whose dependence on the ancestors of white slave owners is almost total in terms of the life saving and life sustaining institutions. The intersectionality of race, gender, and sexuality must be considered when we think about white supremacy. All things considered, the current consumption of Black individuals in the dominant media can erode the respect and dignity of those past and present Black people who represented and represent themselves in ways that resist objectifying and dehumanizing white-male consumption. Without a doubt, all people who believe in fairness, justice, equality, respect for difference, and human dignity cannot rest until these democratic principles are fully realized.

notes

chapter 1

1. Halle Berry winning an Academy Award for her role in *Monster's Ball* can be juxtaposed with Denzel Washington winning an Academy Award for his performance in *Training Day* (2001). Denzel Washington plays the role of a monstrous police officer who trains his white partner in a manner that in antithetical to law and order. It can be argued that Washington symbolically fucks, and fucks over, his white partner. Indeed, Washington becomes characterized as the dangerous Black buck who threatens white society. The issue of miscegenation comes up in many of Washington's films. In a number of his films such as *Pelican Brief* (1993), Washington's concern for Black female viewers and white-male viewers plays itself out in him refraining from sexual roles with white women. Miscegenation is present in *Mississippi Masala* (1991) and *Devil in a Blue Dress* (1995); Washington plays the leading role in these films, but there are no sexual roles with Washington and white women. For a discussion on Washington and his racial concerns, see "Is It Still Taboo for Black and Whites to Kiss in Movies?" *Jet* April 27, 1998), 35–36.

2. In October 1994, Susan Smith of South Carolina claimed that a Black man carjacked her and kidnapped her two children. Susan Smith told another woman, Shirley McCloud, the following story: "I was stopped at the red light

at Monarch Mills and a Black man jumped in and told me to drive. . . . I asked him why was he doing this and he said shut up and drive or I'll kill you." Susan continued and told Shirley that, at the abductor's direction, she drove northeast of Union for about four miles until "he made me stop right past the sign." Shirley confirmed that the sign was for the John D. Long Lake, which was located several hundred yards outside of Shirley's front door. "He told me to get out. He made me stop in the middle of the road. Nobody was coming, not a single car." Susan continued, "I asked him, 'why can't I take my kids?'" Susan told Shirley that the man said, "I don't have time." Susan said that the man pushed her out of the car while he was pointing a gun at her side. Susan continued by telling Shirley that "When he finally got me out he said, 'Don't worry, I'm not going to hurt your kids.'" Susan described how she lay on the ground as the man drove away as both her sons cried out for their mother. Smith later confessed to killing her sons. On October 29, 1989, Charles Stuart of Boston, Massachusetts, claimed that a Black man shot and killed his pregnant wife, Carol Stuart; Charles committed suicide on January 4, 1990, and eventually his brother informed the police that Charles murdered Carol. And Christopher Pittman of Charleston, South Carolina, claimed that a Black man shot and killed his grandparents and set their house on fire. All of these claims were equivocations, but masses of whites (especially law-enforcement individuals) and others initially believed these stories. Charles Stuart's case is particularly disturbing because the Boston police terrorized working-class Black communities in search of a suspect. In his article "The Stuart Case: Race, Class, and Murder in Boston," published in *The Nation*, (February 5, 1990, 153), Andrew Kopkind writes, "Young black men were stopped, searched and detrousered on the street for no cause more reasonable than skin color. The cops called the Blacks 'pussy' and 'faggot,' and sexual humiliation—white male power against Black male impotence—became another disgusting tactic of the occupation" (153). The historical context to these false allegations is the O. J. Simpson trial, the Clarence Thomas Senate Judiciary hearing, the controversy around Michael Jackson, and other Black males in the media connected to issues concerning sexuality.

3. *Monster's Ball* directed by Marc Foster, with actors Billy Bob Thornton, Halle Berry, Peter Boyle, and Heath Ledger, Lions Gates, 2001. All further references will be given parenthetically.

4. Halle Berry's role in *Monster's Ball* recalls another film where the issue of miscegenation as sexual consumption was prominent. That film about interracial relationships was Spike Lee's *Jungle Fever* (1991); here Halle Berry as Vivian played the role of a crack addict and the girlfriend of a crack junkie played by the actor Samuel Jackson. There is the sense that Vivian would do anything sexually for the drug crack. Throughout the film we view the juxtaposition of the drug crack and the white female as two white elements that are destroying

two Black brothers, Flipper Purify (Wesley Snipes) and Gator (Samuel Jackson). Flipper destroys his relationship with his light-skinned Black wife, Drew Purify (Lonette McKee), and his daughter, Ming (Veronica Timbers), when he leaves them for a white-female co-worker Angie Tucci (Annabela Sciorra); and Gator destroys the life of their parents when the father, the Good Reverend Doctor Purify, played by Ossie Davis, shoots and kills him in front of his wife, Lucinda Purify (Rudy Dee), after he rampages the house looking for money to buy drugs. Also, Angie's father beats her when he discovers that she is having a relationship with a Black man.

5. Buck Grotowski expresses his own abusive consumptive behavior when he tells Hank that his mother (Buck's wife) who committed suicide wasn't "shit" and that he has obtained more "pussy" since she has died.

6. The white cowboy hat also relates to an earlier scene where Hank chases two Black boys (friends of his son, Sonny) off his property by firing a rifle into the air. Later, the Black father of the two boys challenges Hank on his cruel behavior and tells him that if he wants to play "cowboy," he should come over to his house. Thus Leticia's gift to Hank reinforces his terrorizing of Black males.

7. The issue of the death penalty in America represents an extremely controversial subject; there is a host of evidence that shows that many individuals regardless of race have been falsely convicted of crimes that they did not commit. However, evidence shows that a disparity exists with regard to the racial identity of those on death row. With the advances in DNA research, some prisoners have been released.

8. The issue of consumption of the Black body is evident here in that the illiterate Jefferson becomes analogous to a hog, especially since one of the main businesses in the town is a slaughterhouse for hogs. Indeed the execution of Jefferson can be viewed as a modern-day lynching. Gaines' repeated use of Jefferson as a hog conjures up thoughts of Claude McKay's poem "If We Must Die." For an analysis of this novel, see Carlyle Van Thompson, "From a Hog to a Black Man: Black Male Subjectivity and Ritualistic Lynching in Ernest J. Gaines' A Lesson Before Dying" CLA Journal XLV. 3. March (2002): 279–310.

9. Other recent films that illustrate miscegenation include Todd Haynes' Far from Heaven (2002), Warren Beatty's Bulworth (1998), Quentin Tarantino's Jackie Brown (1997), John Sayles' Lone Star (1996), Cheryl Dunye's Watermelon Woman (1996), Carl Franklin's One False Move (1992), Anthony Drazan's Zebrahead (1992), Spike Lee's Jungle Fever (1991), and Julie Dash's Daughters of the Dust (1991).

10. Perhaps the most nefarious paradigm of the consumption of the black body can be seen in the circumstances of Saatje Baartman, a South African woman born in 1790, who was exhibited with an animal trainer in 1810 as the infamous "Hottentot Venus" in and around London and Paris for over five years.

After her death in 1815, the anatomist Georges Leopold Curvier dissected her and preserved her genitalia under a bell jar in the Musee de l'Homme in Paris. As Beverly Guy-Sheftall argues in "The Body Politic," Baartman's consumption "underscores a recurring theme in the 'body dramas' that Black women experience. Being Black and female is characterized by the private being made public, which subverts conventional notions about the need to hide and render invisible women's sexuality and private parts. There is nothing sacred about Black women's bodies, in other words. They are not off-limits, untouchable, or unseeable . . . The Black female also came to serve as an icon for Black sexuality in general throughout the nineteenth century as Sandler Gilman cogently argues in his influential work" (18–21).

11. Zora Neale Hurston, *Their Eyes Were Watching God*, 17. All further references will be given parenthetically.

chapter 2

1. Richard Wright, "Between the World and Me" *Partisan Review* 2 (July–August 1935): 18–19. All further references to this text will be given parenthetically.

2. This racist commandant underscores the religious aspect of white supremacy. It is also interesting that the word "Nigger" is capitalized in the same manner that God would be capitalized.

3. Other African American writers and their literary texts that examine lynching are: Countee Cullen's "The Black Christ"; James Weldon Johnson's "Brothers-American Drama"; Claude McKay's "The Lynching"; Langston Hughes' "Song for a Dark Girl," "Christ in Alabama," "Blue Bayou," "Silhouette," "The South," and his short story "Home" in *The Ways of White Folks*; Paul Larence Dunbar's "The Haunted Oak"; Jean Toomer's "Blood-Burning Moon" in *Cane*; and Robert Hayden's "Night, Death, Mississippi."

4. The historical aspect of the lynching connects to older rituals of sacrifice. In Henri Hubert and Marcel Mauss, trans. W. D. Halls, *Sacrifice: Its Name and Function* (Chicago: University of Chicago Press, 1964), the authors illustrated that sacrifice was often if not always a highly ritualized act. Like all ritual, it encompassed drama, celebration, and play. One critical aspect of the sacrificial drama, Hubert and Mauss note, was its "perfect continuity. From the beginning to the end it must continue without interruption and in the ritual order" (28). The apex of this drama was the killing of the victim, at which point there was absolute silence, in marked contrast to the jubilation of later stages. Lastly they note that often there was a common meal at the end of the sacrifice, which in many incidents sublimated for the actual consumption of the sacrificed object.

5. In Philip Dray, *At the Hands of Persons Unknown; The Lynching of Black America,* a most heinous lynching in Valdosta, Georgia, of an African American

woman, Mary Turner, who was eight months pregnant, is described. Dray states: "The sheriff placed her under arrest, possibly for her own protection, but then gave her up to a mob that took her away into the woods near the Little River at a place called Folsom's Bridge. There, before a crowd that included women and children, Mary was stripped, hung upside down by the ankles, soaked with gasoline, and roasted to death. In the midst of this torment, a white man opened her swollen belly with a hunting knife and her infant fell to the ground, gave a cry and was stomped to death" (246).

6. For a discussion of the song "Strange Fruit," which originated as a poem by Abel Meeropol, see David Margolick's *Strange Fruit: Billie Holiday, Café Society, and an Early Cry for Civil Rights.* Here Meeropol states: "I wrote 'Strange Fruit' because I hate lynching and I hate injustice and I hate the people who perpetuate it" (29).

7. Lewis' keynote speech was delivered at Emory University in October 2002.

8. It was during the 1920s that the Klan's membership saw an increase; estimates at the time ranged from three to five million and profits rolled in from the sale of memberships, regalia, costumes, and ritual. The burning cross became their symbol. Although not all whites would go to the extremes of the Ku Klux Klan in terms of the extra-legal violence, many in rural America supported its ideology.

9. White-male subjectivity in this country is too often defined by white males raping or having sex with African American women and by the castration, lynching, and killing of African American men.

10. In Robert F. Williams' *Negroes with Guns,* Williams states: "The majority of white people in the United States have literally no idea of the violence with which Negroes in the South are treated daily—nay hourly. This violence is deliberate, conscious, condoned by the authorities. It has gone on for centuries and is going on today, every day, unceasing and unremitting. It is our way of life. Negro existence in the South has been one long travail, steeped in terror and blood—our blood" (41).

11. For a discussion of the role of white legal authorities in the extra-legal violence against African American people, see Katheryn K. Russell's *The Color of Crime: Racial Hoaxes, White Fear, Black Protectionism, Police Harassment, and other Macroaggressions.*

12. As cited in Dorothy Sterling, *Black Foremothers, Three Lives* (New York: The Feminist Press, 1979), Ida B. Wells wrote; "The city of Memphis has demonstrated that neither character nor standing avails the Negro if he dares to protect himself against the white man or become his rival" (79).

13. This horrific element of the lynching suggests the vampire who feeds on the blood of humans in order to sustain its existence.

14. Currently a group of Black politicians is calling for prosecutors to bring charges for the first time in thee unsolved 1946 lynchings of these four sharecroppers. Rep. Tyrone Brooks, president of the Georgia Association of Black Elected

Officials (this group represents more than eight hundred Black officials), spoke at a news conference calling for the FBI to begin another investigation.

15. In *The Autobiography of Medgar Evers* the death of Mack Charles Parker is explained. "Mack Charles Parker—A black resident of Poplarville, he was charged with raping a white woman. While waiting for trial in jail, he was abducted by a white mob and eventually shot to death in Louisiana. A grand jury returned no indictment on the known suspects, as the judge, Sebe Dale, himself a member of the all-white Citizen's Council, urged the jury to ignore evidence collected by the FBI" (139).

16. In Joyce King's *Hate Crime: The Story of a Dragging in Jasper, Texas*, King, drawing on her own experience in the South and its terror, states: "With this case, I too have graduated to another level of understanding race in America, at least from the perspective of being born and raised in the South. It's part of the world where not that many years ago white lawmen regularly instilled terror in the hearts of law-abiding black citizens, including members of my own family. It was a Sunday afternoon in East Texas when my mother, my aunt, and I took a drive that landed us in jail" (211).

17. The disturbing images of Rodney King and the narrative of Willie Horton have been seared into the minds of most white people in a manner that characterizes them and most African American males as dangerous criminals.

⊕ c h a p t e r   3

1. One of the most heinous attacks by racist whites during the Civil Rights Movement caused the 1964 deaths of James Chaney, Andrew Goodman, and Michael Schwerner, who were murdered by a group of white men organized by Edgar Ray Killen. Their disappearance, and the discovery of their bodies in an earthen dam, galvanized the movement. Edgar Ray Killen, an 80-year-old former Klansman in a wheelchair, was sentenced Thursday, June 23, 2005, to 60 years in prison (20 years for each of the three deaths) by Circuit Judge Marcus Gordon for his role in the deaths of these Civil Rights workers.

2. See Mamie Till-Mobley and Christopher Benson's *Death of Innocence: The Story of the Hate Crime That Changed* America. Here, Till-Mobley relates her viewing of her beloved son's body: "At a glance, the body didn't appear human. I remember thinking it looked like something from outer space, something you might see at one of those Saturday matinees. Or maybe that's only what I wanted to think so that I wouldn't have to admit that this was my son. Suddenly, as I stood there gazing down at the body, something came over me. It was like an electric shock. In fact it was terror. I felt it through every bone in my body. I stiffened. The horror of this moment was as overwhelming as the smell had been before all this, and the sight of the box

before that. And it was not because this body looked like something out of a horror movie. It was because I was getting closer to discovering, to confirming, that this body had once been my son. And I couldn't let anyone in the room know what I was feeling right then. I didn't want them to think even for a moment that I was not up to this. They might try to take this moment away from me. I couldn't let them stop me from going through with it. If I was stopped one more time, I don't know what I would have done. I'm not sure that I could have worked myself back up to it again. I had to steel myself like a forensic doctor. I had a job to do" (134). Keith A. Beauchamp's documentary *The Untold Story of Emmett Louis Till* helped to reopen the unsolved 50-year-old case of Till's murder in Money, MS, leading to the exhumation of his body. *Jet* magazine photographer David Jackson took a picture of Emmett Till's body, after Ms. Mobley insisted on an open casket. It was published in September 1955, a week before an all-white jury acquitted Roy Bryant and J.W. Milam of the murder; three months later, Rosa Parks refused to give up her seat on a bus, and later she linked that decision to her shock at seeing the images of Till's brutalized body. Eight years later in 1963 the world was shocked by the bombing of a Black Birmingham, AL, church in the midst of the Civil Rights protest movement. The bombing killed four Black girls: 11-year-old Denise McNair, and 14-year-olds Addie Mae Collins, Cynthia Wesley, and Carole Robertson. More than a decade passed before a notorious white supremacist, Robert "Dynamite Bob" Chambliss, was convicted of the crime; his alleged co-conspirators were never charged. Spike Lee's film *Four Little Girls* documents this tragedy.

3. In *Notes on the State of Virginia*, Jefferson states: "I advance it therefore as a suspicion only, that the blacks, whether originally a distinct race, or made distinct by time and circumstances, are inferior to the Whites in the endowments both of body and mind. It is not against experience to suppose, that different species of the same genus or varieties of the same species, may possess different qualifications . . . The slave, when made free, might mix with, without staining the blood of his master. But with us a second is necessary, unknown to history. When freed, he is to be removed beyond the reach of mixture" (143).

4. See Cheryl Harris, "Whiteness as Property" *Harvard Law Review*.

5. In Jones' *Labor of Love, Labor of Sorrow*, she states: "White men's persistent violation of black women constituted a more common phenomenon that served as a backdrop for periodic lynchings throughout the South, especially during the years 1890 to 1910. A woman or girl found herself in danger of being attacked whenever she walked down a country road—the poorest type of white man feels at liberty to accost her and follow her and force her." (150). Although she does not address it within her book, there is the possibility that young Black males encountered problems of a sexual nature when they worked in the homes of white people.

6. John Oliver Killens, *Youngblood*: 4–5. All further references to this work will be given parenthetically.

7. For a discussion of an African American females' resistance to sexual violence, see Melton Mclaurin's *Ceila, A Slave*. Celia was 14 when she was purchased by John Newsom. On the journey back to his farm, Newsom raped the young girl, beginning a horrifying pattern of sexual abuse. Finally she confronted him, struck him fatally with a club, was brought to trial, and eventually hanged.

8. See Ralph Ellison, *Invisible Man*: 17–26

9. In "The Half Ain't Never Been Told" (Contemporary Authors Autobiography Series), John Oliver Killens states that "Black manhood and Black womanhood were hazardous pursuits, inflationary expensive," 283–84.

10. For an in-depth discussion of concept of the African American male as a "buck," see Carlyle Van Thompson's *The Tragic Black Buck: Racial Masquerading in the American Literary Imagination*.

11. See Toni Morrison, *Sula*: 71–72.

12. Gilyard relates Killens' historical context for this scene that involved a fight between Black and white students at Pleasant Hill School and the traumatic aftermath. He states: "No White children were apprehended. After the [Black male] children were taken to the courthouse, their mothers were summoned and afforded a choice. Either they could beat their sons in front of the authorities as a lesson not to fight white kids, or they could watch their sons, none of whom was yet a teenager, be carted off to reform school. As much as the mothers hated to do it, every one of them whipped her son to save him from the reformatory" (14).

13. For a discussion of the Rosewood massacre, see Michael D'Orso's *Like Judgment Day: The Ruin and Redemption of a Town Called Rosewood*.

14. For a discussion of the Wallstreet massacre, see Randall Kennedy's *Reconstructing the Dreamland: The Tulsa Race Riot of 1921, Race Reparations, and Reconciliations* (New York: Oxford University Press, 2003); Hannibal B. Johnson's *Black Wall Street: From Riot to Renaissance in Tulsa's Historic Greenwood District* (Marion Koogler McNay Art Museum, 1998); James S. Hirsch's *Riot and Remembrance: The Tulsa Race War and Its Legacy* (New York: Houghton Mifflin, 2002); Tim Madigan's *The Burning: Massacre, Destruction and the Tulsa Riot of 1921* (Thomas Dunne Books, 2001); and Scott Ellsworth's *Death in a Promised Land: The Tulsa Race Riot of 1921*.

15. In Robert F. Williams' *Negroes with Guns*, Williams relates the "Kissing Case" that strongly suggests the incident that Killens describes. This case occurred in October 1958 involving two local black boys, David Simpson, age 7, and Handover Thompson, age 9, who were arrested and charged with rape, which was punishable by death in North Carolina. This incident began when David and Handover were playing "house" with some little white girls. One of the white girls, Sissy Sutton, sat on Handover's lap and suddenly recognized him

as an old playmate (Handover's mother used to be a housekeeper for the Suttons) and kissed him on the cheek. Later on in the afternoon she ran home and told her mother how she had seen Handover and how she was so happy to see him again that she had kissed him. Mrs. Sutton got hysterical when she heard this and she called the police. The two boys were arrested and placed in the county jail; their parents were not immediately notified. The children were sent to the reformatory soon after they were arrested. After much legal battles and the work of the NAACP, the case got national attention. Somebody said something, finally to President Eisenhower, and finally he said something to then-governor Hodges and on February 13, 1959, the children were released (59–61). Along with the Scottsboro Case, which developed from the arrest on March 25, 1931, of nine young blacks in Scottsboro, AL, for the alleged rape of two white girls, this incident represents one of the numerous examples of Black males being falsely accused of raping white females. We can only imagine the psychological trauma that these young Black males, their families, and their communities experienced through these ordeals.

16. The narrative context for Joe Youngblood being shot is that: "Every week this old cracker would short-change him. Fifty cents here and seventy-five cents there. Sometimes he got real bold and went over the dollar mark. Sometimes Joe would mumble something to the cracker, and the cracker would say— 'Go 'long boy, don't waste my time. I don't make no mistakes.' Sometimes Joe wouldn't say a single word and he would feel his whole manhood being robbed from him, draining him of his manhood, like a giant leech sucking all the blood out of him" (208). Here, Killens reveals another element of consumption where the Black man is emasculated and cheated out of his wages; this process was a fundamental aspect of the sharecropping system that kept Black people in another form of enslavement.

chapter 4

1. Gayl Jones, *Corregidora*. All further references to this text will be given parenthetically.

2. By the 1530s, the Portuguese were using African slaves in Brazil. From then until the abolition of the slave trade in 1870, at least ten million Africans were forcibly brought to the Americas: 38 percent to Brazil. The greatest portion of these slaves worked on plantations producing sugar, tobacco, coffee, and rice in the tropical lowlands of Brazil. Slaveholders exerted absolute control over their slaves and the production of crops, and Gayl Jones reinforces the theme of consumption of Black bodies who labor to produce consumable products.

3. The theme of denial of the Black female's voice is evident in both novels. In *Their Eyes Were Watching God*, Jody Starks, in response to a crowd's desire to

hear some encouragement, tells the crowd: "Thank yuh fuh yo' compliments, but mah wife don't know nothin' 'bout no speech-makin'. Ah never married her fo nothin' lak dat. She's uh woman and her place is in de home" (40–41). Jody also forbids Janie from joining the men on the porch who enjoy the art of telling stories. On the other hand, in *Corregidora*, Mutt Thomas dislikes Ursa singing the blues because of the way that men look at his wife; he claims that they are messing with her with their eyes. Interestingly, both Black women have conflict with the Black men in their lives and both have three marriages: Janie marries three different husbands, and Ursa marries Mutt Thomas twice and marries Tadpole once. Lastly, mule talk in *Their Eyes Were Watching God* becomes analogous to the blues in *Corregidora*.

4. The term "flat-footed truths" as explicated in *Flat-Footed Truths: Telling Black Women's Lives*, edited by Patricia Bell-Scott, is a southern saying that means to tell the naked truth. In the foreword, it states: "When we share our stories and seek to unshroud the lives of women who have come before us, the telling empowers us all. We connect the dots between the personal and the political; the individual's truth and the larger realities, women's existence, our people's journey, and the human experience. It can be a painful process, challenging our integrity at every turn as we confront painful truths, less than flattering aspects of our lives and/or the lives of others to maintain the illusion that all of us are brave, that all Black women are strong? How much do we want to know or tell? What to keep? What to share?" (xvi)

5. Both of these novels by African American authors connect miscegenation between white males and Black females to the phenomenon of racial passing. In both novels, the two light-skinned Black male protagonists become reconfigurations of the white male father as they abandon their Black identities.

6. Some white masters, for example, offered a new pig for each child born to a slave family, a new dress to the slave woman for each surviving infant, or no work on Saturdays to Black women who produced six children.

7. As Deborah Gray White argues in *Ar'n't I a Woman? Female Slaves in the Plantation South*, Emancipation and Reconstruction did not end the sexual violence directed at Black women. From the end of the Civil War to the mid-1960s, no Southern white male was convicted of raping or attempting to rape a Black woman; yet, the crime was common. Also, Black woman women had little legal recourse when raped by white men, and many Black women were reluctant to report sexual violence by Black men for fear that Black men would be lynched (188–189).

8. In Melton A. McLaurin's *Celia, A Slave*, there is an example of the sexual violence and one Black woman's response. In 1850, 14-year-old Celia became the property of Robert Newsom, a prosperous and respected Missouri farmer. For the next five years, she was cruelly and repeatedly molested by her abusive master—and bore him two children in the process. But in 1855, driven to the limits of her endurance, Celia fought back. And at the tender

age of 18, the desperate and frightened young Black woman found herself on trial for Newsom's murder. She was found to be guilty of murder and was hanged. Discussing the significance of this incident, McLaurin states: "The life of Celia demonstrates how slavery placed individual, black and white, in specific situations that forced them to make and to act upon personal decisions of a fundamentally moral nature. Such decisions involved, and inevitably affected, the lives of both the decision maker and the individuals caught in the moral dilemma about which decisions were made. Ultimately, each of these individual decisions was also a judgment about the morality of the institution of slavery itself" (xiii).

9. In *Their Eyes Were Watching God*, Janie Crawford's relationship with her second husband, Jody Starks, begins when he notices her long, flowing hair. The novel states: "He didn't look her way nor no other way except straight ahead, so Janie ran to the pump and jerked the handle hard while she pumped it. It made a loud noise and also made her heavy hair fall down" (26). Frustrated with her relationship with Logan, Janie takes up with Jody, but she becomes a beautiful trophy who never realizes her sexual subjectivity in this marriage. Indeed her "beautiful" features and especially her hair become critical attractions to Black men. Janie's hair becomes analogous to her sexuality and Jody at some point forces her to tie up her hair so that other cannot see it or feel it.

10. In Spike Lee's *Jungle Fever*, there is a power scene between Flipper Purify and Drew Purify that highlights the issue of intra-racial color hegemony. Drew confronts Flipper on his color prejudice and informs him of the names she was called by other Blacks; she states: "What I mean is that you've got a complex about color. You've always had it. I never wanted to believe it until now . . . I told you what happened to me when I was growing up . . . I told you how they called me high yella, yellow bitch, white honky, honky white, white nigger, nigger white, octoroon, quadroon, half-breed, mongrel." Drew's ultimate argument is that a light-skinned Black woman has not been enough for Flipper. She believes that his relationship with Angie represents the fulfillment of that desire. Within a white-supremacist culture, the white female represents the forbidden fruit that some Black men seek and by having sexual relations with the white females they are challenging white-male domination.

11. This sexual assault on Ursa by Jeffy illustrates the idea that Ursa is an object of sexual desire by both male and females; they both misread Ursa's body as a site of sexual consumption.

12. Stu Segall's film *Illegal in Blue* (1995) relates the story of Kari Truitt (Stacey Dash), a dangerously seductive blues singer. While singing the blues in a club, Kari tracks down the white men who killed and destroyed her baby sister. She blames these men for her sister's suicide and tells an ex-police officer, Chris Morgan (Dan Gauthier), that "They didn't just kill her, they destroyed

her. They destroyed her. They made her hate herself so much that she didn't want to live anymore." In a seductive scene with one of the men responsible for Kari's sister's death, Mickey Fuller (Trevor Goddard) tells the blue-bra-and-panties clad Kari that: "I want to lick every inch of you." Kari leans forward to embrace him, pulls out a small pistol, and then shoots him in the head. In another scene with Chris, Kari tells him that she had encountered problems with the owner of the club because she will not fuck him. Like Ursa, Kari faces male hegemony and uses the blues to provide a foundation for her quest for redemption for the death of her sister.

13. In Alice Walker's *The Color Purple*, the intra-racial violence is matched by the interracial violence. When Sofia tells the mayor's wife, "Hell no" in response to her working for her, the mayor slaps Sofia. A physical confrontation ensues and Sofia is arrested. Celie relates the tragic aftermath: "When I see Sofia I don't know why she still alive. They crack her skull, they crack her ribs. They tear nose loose on one side. They blind her in one eye. She swole from head to foot. Her tongue the size of my arm, it stick out tween her teef life a piece of rubber. She can't talk. And she just about the color of a eggplant" (86–87). For cussing the mayor's wife and for hitting the mayor, Sofia is sentenced to twelve years in prison. "They put Sofia to work in the prison laundry. All day long from five to eight she washing clothes. Dirty convict uniforms, nasty sheets and blankets piled way over her head. Her face yellow and sickly, her fingers look like fatty sausage. Everything nasty her, she say, even the air. Food bad enough to kill you with it. Roaches here, mice, flies, lice and even a snake or two. If you say anything they strip you, make you sleep on a cement floor without a light" (88). In many ways the penal system under Jim Crow segregation was analogous to slavery.

14. In Robert Hayden's poem "Runagate, Runagate" the lines "If you see my Pompey, 30 yrs of age,/new breeches, plain stocking, negro shoes;/if you see my Anna, likely young mulatto/branded E on the right cheek, R on the left" illustrates the physical violence that slave masters used to control their Black slave property.

15. Gayl Jones' naming of some male characters reinforces the concept that Ursa is an object of consumption. Mutt's name reinforces the idea that he is a hungry dog in search of meat, and Tadpole's name suggests a frog in constant search of wetness.

16. In the foreword of Albert Murray's *Train Whistle Guitar*, Robert G. O'Meally explicates a description of the blues that relates the heroic aspects of Ursa Corregidora's journey to redemption with Mutt Thomas. O'Meally, discussing the improvisational aspect of the blues, states: "Its keystone strategies for perseverance are *confrontation* of the low, dirty fact, implied in most blues lyrics, that things are not necessarily going to work out for the best, and *improvisation* in the face of this unhappy truth, swinging with style and flexibility no matter how tricky the key or time changes, no matter how crazily the

background voices [memories] (be they horns, cymbals, or a galloping piano) may holler and hoot. In this ritual drama of Saturday night, the action of the dancer, the musician, and even the music itself can suggest the role of the hero. And although even blues and blue-steel heroes cannot always win (life is so low-down and rotten), at least they can go down swinging" (viii).

17. For some African American writers, Brazil represented an escape from the suffocating grip of white supremacy. For example, Nella Larsen's *Passing* (1929) describes a Black physician, Brian Redfield, as an individual who seeks to go to Brazil to escape the racism in America. In the novel, Irene Redfield contemplates the strain in her marriage: "That strange, and to her fantastic, notion of Brian's of going off to Brazil, which, though unmentioned, yet lived within him; how it frightened her, and—yes, angered her!" And later, Irene's "voice had been even and her step was firm, but in her there was no slackening of the agitation, of the alarms, which Brian's expression of discontent had raised. He had never spoken of his desire since that long-ago time of storm and strain, of hateful and nearly disastrous quarreling, when she had so firmly opposed him, so sensibly pointed out its utter impossibility and its probable consequences to her and the boys, and had even hinted at a dissolution of their marriage in the event of his persisting in his idea. No, there had been, in all the years that they had lived together since then, no other talk of it, no more than there had been any other quarreling or any other threats. But because, so she insisted, the bond of flesh and spirit between them was so strong, she knew, had always known that his dissatisfaction had continued, as had his dislike and disgust for his profession and his country" (217–218). In the final section of the novel, Irene reveals her frustration with Clare Kendry-Bellow, who appears to be a threat to her marriage with Brian: "Could think again of ways to keep Brian by her side, and in New York. For she would not go to Brazil. She belonged in this land of rising towers. She was an American. She grew from this soil, and she would not be uprooted. Not even because of Clare Kendry, or a hundred Clare Kendrys" (267).

chapter 5

1. While Octavia Butler's novel addresses only the rape of Black women by white males, it is important to consider that Black men were also victims of sexual violence. They could be forced to perform nonconsensual sexual acts or suffer the violent consequences.

2. Octavia Butler's *Kindred*, 109. All further references to this text will be given parenthetically.

3. Avatara "Avey" Johnson is a middle-aged, middle-class African American widow who gains the American Dream but loses her soul. The novel traces

her quest to recover her lost identity, which is only possible through the sacrifice of her middle-class trappings and the recovery of the rituals of her family and the other people of the African Diaspora.

4. Frederick Douglass' *Narrative of the Life of Frederick Douglass, an American Slave Written by Himself*, 17. All further references to this text will be given parenthetically. This scene is often quoted to illustrate Black suffering, but I am also concerned with the analogy of the Black body and commodities of consumption. This whipping takes place in the kitchen and Aunt Hester is hung up in the same manner as a piece of meat. Returning to the spectacular image of suffering, Saidiya V. Hartman in *Scenes of Subjection: Terror, Slavery and Self-Making in Nineteenth-Century America* states: "I have chosen not to reproduce Douglass's account of the beating of Aunt Hester in order to call attention to the ease with which such scenes are usually reiterated, the casualness with which they are circulated and the consequences of this routine display of the slave's ravaged body . . . and especially because they reinforce the spectacular character of black suffering" (3). While Hartman makes a good point about the casualness of this violence, she misses the point that the slave master becomes an inhuman beast in this process. In the slave master's attempt to destroy another human being, he destroys himself. Both the slave master and the slave become traumatized.

5. White males involved in the business of catching slaves were an industry. Armed community slave patrols, paid slave catchers, and slave hunters with bloodhounds played a significant part in keeping Black people in a state of terror. However, the success of Harriet Tubman and the thousands of Blacks who escaped illustrates that Black people were relentless in their determination to obtain freedom.

6. The role-playing that Kevin and Dana must perform signifies the slave narrative by William and Ellen Craft *Running a Thousand Miles to Freedom* (1848). Here husband-and-wife Georgia slaves devise a plan to escape from slavery. In their plan, Ellen being light-skinned would transform her race, gender, and class and masquerade as a white slave master going North for medical treatment accompanied by "his" slave, William, who masquerades as his master's slave. Here the wife becomes the master and the husband becomes his wife's slave. They were successful and eventually escape to Canada. Discussing their ensuing performances, Dana tells Kevin: "'We're going to have to fit in as best we can with the people here for as long as we have to stay. That means we're going to have to play the roles you gave us'" (65).

7. Hegel's theory of the master and slave dialectic is useful here because despite the inhuman conditions of slavery, relationships between masters and slaves developed. Like any human relationship, relationships between master and slaves were complex in the content of shifting power. Masters manipulated their slaves and slaves manipulated their masters.

8. Douglass experienced many of the horrors that Butler described, and his speech links the present with the past because Kevin joins friends for a holiday celebration.

chapter 6

1. Abner Louima thought that a toilet plunger was used to sodomize him, but court testimony reveals that Justin A. Volpe used a broomstick to sodomize Louima in his anus.
2. It should be noted that the lawyer, Johnny Cochran, played a critical role in the nine million dollar settlement that Abner Louima received, as well as an attempt to change the New York City Police Department's policy that led up to this assault and the cover-up that ensued.

conclusion

1. On February 8 and 9, 2005, I had the honor of giving post-performance discussion of James Suggs' one-man play *Disposable Men* performed at the HERE Arts Center in downtown Manhattan. Suggs examines the role of Black males in popular culture based on *The Birth of a Nation* and other films where "monsters" are present. James Scruggs' high-tech lynching play represents an innovative technological illustration of the Black man as a disposable individual and the commodification of those Black men who no longer serve any useful function for a society governed by white-male supremacy. Drawing on films and historical documents, this play examines how Black men are represented in popular culture. Black men become consumable commodities by others and engage in behavior where they consume themselves. Moreover, I view his work as an attempt to struggle with issues of Black manhood in a way that respects the debates about Black masculinities within African American culture; that is, the way in which they deal with the real crises of young and old Black males. However, by articulating the political, social, economic, and domestic consequences of Black male suffering, he by no means suggests that Black women are not suffering as well. What he is suggesting is that the immediate consequences of the devastation that Black men face amounts to a palpable threat to the survival and flourishing of Black communities. Thus Black males can be viewed as perpetual enemies of the state. Accordingly many Black males have a perpetual rage against this society for its past, present, and future plans to make them an endangered species. Old-fashioned storytelling pairs with new media in *Disposable Men*. Using humor this solo work presents a series of interactive

monologues demonstrating the flippant irreverence with which the popular media treats the disposability of African American men. With witty sardonicism, Scruggs plays characters as varied as a waiter at a theme restaurant that features customized lynchings, a modern-day minstrel performing at kids' parties, and more. This is all performed with an underlying motif of the shockingly close relationship that Hollywood monsters and African American men share, especially the imaginative, over-the-top ways both are feared, killed, and ultimately disposed of.

2. Federal regulators fined CBS a record $550,000 for Janet Jackson's "wardrobe malfunction." The Federal Communications Commission voted unanimously to penalize each of the 20 CBS-owned television stations with the maximum indecency violation of $27,500. Discussing the penalty, FCC Chairman Michael Powell states: "As countless families gather around the television to watch one of the nation's most celebrated events, they were rudely greeted with a halftime show stunt more fitting for a burlesque show. This show clearly intended to push the limits of prime-time television."

3. Spike Lee's satirical film *Bamboozle* (2000) was quite provocative in illustrating the modern-day minstrel performances that too many Black actors participate in at the expense of their own self-worth and dignity. Here a frustrated television writer named Delacroix (Damon Wayans), unable to break his contract with his company, tries to get fired by proposing a new minstrel show, complete with dancers in blackface. But the network loves the idea, and Delacroix hires two street performers (Savion Glover, who is truly one of the finest tap dancers, and Tommy Davidson) whose hunger for success and ignorance of history combine to make them accept the blackface. Despite protests, the show is a huge success—but gradually, the mental balance of everyone involved starts to crumble. Also, Lee illustrates parallels between minstrel and contemporary hip-hop personas.

4. The concept of the Black female as a wanton individual is evident in the 1915 movie *The Birth of a Nation*; here Lydia Brown is a mulatto character who is the mistress of the white character, Senator Stoneman. Lydia is characterized as savage, corrupt, and lascivious; she uses her femininity to seduce white males.

5. Michael Jackson's two marriages to two white women, Debbie Rowe and Priscilla Presley, also reveal the issues of miscegenation, despite the fact that Jackson appears to be more white than African American. With a ghostly white face, straight hair, and numerous plastic surgeries, Jackson appears to be consumed with the desire to be white and embrace whiteness. This consumption of whiteness also manifests in that Jackson is accused of having inappropriate sexual relations with young boys.

6. It interesting to note that during the week of the Central Park rape, 28 other first-degree rapes or attempted rapes were reported in New York City. Nearly all the reported rapes involved Black women or Latinas. However, as Don

Terry wrote in the *New York Times*, most went unnoticed by the public. See "A Week of Rapes: The Jogger and 28 Not in the News."

7. The victim, now 42 years old, married, and living in Connecticut, has not made any statement about the latest developments in the case. Her book entitled *I Am the Central Park Jogger: A Story of Hope and Possibility* focuses on her recovery rather than the assault itself.

8. Clarence Thomas was nominated to the Supreme Court by President George Bush and supported by Senator John C. Danforth. Paradoxically Clarence Thomas was to replace Supreme Court Judge Thurgood Marshall, the lawyer who successfully argued the *Brown vs. Board of Education* decision.

9. The themes of miscegenation and sexual desire are also present in the film *Ruby's Bucket of Blood* (2002), starring Angela Bassett, Brian Stokes Mitchell, and Kevin Anderson. Bassett plays the role of Ruby Delacroix, a juke joint owner (she inherited it from her mother) whose Black husband, Earl Delacroix (Brian Stokes Mitchell) deserts her and she becomes involved with a married white man, Billy Dupre (Kevin Anderson) who comes to sing at her juke joint. Even though their affair could be a fatal mistake in the racist South of the early 1960s, the couple cannot resist temptation. After his white wife, Betty Dupre (Angelica Torn), discovers the affair, an altercation leaves Billy dead; Ruby takes her daughter, Emerald Delacroix (Jurnee Smollett), and leaves. Like most narratives of illicit miscegenation, this film ends with tragedy and the possibility for redemption. In one of the film's most important scenes, Ruby talks to her daughter, Emerald, about the realities of life in the South for a Black woman. Ruby tells her the worse thing in the world is a colored woman. Also, Ruby, articulating a discourse of racial and gender essentialism, says when the world looks at her they see a nursemaid, a whore, and a mule all rolled into one "and wondering why she ain't serving them." Despite the fact that she pays more taxes than most folks, whites folks seek to conduct business with her husband (when he's not away on the Texaco oil-rig job), and with her attitude they view her as being in need of a good whipping. Thus she encourages her daughter to "stay low." Like Zora Neale Hurston's *Their Eyes Were Watching God*, this film synthesizes the racism and sexism that most Black women encountered during this period. Ruby in her attempts to protect her daughter suggests that she marginalize herself. Like Janie, Emerald's response is that her mother's discourse is that of slavery and that she will not "stay low." Ruby's discourse is also influenced by the white sheriff, who looks at her in a manner that suggests female decapitation. For the white sheriff, she is a sexual object that he would like to consume. Thus the mother-and-daughter conflict illustrates that Black women are viewed as commodities of consumption by racist white males.

10. Angela Bassett was initially approached for the role of Leticia Musgrove in the film, but she rejected the role because she thought that it was too demeaning. "I wasn't going to be a prostitute on film," Bassett said when asked by

Newsweek why she had turned down the role. "I couldn't do that because it's such a stereotype about black women and sexuality." However, Lions Gate Production president Michael Paseornek and the film's producer, Lee Daniels, rebut Bassett, stating that she was never even offered the role and was committed to another film. Despite this denial, Bassett makes a fundamental point that *Monster's Ball* represents a leering and absurd look at interracial sex from a white-male perspective. It attempts to reverse the sexual violence of slavery by having the Black female seduce the unsuspecting white male; this sexual stereotype was forged during slavery. Also Vanessa L. Williams was offered the role of Leticia but turned it down because of the full frontal nudity, and Queen Latifah was considered for the role of Leticia.

11. In my mind, the name of this high-tech robot suggests the absent Black male character. The direct reference in the film is that Fly Boy represents a World War I fighter pilot who crashed and burned. However, being a robot in space that is always clothed in Black attire, the robot suggests Gordon Parks Jr.'s film *Superfly* (1972) that chronicles the exploits of Youngblood Priest (played by the actor Ron O'Neal), the flamboyantly dressed cocaine drug dealer and sexual stud in Harlem, New York. The robot has beyond-human abilities, and of course he is flying around in space like the other members of the *Nightingale 229* crew. A problematic aspect of the name "Fly Boy" with regard to Black males is that the signifier "boy" echoes the racism of the Jim Crow segregation period, where all Black men were referred to as boys.

12. The issue of Black male characters being absent represents a critical issue in this film. With the idea of Black males being an endangered species, we wonder if this futuristic world represents the reality of this idea. Karl's statement of rescuing Kaela suggests some absence in her life. Considering the legacy of white supremacy's violence of lynching Black males and raping Black females, one ensures the absence of the Black body and the other requires the presence of the Black body.

13. It should be noted that Angela Bassett in the role of Dr. Kaela Evers has a majestic presence in the film. Even in her most desperate moments with Karl, Kaela never loses control, and the camera angles capture her sexuality and power in a dignified manner. This is especially true in the film's final scene with Nick, where he and Kaela debate the possibilities of them sharing the single-dimension stabilization unit. At no point does Kaela acquiesce to either Karl or Nick. While Karl and Nick may have sexual consumption in mind when they interact with Kaela, Kaela is never characterized as a victim of their sexual desires. From the beginning of the film to the end, Dr. Kaela Evers' majestic subjectivity remains intact.

14. Dr. Myrlie Evers-Williams is a Civil Rights activist and the previous chairperson of the NAACP (1995–1998). Evers-Williams was the first woman to lead the nation's oldest Civil Rights organization in 1995, a time when it

had been surrounded by scandal and controversy. Evers-Williams' positive reputation among Civil Rights leaders and African Americans in general, made her election a cause for renewed optimism among NAACP support- ers. With her husband, Medgar Evers, in 1954, Myrlie Evers served as sec- retary for the NAACP office in Jackson, Mississippi. In that capacity she served a critical role in advancing the cause of Civil Rights. During the next nine years, they led other Blacks in challenging racial segregation and discrimination in what was considered the most racist state in the nation. In June 1963, Medgar Evers was killed outside his home in Jackson; his murder brought national attention to racism in the South, especially Mississippi. Clearly devastated by the loss, Myrlie became a symbol of courage and trag- edy in the Civil Rights Movement. In 1964, Myrlie Evers moved to Cali- fornia with her three children and obtained her BA degree from Pomona College in 1968. She remained active in Civil Rights and politics while receiving honorary doctorial degrees. In Myrlie Evers-Williams' *Watch Me Fly* (New York: Little Brown and Company, 1999), she states: "Life is never without struggle. For thirty years I had painstakingly transformed myself, trading in my mantle of widowhood for a cloak of increasing independence . . . The qualities that helped me stay the battle and strive for justice—not only my faith, but my stubborn perseverance, my unwillingness to embrace conventional wisdom, my reluctance to be identified solely by Medgar's memory while, at the same time, honoring it—helped me survive every- thing that transformed in my life from the moment Beckwith's bullet found its mark" (11–12).

15. Apprehensions around miscegenation were fundamental to many of Strom Thurmond's earlier views on segregation. He stated: "I want to tell you that there's not enough troops in the army to force the southern people to break down segregation and admit the Negro race into our theaters, into our swim- ming pools, into our homes, and into our churches." On another occasion, Thurmond's discourse appears to come from a Ku Klux Klan individual when he stated: "If the segregation program of the president is enforced, the results of civil strife may be horrible beyond imagination. Lawlessness will be ram- pant. Chaos will prevail. Our streets will be unsafe. And there will be the greatest breakdown of law enforcement in the history of the nation." For a discussion on the subject of Strom Thurmond having a Black daughter, see Essie Mae Washington-Williams and William Stadiem's *Dear Daddy: A Memoir by the Daughter of Strom Thurmond* (Regan Books, 2005). Discussing the paradoxical legacy of her father, Essie Mae Washington-Williams states: "I tried to feel peace with the passing of my father, but I couldn't. If life was a game, then Strom Thurmond had won it, big time. He lived 100 years, with almost perfect health. He had enormous, success, wielded inestimable power, and served his country with great honor both at war and peace. Yes, he had changed, and so had the world. He had beautiful wives, beautiful children, a

beautiful life, as well as a prominent place in history. Why was I so unsettled, so discontent? It was because he and I had never really made our peace. Yes, he had changed, and so had the world, but he and I never so much as sat down together for a meal. We had never said 'I love you' to each other. We had never confronted the reality of our relationship. Too much remained unsaid. I was so grateful just to have a father that I had never been brave enough to risk losing him by rocking the boat. Now I was seventy-eight years old. This was no time to start rocking" (212).

16. William Loren Katz, David R. Roediger, George Lipsitz, and Tim J. Wise are just four of the white scholars who are relentless in their challenges to the philosophy of white-male supremacy (white privilege), and their scholarship has had a profound effect in the academy and in the public sector. However, the white people who are in denial are not alone, because there are many Black people and Black intellectuals who believe that racism is not a serious problem in American society. Significant number of Black men and women in prisons; the high number of Black children in foster care; high infant-mortality rates; dramatic increases in the number of Blacks with AIDS, cancer, and heart attacks; Black homelessness; Black unemployment; and single-female–headed households are all examples of the enduring impact of racism.

17. For an intensive discussion of the Enron financial scandal, see Bethany McClean and Peter Elkind's *The Smartest Guys in the Room: The Amazing Rise and Scandalous Fall of Enron* (2004). The WorldCom $11-billion scandal is another example of the numerous recent financial frauds done by white-male business leaders.

18. The film provides a flashback of Jack coming up the stairs to his apartment with a dozen roses and discovering his then-fiancée, Fatima, having sexual relations with another woman, some weeks before they are supposed to be married. During this encounter, Jack discovers the strap-on dildo that the woman uses to fuck Fatima. Four years later, when Jack and Fatima have a chance to discuss the incident that has destroyed their relationship, he asks her what she learned from this first experience with another woman. Fatima responds: "I learned that I love pussy too."

19. Spike provides an anecdotal story with regard to sperm clinics when the character of Simona relates the story of the head of a sperm clinic, Dr. Cecil B. Jacobson, who used his own sperm to impregnate 70 of his female patients. The women were unaware that the sperm was from the doctor.

20. Here Spike Lee makes the point that young white males' buying and consuming Black hip-hop music has not lessened the racism and xenophobia in the society. Many white people embrace Black culture, but find it difficult to embrace Black people.

21. Approximately one of every nine African American males under the age of 35 is in prison or jail (Black males on probation is another significant issue),

whereas Black men make up more than 50 percent of all prison inmates. This represents a systematic removal of Black individuals from their respective communities into the criminal justice system. Decreases in funding for construction of schools and colleges are related to the increase in funding for the construction of prisons and detention facilities. The incarceration of Black males provides employment for judges, attorneys, court officers, and prison guards; also those businesses that supply food, toilet paper, water, and other supplies make significant profits on high incarceration rates. Transportation and telephone companies also make significant profits when relatives visit or communicate with their loved ones. Simply put, there is a great deal of money to be made by high incarceration rates. White-male politicians, among others, are driving this public policy. A direct consequence of this public policy is a rise in the number of Black males who come in contact with the criminal justice system and who are charged with a felony conviction. A felony conviction frustrates rehabilitation measures because significant burdens are placed on an individual's ability to re-enter society. All felons are disenfranchised politically, socially, and economically, as they are prevented from voting in elections, from living in public housing, and of course from finding and keeping employment. A possible 13 percent of all African American males have lost their right to vote. Indeed, in Richard Wright's former state, Mississippi, more than 30 percent of Black men are disenfranchised. Thus this consumption of Black males has direct benefits to the white male-dominated society, and disastrous consequences for the Black community. It would also be fair to state that too many Black males do not take responsibility for their actions and behave in manners that are antithetical to the construction of healthy families and communities. Many Black males have bought into the ludicrous idea that the pursuit of education, literacy, and knowledge is somehow an attempt to be white. By accepting this notion, they place themselves in desperate situations where hopelessness and despair seep into their consciousness; antisocial behavior is often a result. Actions based on nihilism feed the prevailing stereotypes that exist in many of the minds of those white males who tend to dominate the fields of politics, business, law, and education. It should be noted that currently the increase in Black women in prison is increasing at a greater level than Black men in prison; the current percentage of increase is about 700. The numerous points that I am making here connect to the literature and the incidents of police brutality because the consumption by whites of Black people's ideas, labor, inventions, and culture has been a fundamental aspect of white-supremacist culture.

22. In Damien Cave's "Scrutinizing the State of the African-American Male, and How to Improve It" (*New York Times*, June 19, 2005: 27), he reports on a conference on Black males held on June 18, 2005, at the New York University School of Law. Cave writes: "Several speakers cited a study, released last

week by two Princeton University professors, that found that white men with prison records are far more likely to receive offers for entry-level jobs than black men with identical criminal histories, and sometimes even black men who have never been arrested."

23. Here this applies to nonviolent crimes, especially that involving drug use. The Rockefeller drug laws have been particularly devastating to Black and Latino communities.

bibliography

Aaron, Daniel. "The 'Inky Curse': Miscegenation in the White American Literary Imagination." *Social Sciences Information* 22 (1983): 169–190.

Abraham, Nicolas, and Maria Torok. *The Shell and the Kernel: Renewals of Psychoanalysis.* Trans. and ed. Nicholas Rand. Chicago: University of Chicago Press, 1984.

Abrahams, Roger D. *Singing the Master: The Emergence of African American Culture in the Plantation South.* New York: Penguin Books, 1992.

Adoff, Arnold. *I Am the Darker Brother: An Anthology of Modern Poems by African Americans.* New York: Simon Pulse, 1997.

Akbar, Na'im. *Breaking the Chains of Psychological Slavery.* Tallahassee, FL: Mind Productions & Associates Inc., 1996.

——. *Chains and Images of Psychological Slavery.* Jersey City: New Mind Productions, 1984.

Allen, Denia Elizabeth. "The Role of the Blues in Gayl Jones's *Corregidora.*" *Callaloo* 25.1 (2002): 257–273.

Amoah, Jewel D. "Back on the Auction Block: A Discussion of Black Women and Pornography." *National Black Law Journal* 14.2 (Spring 1997): 204–221.

Anderson, Claude. *Black Labor, White Wealth: The Search for Power and Economic Justice.* Edgewood, MD: Duncan & Duncan Inc., 1994.

——. *Dirty Little Secrets about Black History, Its Heroes and Other Troublemakers.* Bethesda: PowerNomics Corporation of America, 1997.

Anderson, Karen. *Changing Woman: A History of Racial Ethnic Women in Modern America.* New York: Oxford University Press, 1996.

Anderson, Lisa M. *Mammies No More: The Changing Image of Black Women on Stage and Screen.* Lanham, MD: Rowman & Littlefield, 1997.

Andrews, William L. "The Conversation of Race." *Black American Literature Forum* 23 (1989): 37–60.

———. "Miscegenation in the Late Nineteenth-Century Novel." *Southern Humanities Review* 17 (1974): 13–24.

———. Race. *Key Words in Contemporary Literary Studies,* eds. Frank Lentricchia and Tom McLaughlin, 247–287. Chicago: Chicago University Press, 1989.

———. "Racisms." *Anatomy of Racism,* ed. David Theo Goldberg, 3–17. Minneapolis: University of Minnesota Press, 1990.

———, ed. "The Representation of Slavery and the Rise of Afro-American Literary Realism, 1865–1920." *African American Autobiography: A Collection of Critical Essays,* 77–89. Englewood Cliffs: Prentice Hall, 1993.

———. *To Tell a Free Story: The First Century of Afro-American Autobiography, 1760–1865.* Urbana: University of Illinois Press, 1986.

———, and Amy Gutman. *Color Conscious: The Political Morality of Race.* Princeton: Princeton University Press, 1996.

Avant, John Alfred. Review of *Corregidora. The New Republic* (June 28, 1975): 27–28.

Baker Jr., Houston A. *Blues, Ideologies, and Afro-American Literature: A Vernacular Theory.* Chicago: University of Chicago Press, 1984.

Baldwin, James. *The Devil Finds Work.* New York: The Dial Press, 1976.

———. *Going to Meet the Man.* 1965. New York: Vintage Books, 1995.

———. *No Name in the Street.* New York: The Dial Press, 1972.

Balibar, Etienne, and Immanuel Wallerstein. *Race, Nation, Class: Ambiguous Identities.* Trans. of Etienne Balibar by Chris Turner. London: Verso, 1991.

Bambara, Toni, ed. *The Black Woman: An Anthology.* New York: New American Library, 1970.

Barksdale, Richard K. *Praisesong of Survival: Lectures and Essays, 1957–1989.* Urbana: University of Illinois Press, 1992.

Beal, Frances M. "Black Woman and the Science Fiction Genre: Interview with Octavia Butler." *Black Scholar* 17 (March–April 1986): 14–18.

———. "Double Jeopardy: To Be Black and Female." *The Black Woman: An Anthology,* ed. Toni Cade, 90–100. New York: New American Library, 1970.

Bell, Bernard W. *The Afro-American Novel and Its Tradition.* Amherst: University of Massachusetts Press, 1987.

———. *The Contemporary African American Novel: Its Folk Roots and Modern Literary Branches.* Amherst: University of Massachusetts Press, 2004.

Bell, Derrick A. *Faces at the Bottom of the Well: The Permanence of Racism.* New York: Basic Books, 1992.

———. "Interracial Sex and Marriage." *Race, Racism, and American Law,* 53–81. Boston: Little Brown, 1973.

————. "Property Rights in Whiteness." *Critical Race Theory: The Cutting Edge*, ed. Richard Delagado, 75–83. Philadelphia: Temple University Press, 1995.

Bell, Roseann Pope. "Gayl Jones Takes a Look at *Corregidora*—An Interview." *Sturdy Black Bridges: Visions of Black Women in Literature*, eds. Roseann P. Bell, Bettye J. Parker, and Beverly Guy-Shetfall, 282–87. Garden City: Anchor, 1979.

Bell-Scott, Patricia ed. *Flat-Footed Truths: Telling Black Women's Lives*. New York: Henry Holt and Company, 1998.

Belton, Don. *Speak My Name: Black Men on Masculinity and the American Dream*. Boston: Beacon Press, 1995.

Benston, Kimberly W. "I Yam What I Am: The Topos of Un(naming) in Afro-American Literature." *Black Literature and Literary Theory*, ed. Henry Louis Gates Jr., 151–172. New York: Methuen, 1984.

Berlin, Ira. *Generations of Captivity: A History of African-American Slaves*. Cambridge: Belknap Press of Harvard University Press, 2003.

Berzon, Judith R. *Neither Black nor White: The Mulatto Character in American Fiction*. New York: New York University Press, 1978.

Blassingame, John W. *The Slave Community: Plantation Life in the Antebellum South*. New York: Oxford University Press, 1972.

Blount, Marcellus, and George P. Cunningham, eds. *Representing Black Men*. New York: Routledge, 1996.

Brandt, Joseph. *Dismantling Racism: The Continuing Challenge to White America*. Minneapolis: Augsberg Fortress, 1991.

Brodie, Fawn M. *Thomas Jefferson: An Intimate History*. New York: Bantam Books, 1974.

————. "The Great Jefferson Taboo." *American Heritage* 22 (1972): 49–57, 97–100.

Brundage, W. Fitzhugh. *Lynching in the New South: Georgia and Virginia, 1880–1930*. Chicago: University of Illinois Press, 1993.

Butler, Octavia. *Kindred*. Boston: Beacon Press, 1979.

Byerman, Keith E. *Fingering the Jagged Grain: Tradition and Form in Recent Black Fiction*. Athens: University of Georgia Press, 1985.

Caldwell, Earl. "Police Sodomy in Queens: The Column the *Daily News* Killed." *New York Amsterdam News* 34 (August 21–27, 1997): 12.

Callahan, John F. *In the African-American Grain: Call and Response in Twentieth-Century Black Fiction*. Middletown: Wesleyan University Press, 1989.

Camper, Carol. "Into the Mix." *Miscegenation Blues: Voices of Mixed Race Women*, ed. Carol Camper. Toronto: Sister Vision: Black Women and Women of Colour Press, 1994.

Carby, Hazel V. "It Jus Be's Dat Way Sometimes: The Sexual Politics of Women's Blues." *The Jazz Cadence of American Culture*, ed. Robert G. O'Meally, 469–482. New York: Columbia University Press, 1998.

————. *Reconstructing Womanhood: The Emergence of the Afro-American Woman Novelist*. New York: Oxford University Press, 1987.

Caruth, Cathy. *Unclaimed Experiences: Trauma, Narrative, and History*. Baltimore: Johns Hopkins University Press, 1996.

Cash, W.J. *The Mind of the South*. New York: A.A. Knopf, 1957.

Cassuto, Leonard. *The Inhuman Race: The Racial Grotesque in American Literature*. New York: Columbia University Press, 1987.

Chafe, William H., ed. *Remembering Jim Crow: African Americans Tell about Life in the Segregated South*. New York: The New Press, 2001.

Chesnutt, Charles. *The House Behind the Cedars*. 1900. Reprint. Introduction by Donald B. Gibson. New York: Penguin Books, 1993.

Chodorow, Nancy. *The Reproduction of Motherhood: Psychoanalysis and the Sociology of Gender*. Berkeley: University of California Press, 1978.

Chrisman, Robert, and Robert L. Allen. *Court of Appeal: The Black Community Speaks Out on the Racial and Sexual Politics of Clarence Thomas vs. Anita Hill*. New York: Ballentine Books, 1992.

Cochran, Johnnie, and David Fisher. *A Lawyer's Life*. New York: Thomas Dunne Books, 2002.

Cohen, Janet Langhart, with Alexander Kopelman. *From Rage to Reason: My Life in Two Americas*. New York: Kensington Publishing Corp., 2004.

Cohen, Jeffrey Jerome, ed. *Monster Theory: Reading Culture*. Minneapolis: University of Minnesota Press, 1996.

Coleman, Beth. "Pimp Notes on Autonomy." *Everything but the Burden: What White People Are Taking from Black Culture*, ed. Greg Tate, 68–80. New York: Broadway Books, 2003.

Colie, Rosalie. *Paradoxia Epidemica: The Renaissance Tradition of Paradox*. Princeton: Princeton University Press, 1966.

Collins, Janelle. "'Intimate History': Storyteller and Audience in Gayl Jones's *Corregidora*." *CLA Journal* XLVII.1 (2003): 1–31.

Collins, Patricia Hill. *Black Sexual Politics: African Americans, Gender and the New Racism*. New York: Routledge, 2004.

———. *Black Feminist Thought: Knowledge, Consciousness, and the Politics of Empowerment*. Boston: Unwin Hyman Inc., 1990.

Cone, James H. *The Spiritual and the Blues*. Maryknoll: Orbis Books, 1972.

Conrad, Robert Edgar. *Children of God's Fire: A Documentary History of Black Slavery in Brazil*. Princeton: Princeton University Press, 1983.

Cooke, Michael C. *Afro-American Literature in the Twentieth Century: The Achievement of Intimacy*. New Haven: Yale University Press, 1984.

Courtney, Susan. *Hollywood Fantasies of Miscegenation: Spectacular Narratives of Gender and Race*. Princeton: Princeton University Press, 2004.

Crenshaw, Kimberle. "Whose Story Is It, Anyway? Feminist and Antiracist Appropriations of Anita Hill." *Race-ing Justice, En-gendering Power: Essays on Anita Hill, Clarence Thomas, and the Construction of Social Reality*, ed. Toni Morrison, 402–440. New York: Pantheon, 1992.

Crouch, Stanley. "Racial Mixing Has Been with Us from Start." *Daily News* (May 19, 1999): 39.

D' Orso, Michael. *Like Judgment Day: The Ruin and Redemption of a Town Called Rosewood*. New York: Putnam Publication Group, 1996.

Danner, Mark. *Torture and Truth: America, Abu Ghraib and the War on Terror.* New York: New York Review of Books, 2004.

Dassin, Joan. *Torture in Brazil.* New York: Vintage Books, 1986.

Davis, Angela. *Blues Legacies and Black Feminism: Gertrude "Ma" Rainey, Bessie Smith, and Billie Holiday.* New York: Pantheon Books, 1998.

———. "Rape, Racism, and the Capitalist Setting." *Black Scholar* 9.7 (1978): 24–30.

———. "Reflections on the Black Women's Role in the Community of Slaves." *Black Scholar* 3 (December 1971): 2–15.

———. *Women, Race, and Class.* New York: Vintage Books, 1983.

———. *Women, Culture, and Politics.* New York: Random House, 1984.

Davis, Arthur P. *From the Dark Tower: Afro-American Writers 1900 to 1960.* Washington, DC: Howard University Press, 1974.

Davis, David Brion. *The Problem of Slavery in Western Culture.* Ithaca, NY: Cornell University Press, 1966.

Day, Beth. *Sexual Life between Blacks and Whites: The Roots of Racism.* New York: World Publishing, 1972.

Deburg, William L. Van. *The Slave Drivers: Black Agriculture Labor Supervisors in the Antebellum South.* New York: Oxford University Press, 1979.

Degler, Carl N. *Neither Black nor White: Slavery and Race Relations in Brazil and the United States.* Madison: University of Wisconsin Press, 1971.

Demarest, David P. "Richard Wright: The Meaning of Violence." *Negro American Forum* 8.3 (1974): 236–239.

Dixon, Melvin. *Ride Out the Wilderness: Geography and Identity in Afro-American Literature.* Urbana: University of Chicago Press, 1987.

———. "Sing a Deep Song: Language as Evidence in the Novels of Gayl Jones." *Black Woman Writers (1950–1980): A Critical Evaluation,* ed. Mari Evans, 236–248. Garden City: Anchor, 1984.

Dixon, Thomas. *The Clansman: An Historical Romance of the Ku Klux Klan.* Ridgewood, NJ: Gregg Press, 1967.

Douglas, Mary. *Purity and Danger.* London: Routledge, 1966.

Douglass, Frederick. *My Bondage and My Freedom.* New York: Penguin Books, 2003.

———. *Narrative of the Life of Frederick Douglass, An American Slave Written by Himself.* 1845. Reprint: eds. John W. Blassingame, John R. McKivigan, and Peter P. Hinks. New Haven: Yale University Press, 2001.

———. "Oration, Delivered in Corinthian Hall, Rochester, July 5, 1852." *Black Writers of America: A Comprehensive Anthology,* eds. Richard Barksdale and Keneth Kinnamon, 89–101. New York: Macmillan Publishing Company, 1972.

Doyle, Bertram Wilbur. *The Etiquette of Race Relations: A Study in Social Control.* 1937. Reprint: New York: Schocken Books, 1971.

Dray, Philip. *At the Hands of Persons Unknown: The Lynching of Black America.* New York: Random House, 2002.

Dubey, Madhu. *Black Women Novelist and the Nationalist Aesthetic.* Bloomington: Indiana University Press, 1994.

Du Bois, W.E.B. *Black Reconstruction in America, 1860–1880*. 1935. New York: Atheneum, 1962.

duCille, Ann. "The Occult of True Black Womanhood: Critical Demeanor and Black Feminist Studies." *Signs* 19.3 (1994): 591–629.

———. "Phallus(es) of Interpretation: Toward Engendering the Black Critical 'I.'" *Callaloo* 16 (1993): 559–573.

———. *Skin Trade*. Cambridge: Harvard University Press, 1998.

———. "The Unbearable Darkness of Being; 'Fresh' Thoughts on Race, Sex, and the Simpsons." *Birth of a Nation'hood: Gaze, Script, and Spectacle in the O.J. Simpson Case*, eds. Toni Morrison and Claudia Brodsky Lacour, 293–338. New York: Pantheon Books, 1997.

Dworkin, Andrea. *Intercourse*. New York: The Free Press, 1987.

Dyson, Michael Eric. "Be Like Mike?: Michael Jordan and the Pedagogy of Desire." *The Jazz Cadence of American Culture*, ed. Robert G. O'Meally, 372–380. New York: Columbia University Press, 1998.

———. *Open Mike: Reflections on Philosophy, Race, Sex, Culture, and Religion*. New York: Basic Books, 2003.

———. *Race Rules: Navigating the Color Line*. New York: Vintage Books, 1997.

Edelman, Lee. *Homographesis*. New York: Routledge, 1994.

Eliberg-Schwartz, Howard, and Wendy Doniger. *Off with Her Head: The Denial of Women's Identity in Myth, Religion, and Culture*. Berkeley: University of California Press, 1995.

Ellison, Ralph. *Going into the Territory*. New York: Vintage, 1987.

———. *Invisible Man*. 1952. Reprint: New York: Vintage Books, 1985.

———. *Shadow and Act*. New York: Vintage, 1964.

Ellsworth, Scott. *Death in a Promised Land: The Tulsa Race Riot of 1921*. Baton Rouge: Louisiana State University Press, 1982.

Evers-Williams, Myrlie, with Melinda Blau. *Watch Me Fly: What I Learned on the Way to Becoming the Woman I Was Meant To Be*. New York: Little Brown and Company, 1999.

———. & Manning Marable eds. *The Autobiography of Medgar Evers: A Hero's Life and Legacy Revealed Through His Writings, Letters, and Speeches*. New York: Basic Books, 2005.

Eyerman, Ron. *Cultural Trauma: Slavery and the Formation of African American Identity*. Cambridge: Cambridge University Press, 2003.

Fanon, Frantz. *Black Skin, White Masks*. New York: Grove Press, 1967.

Feagin, Joe R., and Herman Vera. *White Racism: The Basics*. New York: Routledge, 1995.

Ferguson, Ann. *Blood at the Root: Motherhood, Sexuality, and Male Dominance*. London: Pandora Press, 1989.

Fernandes, Florestan. *The Negro in Brazilian Society*, ed. Phyllis B. Eveleth; trans. Jacqueline D. Skiles, A. Brunel, and Arthur Rothwell. New York: Atheneum, 1971.

Fields, Barbara. "Slavery, Race, and Ideology in the United States of America." *New Left Review* 181 (1990): 95–119.

Fish, Jefferson M. "Mixed Blood." *Psychology Today* (Nov./Dec. 1995): 55–61, 76, 80.

Fitzgerald, F. Scott. *The Great Gatsby*. 1925. Reprint: New York: Simon and Schuster, 1995.

Foucault, Michel. *Discipline and Punish: The Birth of the Prison*; trans. from French by Alan Sheridan. New York: Vantage Books, 1979.

Fox-Genovese, Elizabeth. *Within the Plantation Household: Black and White Women of the Old South*. Chapel Hill: University of North Carolina Press, 1988.

Frankenberg, Ruth. *White Women, Race Matters: The Social Construction of Whiteness*. Minneapolis: University of Minnesota Press, 1993.

Franklin, John Hope, and Alfred E. Moss. *From Slavery to Freedom: A History of Negro Americans*. 1947. Reprint: New York: Alfred A. Knopf, 1988.

———. "'Birth of a Nation': Propaganda as History." *Massachusetts Review* 20.3 (1979): 417–433.

———. "Introduction: Color and Race in the Modern World." *Color and Race*, ed. John Hope Franklin, vii–xvi. Boston: Houghton Mifflin Co., 1968.

Fredrickson, George M. *The Arrogance of Race: Historical Perspectives on Slavery, Racism, and Social Inequality*. Middletown, CT: Wesleyan University Press, 1988.

———. *The Black Image in the White Mind: The Debate on Afro-American Character and Destiny 1817–1914*. New York: Harper and Row, 1972.

———. *White Supremacy: A Comparative Study in American and South African History*. New York: Oxford University Press, 1982.

Freyre, Gilberto. *The Master and the Slaves: A Study in the Development of Brazilian Civilization*. Trans. Samuel Putman. New York: Knopf, 1964.

Fuller Jr., Neely. "Understanding Racism: The Opinions of Neely Fuller Jr." *African Business & Culture* 2.17 (2002): 25-27.

Fuss, Diana. *Essentially Speaking*. London: Routledge, 1989.

Gaines, Ernest J. *A Lesson Before Dying*. New York: Vintage, 1993.

Giddings, Paula. *When and Where I Enter: The Impact of Black Women on Race and Sex in America*. New York: William Morrow, 1984.

Gilman, Sander L. "Black Bodies, White Bodies: Toward an Iconography of Female Sexuality in Late Nineteenth-Century Art, Medicine, and Literature." *Race, Writing, and Difference*, ed. Henry Louis Gates Jr., 223–261. Chicago: University of Chicago Press, 1986.

———. *Difference and Pathology: Stereotypes of Sexuality, Race, and Madness*. Ithaca: Cornell University Press, 1985.

Gilyard, Keith. *Liberation Memories: The Rhetoric and Poetics of John Oliver Killens*. Detroit: Wayne State University Press, 2003.

Ginzburg, Ralph. *100 Years of Lynchings*. 1962. Baltimore: Black Classic Press, 1988.

Giroux, Henry. *Border Crossings: Cultural Workers and the Politics of Education*. New York: Routledge, 1992.

Goldberg, David Theo. *Racist Culture: Philosophy and the Politics of Meaning*. Cambridge: Blackwell Publishers, 1993.

———. "Introduction." *Anatomy of Racism*, ed. David Theo Goldberg, xi–xxiii. Minneapolis: Minnesota University Press, 1990.

Golden, Bernette. "Review of *Corregidora*." *Black World* (February 1976): 82.

Goodman, James E. *Stories of Scottsboro*. New York: Vintage Books, 1995.

Gordon, Avery F. *Ghostly Matters: Haunting and the Sociological Imagination*. Minneapolis: University of Minnesota, 1997.

Gordon-Reed, Annette. *Thomas Jefferson and Sally Hemings: An American Controversy*. Charlottesville: University Press of Virginia, 1997.

Gottfried, Amy. "Angry Acts: Silence, Speech, and Song in Gayl Jones' *Corregidora*." *African American Review* 28 (1994): 559–570.

Gubar, Susan. *Racechanges: White Skin, Black Face in American Culture*. New York: Oxford University Press, 1997.

Gunning, Sandra. *Race, Rape, and Lynching: The Red Record of American Literature 1890–1912*. New York: Oxford University Press, 1996.

Guy-Sheftall, Beverly. "The Body Politic: Black Female Sexuality and the Nineteenth-Century Euro-American Imagination." *Skin Deep, Spirit Strong: The Black Female Body in American Culture*, edited by Kimberly Wallace-Sanders, 13-35. Ann Arbor: The University of Michigan Press, 2002.

Hacker, Andrew. *Two Nations: Black and White, Separate, Hostile, Unequal*. New York: Scribner's Sons, 1992.

Hall, Calvin S. and Gardner Lindzey. *Theories of Personality*. New York: John Wiley & Sons Inc., 1970.

Hall, Jacqueline Dowd. *Revolt Against Chivalry: Jessie Daniel Ames and the Women's Campaign Against Lynching*. New York: Columbia University Press, 1979.

Harper, Michael. "Gayl Jones: An Interview." *Chant of Saints: A Gathering of Afro-American Literature, Art, and Scholarship*, eds. Harper and Robert B. Stepto, 352–375. Urbana: University of Illinois Press, 1979.

Harris, Cheryl. "Whiteness as Property." *Harvard Law Review* 106.8 (1993): 1,705–1,791.

Harris, Janice. "Gayl Jones' *Corregidora*." *Frontiers* 3 (1980): 1–5.

Harris, Trudier. *Exorcising Blackness: Historical and Literary Lynching and Burning Rituals*. Bloomington: Indiana University Press, 1984.

Harrison, Daphne Duval. *Black Pearls: Blues Queens of the 1920s*. Brunswick: Rutgers University Press, 1990.

Hartman, Saidiya V. *Scenes of Subjection: Terror, Slavery, and Self-Making in Nineteenth-Century America*. New York: Oxford University Press, 1997.

Hayden, Robert. *Collected Poems*, ed. Frederick Glaysher. New York: Liveright Publishing Corporation, 1985.

Henderson, Mae G. "Speaking in Tongues: Dialogics, Dialectics, and the Black Woman Writer's Tradition." *Changing Our Own Words: Essays on Criticism, Theory, and Writing by Black Woman*, ed. Cheryl Wall, 16–37. New Brunswick: Rutgers University Press, 1989.

Herbert, Bob. "A Cop's View." *New York Times* (March 18, 1998): 17.

———. "Lifting the Censor's Veil on the Shame of Iraq." *New York Times* (May 5, 2005): 35.

———. *Promises Betrayed: Waking up from the American Dream.* New York: Henry Holt Company, 2005.

Herman, Judith Lewis. *Trauma and Recovery: The Aftermath of Violence from Domestic Abuse to Political Terror.* New York: Basic Books, 1997.

Hersh, Seymour M. *Chain of Command: The Road from 9/11 to Abu Ghraib.* New York: HarperCollins Publishers, 2004.

Hine, Darlene Clark. "Female Slave Resistance: The Economics of Sex. *Western Journal of Blacks Studies* 3 (1979) 1–10.

Hoch, Paul. *White Hero, Black Beast: Racism, Sexism and the Mask of Masculinity.* London: Pluto Press, 1979.

Hogue, W. Lawrence. *Discourse and the Other: The Production of the Afro-American Text.* Durham: Duke University Press, 1986.

Holland, Sharon Patricia. *Raising the Dead: Readings of Death and (Black) Subjectivity.* Durham: Duke University Press, 2000.

Holloway, Karla F. C. *Codes of Conduct: Race, Ethics, and the Color of Our Character.* New Brunswick: Rutgers University Press, 1972.

———. *Passed On: African American Mourning Stories.* Durham: Duke University Press, 2002.

hooks, bell. *Ain't I a Woman: Black Women and Feminism.* Boston: South End Press, 1981.

———. *Black Looks: Race and Representation.* Boston: South End Press, 1992.

———. *We Real Cool: Black Men and Masculinity.* New York: Routledge, 2004.

———. *Yearning.* Toronto: Between the Lines, 1990.

Huff, Rance E. "Waiting for Justice." *The Black Reign* (May 13–26, 1999): 1.

Hughes, Langston. Selected *Poetry of Langston Hughes.* 33-49. New York: Vintage Books, 1990.

———. "Home." *The Ways of White Folks.* 1933. Reprint. New York: Vintage Books, 1962.

Human Rights Watch. *No Escape: Male Rape in U.S. Prisons.* New York: Human Rights Watch, 2001.

Hurston, Zora Neale. *Their Eyes Were Watching God.* 1937. Reprint: New York: Harper & Row, 1990.

Hutchison, George. "Toomer and American Racial Discourse." *Texas Studies in Literature and Language* 35 (Summer 1993): 226–250.

Irigaray, Luce. *This Sex Which Is Not One,* trans. Catherine Porter, with Carolyn Burke. Ithaca: Cornell University Press, 1985.

Jacobs, Harriet A. *Incidents in the Life of a Slave Girl, Written By Herself.* 1861. Reprint: Mineola, New York: Dover Press, 2001.

Jefferson, Margo. "Making Generations." *Newsweek* (May 19, 1975): 84–85.

Jefferson, Thomas. *Notes on the State of Virginia.* 1782. Reprint: New York: W.W. Norton & Co., 1987.

Johnson, James Weldon. *The Autobiography of an Ex-Coloured Man.* 1912. Reprint: New York: Hill and Wang, 1960.

Jones, Gayl. *Corregidora*. 1975. Boston: Beacon Press, 1986.

———. *The Hermit Woman*. Detroit: Lotus, 1981.

———. *Liberating Voices: Oral Tradition in African American Literature*. Cambridge: Harvard University Press, 1991.

Jones, Jacqueline. *Labor of Love, Labor of Sorrow: Black Women, Work, and the Family from Slavery to the Present*. New York: Vintage Books, 1986.

Jordan, Winthrop D. *The White Man's Burden: Historical Origins of Racism in the United States*. New York: Oxford University Press, 1974.

———. *White over Black: American Attitudes toward the Negro, 1550–1812*. New York: W.W. Norton & Co., 1968.

Joyce, Joyce Ann. *Richard Wright's Art of Tragedy*. Iowa: University of Iowa Press, 1986.

Katz, William Loren. *The Invisible Empire: The Ku Klux Klan Impact on History*. Seattle: Open Hand Publishing Inc., 1986.

Kelly, Robin D.G. *Freedom Speaks: The Black Radical Imagination*. Boston: Beacon Press, 2002.

Kennedy, Randall. *Interracial Intimacies: Sex, Marriage, Identity, and Adoption*. New York: Pantheon Books, 2003.

Kent, R.K. "Palmares: An African State in Brazil." *Maroon Societies: Rebel Slave Communities in the Americas*, ed. with a new afterword by Richard Price, 170–190. Baltimore: Johns Hopkins University Press, 1979.

Killens, John Oliver. "The Half Ain't Never Been Told." *Contemporary Authors Autobiography Series*, ed. Adel Sarkissian. Detroit: Gale, 1985.

———. *Youngblood*. 1954. Reprint: Athens: Georgia University Press, 1982.

King, Joyce. *Hate Crime: The Story of a Dragging in Jasper, Texas*. New York: Pantheon Books, 2002.

Kopkind, Andrew. "The Stuart Case: Race, Class, and Murder in Boston." *The Nation* 5 (February 1990): 153.

Kovel, Joel. *White Racism: A Psychohistory*. 1970. Reprint New York: Columbia University Press, 1984.

Kubitschek, Missy Dehn. *Claiming the Heritage: African-American Novelists and History*. Jackson: University Press of Mississippi, 1991.

Larsen, Nella. *Passing*. 1929. Reprint. In *An Intimation of Things Distant: The Collected Fiction of Nella Larsen*, ed. and with Introduction by Charles R. Larson. New York: Anchor Books, 1992.

Lemire, Elise. *"Miscegenation": Making Race in America*. Philadelphia: University of Pennsylvania Press, 2002.

Lerner, Gerda. *The Creation of Patriarchy*. New York: Oxford University Press, 1986.

Levine, Lawrence W. *Black Culture and Black Consciousness: Afro-American Folk Thought from Slavery to Freedom*. New York: Oxford University Press, 1977.

Lipsitz, George. *The Possessive Investment in Whiteness: How White People Profit from Identity Politics*. Philadelphia: Temple University Press, 1992.

Litwack, Leon F. *Trouble in Mind: Black Southerners in the Age of Jim Crow*. New York: Alfred J. Knopf, 1998.

Lombardo, Paul A. "Miscegenation, Eugenics, and Racism: Historical Footnotes to *Loving v. Virginia*." *University of California Davis Law Review* 21.2 (1988): 421–452.

Lott, Eric. *Love and Theft: Blackface Minstrelsy and the American Working Class*. New York: Oxford University Press, 1993.

MacLean, Nancy. *Behind the Mask of Chivalry: The Making of the Second Ku Klux Klan*. New York: Oxford University Press, 1994.

Madhubuti, Haki R. *Tough Notes: A Healing Call for Creating Exceptional Black Men*. Chicago: Third World Press, 2002.

Madison, James H. *A Lynching in the Heartland: Race and Memory in America*. New York: Palgrave, 2001.

Margolick, David. *Strange Fruit: Billie Holiday, Café Society, and an Early Cry for Civil Rights*. Philadelphia: Running Press, 2000.

Marshall, Paule. *Daughters*. New York: Atheneum, 1991.

———. *Praisesong for the Widow*. 1983. Reprint: New York: Plume, 1992.

Marx, Karl. *The Eighteenth Brumaire of Louis Bonaparte*. New York: International, n.d.

Maultsby, Portia K. " Africanisms in African-American Music." *Africanisms in American Culture*, ed. Joseph E. Holloway, 185–210. Bloomington: Indiana University Press, 1990.

Mayer, Jane. "The Experiment: Is the Military Devising New Methods of Interrogation at Guantanamo?" *The New Yorker* (July 11/18, 2005): 60–71.

———, and Jill Abramson. *Strange Justice: The Selling of Clarence Thomas*. New York: Houghton Mifflin Co., 1994.

Mayer, Milton. "The Issue Is Miscegenation." *White Racism: Its History, Pathology, and Practice*, eds. Barry Schwartz and Robert Disch, 207–217. New York: Dell, 1970.

McClintock, Anne. *Imperial Leather: Race, Gender, and Sexuality in the Colonial Contest*. New York: Routledge, 1995.

McKay, Claude. *Selected Poems of Claude McKay*. New York: Harcourt, Brace and World, 1953.

McKible, Adam. "'These are the facts of the darky's history': Thinking History and Reading Names in Four African American Texts." *African American Review* 28.2 (1994): 223–235.

McKinney, James. *Amalgamation!: Race, Sex and Rhetoric in the Nineteenth-Century American Novel*. Westport: Greenwood Press, 1985.

Mclaurin, Melton. *Celia, A Slave*. New York: Avon Books, 1993.

McLean, Bethany, and Peter Elkind. *The Smartest Guys in the Room: The Amazing Rise and Scandalous Fall of Enron*. New York: Penguin Group, 2004.

Mencke, John G. *Mulattoes and Race Mixture: American Attitudes and Images, 1865–1918*. Ann Arbor: UMI Research Press, 1979.

Michaels, Walter Benn. "The No-Drop Rule." *Identities*, eds. Kwame Anthony Appiah and Henry Louis Gates Jr. Chicago: University of Chicago Press, 1995. 401–412.

———. *Our America: Nativism, Modernism, and Pluralism*. Durham: Duke University Press, 1995.

———. "Race into Culture: A Critical Genealogy of Cultural Identity." *Critical Inquiry* 18.4 (1992): 655–685.

———. "The Souls of White Folk." *Literature and the Body: Essays on Population and Persons*, ed. Elaine Scarry. Baltimore: Johns Hopkins University Press, 1988. 185–209.

Miller, Anita, ed. *The Complete Transcripts of the Clarence Thomas—Anita Hill Hearings, October 11, 12, 13, 1991*. Preface by Nina Totenberg. Chicago: Academy Chicago Publishers, 1994.

Minh-ha, Trinh T. *Women, Native, Other: Writing Postcoloniality and Feminism*. Bloomington: Indiana University Press, 1989.

Mizruchi, Susan L. *The Science of Sacrifice: American Literature and Modern Social Theory*. Princeton: Princeton University Press, 1998.

Morgenstern, Naomi. "Mother's Milk and Sister's Blood: Trauma and the Neoslave Narrative." *Differences* 8.2 (1996): 101–126.

Morrison, Toni. *Beloved*. New York: Plume, 1987.

———. "Introduction." *Birth of a Nation'hood" Gaze, Script, and Spectacle in the O.J. Simpson Case*, eds. Toni Morrison and Claudia Brodsky Lacour. New York: Pantheon Books, 1997.

———. *The Bluest Eye*. New York: Washington Square Press, 1970.

———. *Conversations with Toni Morrison*. Jackson: University Press of Mississippi, 1994.

———. *Playing in the Dark: Whiteness and the Literary Imagination*. Cambridge: Harvard University Press, 1992.

———, ed. *Race-ing, Justice, Engendering Power: Essays on Anita Hill, Clarence Thomas, and Construction of Social Reality*, ed. and with Introduction by Toni Morrison. New York: Pantheon Books, 1992.

———. "Rootedness: The Ancestor as Foundation." *Black Women Writers (1950–1980): A Critical Evaluation*, ed. Mari Evans, 339–345. Garden City: Anchor Books, 1984.

———. *Sula*. 1973. New York: Penguin Group, 1982.

———. "Unspeakable Things Unspoken: The Afro-American Presence in American Literature." *Criticism and the Color Line: Desegregating American Literary Studies*, ed. Henry B. Wonham, 16–29. New Brunswick: Rutgers University Press, 1996.

Murray, Albert. *The Blue Devils of Nada: A Contemporary American Approach to Aesthetic Statement*. New York: Vintage Books, 1997.

———. *The Omni-Americans: New Perspectives on Black Experience and American Culture—Some Alternatives to the Folklore of White Supremacy*. New York: Outerbridge & Dienstfrey, 1970.

———. *South to a Very Old Place*. 1971. Reprint: New York: The Modern Library, 1995.

———. *Train Whistle Guitar*, with Foreword by Robert G. O'Meally. Boston: Northeastern University Press, 1989.

Myrdal, Gunnar. *An American Dilemma: The Negro Problem and Modern Democracy*. 1944. Reprint. New York: Harper and Row, 1960.

Nascimento, Abdias do. *Brazil: Mixture or Massacre?: Essays in the Genocide of a Black People*. Trans. Elisa Larkin Nascimento, 2nd rev. ed. Dover, MA: Majority Press, 1989.

Nash, Gary B. *Forbidden Love: The Secret History of Mixed-Race America*. Henry Holt and Co. Inc., 1999.

Neal, Angela M., and Midge L. Wilson. "The Role of Skin Color and Features in the Black Community: Implications for Black Women and Therapy." *Clinical Psychology Review* 9 (1989): 323–333.

Nelson, Jill, ed. "Introduction." *Police Brutality: An Anthology*. New York: W.W. Norton & Co., 2000.

Newby, I.A. *Jim Crow Defense: Anti-Negro Thought in America, 1900–1930*. Baton Rouge: Louisiana State University Press, 1965.

Niro, Brian. *Race*. New York: Palgrave Macmillan, 2003.

Njeri, Itabari. *The Last Plantation: Color, Conflict and Identity: Reflections of a New World Black*. New York: Houghton Mifflin Co., 1997.

Nowatzki, Robert. "Race, Rape, Lynching, and Manhood Suffrage: Construction of White and Black Masculinities in Turn-of-the-Century White Supremacist Literature." *Journal of Mens Studies: A Scholarly Journal about Men and Masculinities* 3.2 (1994): 161–170.

Oakley, Giles. *The Devil's Music: A History of the Blues*. New York: Harvest/HBJ Books, 1976.

Oliver, William. *The Violent Social World of Black Men*. New York: Lexington Books, 1994.

Outlaw, Lucius. "Toward a Critical Theory of Race." *Anatomy of Racism*, ed. David Theo Goldberg, 58–84. Minneapolis: University of Minnesota Press, 1990.

Patterson, Orlando. *Rituals of Blood: Consequences of Slavery in Two American Centuries*. Civitas/Counterpoint: Washington, DC, 1998.

———. *Slavery and Social Death: A Comparative Study*. Cambridge: Harvard University Press, 1982.

Peterson, Carla L. "Foreword: Eccentric Bodies." *Recovering the Black Female Body: Self-Representations by African American Women*, eds. Michael Bennett and Vanessa D. Dickerson, ix–xvi. New Brunswick: Rutgers University Press, 2001.

Phelps, Timothy M., and Helen Winternitz. *Capitol Games: The Inside Story of Clarence Thomas, Anita Hill, and a Supreme Court Nomination*. New York: HarperPerennial 1992.

Philip, Marlene Nourbese. *Genealogy of Resistance*. New York: Insomniac Group, 1997.

Ragan, Sandra L., Dianne G. Bystron, Lynda Lee Kaid, and Christina S. Beck. *The Lynching of Language: Gender, Politics and Power in the Hill–Thomas Hearings*. Urbana: University of Illinois Press, 1996.

Reed, Tennessee. "Being Mixed in America." *MultiAmerica: Essays on Cultural Wars and Cultural Peace*, ed. Ishmael Reed, 113–115. New York: Viking Books, 1997.

Reilly, John. *Richard Wright: The Critical Reception*. New York: Burt Franklin, 1978.

Reuter, Edward Byron. *The Mulatto in the United States: Including a Study of the Role of Mixed Blood Races Throughout the World*. Boston: Richard Badger. Reprint: New York: Negro University Press, 1969.

Rich, Adrienne. "Rape." *Poems Selected and New: 1950–1974*. New York: W.W. Norton, 1994.

Richter, Gregory C. *The Incest Theme in Literature and Legend: Fundamentals of a Psychology of Literary Creation*, trans. and introduction by Peter Rudnytsky. Baltimore: Johns Hopkins University Press, 1992.

Roberts, Dorothy. *Killing the Black Body: Race, Reproduction, and the Meaning of Liberty.* New York: Vintage Books, 1999.

Robeson Jr., Paul. "The Choice Between Two Americas." *The Amsterdam News.* (September 29–October 5, 2005): 13, 30.

Robinson, Sally. *Engendering the Subject: Gender and Self-Representation in Contemporary Women's Fiction.* Albany: State University of New York Press, 1991.

Rothenberg, Paula, ed. *Racism and Sexism: An Integrated Study.* New York: St. Martin's Press, 1988.

Rowell, Charles. "An Interview with Gayl Jones." *Callaloo* 5.3 (1982): 32–53.

Rushdy, Ashraf H.A. "Families of Orphans: Relation and Disrelation in Octavia Butler's *Kindred.*" *College English* 55:2 (February 1993): 135-157.

———. "'Relate Sexual to Historical': Race, Resistance, and Desire in Gayl Jones' *Corregidora.*" *African American Review* 34.2 (2000): 273–97.

Russell, Katheryn K. *The Color of Crime: Racial Hoaxes, White Fear, Black Protectionism, Police Harassment, and Other Macroaggressions.* New York: New York University Press, 1998.

Russell, Kathy, Midge Wilson and Ronald Hall. *Color Complex: The Politics of Skin Color among African Americans.* New York: Harcourt Brace Jovanovich, Publishers, 1992.

Saar, Erik, and Viveca Novak. *Inside the Wire: A Military Intelligence Soldier's Eyewitness Account of Life at Guantanamo.* New York: Penguin Press, 2005.

Saks, Eva. "Representing Miscegenation Law." *Raritan: A Quarterly Review* 8.2 (1988): 39–69.

Scarry, Elaine. *The Body in Pain.* Oxford: Oxford University Press, 1985.

Schechter, Patricia A. "Unsettled Business: Ida B. Wells against Lynching, or How Antilynching Got Its Gender." *Under Sentence of Death: Lynching in the South*, ed. W. Fitzhugh Brundage. Chapel Hill: The University of North Carolina Press, 1997.

Schwenk, Katrin. "Lynching and Rape: Border Cases in African American History and Fiction." *The Black Columbian: Defining Moments in African American Literature and Culture*, eds. Werner Sollors and Maria Diedrich, 312–324. Cambridge: Harvard University Press, 1994.

Scott, James. *Domination and the Arts of Resistance.* New Haven, CT: Yale University Press, 1990.

Semmes, Clovis E. *Racism, Health, and Post-Industrialism: A Theory of African American Health.* New York: Praeger Publications, 1996.

Shapiro, Thomas M. *The Hidden Cost of Being African American: How Wealth Perpetuates Inequality.* New York: Oxford University Press, 2004.

Sharpley-Whiting, Denean T. *Black Venus: Sexualized Savages, Primal Fears and Primitive Narratives in French.* Durham: Duke University Press, 1999.

Simon, Bruce. "Traumatic Repetition in Gayl Jones's *Corregidora.*" *Race Consciousness: African-American Studies for the New Century*, eds. Judith Jackson Fossett and Jeffrey A. Tucker, 93–112. New York: New York University Press, 1996.

Smith, Barbara. *The Truth That Never Hurts: Writings on Race, Gender, and Freedom.* New Brunswick: Rutgers University Press, 1998.

Smith, Barbara Herrnstein. *Contingencies of Value Alternatives Perspectives for Critical Theory*. Cambridge: Harvard University Press, 1988.

Smith, Valerie. *Not Just Race, Not Just Gender: Black Feminist Readings*. New York: Routledge, 1998.

Snead, James A. "Repetition as a Figure of Black Culture." *Out There*, eds. Russell Ferguson et al., 213–232. Cambridge: MIT Press, 1992.

Sollors, Werner. *Interracialism: Black–White Intermarriage in American History, Literature, and Law*. New York: Oxford University Press, 2000.

———. *Neither Black Nor White Yet Both: Thematic Explorations of Interracial Literature*. Cambridge: Harvard University Press, 1997.

———. "'Never Was Born': The Mulatto, an American Tragedy?" *Massachusetts Review* 27 (1986): 293–316.

Sowell, Thomas. *The Economics and Politics of Race*. New York: Quill, 1983.

Spencer, Jon Michael. *Blues and Evil*. Knoxville: University of Tennessee Press, 1993.

Spillers, Hortense J. "Introduction: Who Cuts the Border? Some Readings on America." *Comparative American Identities: Race, Sex, and Nationality in the Modern Text*, ed. Hortense J. Spillers, 1–25. New York: Routledge, 1991.

———. "Mama's Baby, Papa's Maybe: An American Grammar Book." *Diacritics* 17 (1987): 65–81.

———. "'The Permanent Obliquity of an In(pha)llibly Straight': In the Time of the Daughters and the Fathers." *Changing Our Own Words: Essays on Criticism, Theory, and Writing by Black Women*, ed. Cheryl A. Wall, 127–149. New Brunswick: Rutgers University Press, 1989.

St. Jean, Yanick, and Joe R. Feagin. *Double Burden: Black Women and Everyday Racism*. Armonk, NY: M.E. Sharpe Inc., 1998.

Stammp, Kenneth. *The Peculiar Institution: Slavery in the Ante-Bellum South*. New York: Vintage Books, 1956.

Starling, Marion Wilson. *The Slave Narrative: Its Place in American History*. Boston: Hall, 1981.

Stepto, Robert B. *From Behind the Veil: A Study of Afro-American Narrative*. Chicago: University of Illinois Press, 1979.

Stevenson, Brenda E. *Life in Black and White: Family and Community in the Slave South*. New York: Oxford University Press, 1996.

Stolberg, Sheryl Gay. "The Senate Apologizes, Mostly." *New York Times* (June 19, 2005): 3.

Stone, Robin D. *No Secrets, No Lies: How Black Families Can Heal from Sexual Abuse*. New York: Broadway Books, 2004.

Street, James. *Look Away! A Dixie Notebook*. New York: Viking Press, 1936.

Suggs, Jon-Christian. *Whispered Consolations: Law and Narrative in African American Life*. Ann Arbor: University of Michigan Press, 2000.

Sundquist, Eric J. *The Hammers of Creation: Folk Culture in Modern African American Fiction*. Athens: University of Georgia Press, 1992.

———. *To Wake the Nations: Race in the Making of American Literature*. Cambridge: Harvard University Press, 1993.

Tate, Claudia. "*Corregidora*: Ursa's Blues Medley." *Black American Literature Forum* 13 (1979): 139–141.

———. "An Interview with Gayl Jones." *Black American Literature Forum* 13 (1979): 142–148.

Tate, Greg. "Introduction." *Everything but the Burden: What White People Are Taking from Black Culture*, ed. Greg Tate. New York: Broadway Books, 2003.

Taussig, Michael. *Shamanism, Colonialism, and the Wild Man: A Study in Terror and Healing*. Chicago: University of Chicago Press, 1987.

Temple-Raston, Dina. *A Death in Texas: A Story of Race, Murder, and a Small Town's Struggle for Redemption*. New York: Henry Holt and Company, 2002.

Terry, Don. "A Week of Rapes: The Jogger and 28 Not in the News." *New York Times* (May 29, 1989): 25.

Thompson, Carlyle Van. *The Tragic Black Buck: Racial Masquerading in the American Literary Imagination*. New York: Peter Lang Publishing, 2004.

Thompson, Robert Farris. *Flash of the Spirit: African and Afro-American Art and Philosophy*. New York: Random House, 1983.

Till-Mobley, Mamie, and Christopher Benson. *Death of Innocence: The Story of the Hate Crime That Changed America*. New York: Random House, 2003.

Tolnay, Stewart, and E.M. Beck. *Festival of Violence: An Analysis of Southern Lynchings, 1882–1930*. Chicago: University of Illinois Press, 1995.

Toomer, Jean. *Cane*. 1923. Reprint, with Introduction by Darwin T. Turner. New York: W.W. Norton, 1988.

Trelease, Allen W. *White Terror: The Ku Klux Klan Conspiracy and Southern Reconstruction*. Baton Rouge: Louisiana State University Press, 1971.

Vachss, Andrew. "Unsafe at Any Age." *New York Times* (June 15, 2005): A23.

Vance, Carole S., ed. *Pleasure and Danger: Exploring Female Sexuality*. Boston: Routledge & Kegan Paul, 1985.

Wallace-Sanders, Kimberly. *Skin Deep Spirit Strong: The Black Female Body in American Culture*. "Introduction." Ed. Kimberley Wallace-Sanders. 1-10. Ann Arbor: University of Michigan Press, 2002.

Walker, Alice. *The Color Purple*. 1970. Reprint: New York: Harcourt, 1982.

Watt, Gail Elizabeth. *Stolen Women: Reclaiming Our Sexuality, Taking Back Our Lives*. New York: John Wiley & Sons, 1997.

Webster, Ivan. "Really the Blues." *Time* (June 16, 1975): 79.

Wells-Barnett, Ida B. *On Lynching*. 1892. Reprint: New York: Arno, 1969.

West, Cornel. *Democracy Matters: Winning the Fight against Imperialism*. New York: Penguin Press, 2004.

———. *Race Matters*. Boston: Beacon Press, 1993.

Wexler, Laura. *Fire in a Canebrake: The Last Mass Lynching in America*. New York: Scribner, 2003.

White, Deborah Gray. *Ar'n't I a Woman? Female Slaves in the Plantation South*. New York: W.W. Norton, 1985.

White, Mimi. *"The Birth of a Nation*: History as Pretext." *The Birth of a Nation*, ed. Robert Lang, 214–224. New Brunswick: Rutgers University Press, 1994.

White, Walter. *Rope and Faggot*. 1929. New York: Arno Press and the New York Times, 1969.

Wideman, John Edgar. "Defining the Black Voice in Fiction." *Black American Literature Forum* 11 (1977): 79–82.

Wiegman, Robyn. *American Anatomies: Theorizing Race and Gender*. Durham: Duke University Press, 1995.

———. "Anatomy of Lynching." *Journal of the History of Sexuality* 3.3 (1993): 445–467.

Williams, Andrea. "Something to Talk About." *Sauti Mpya* 9 (Winter 2001): 30.

Williams, Patricia. *The Rooster's Egg: On the Persistence of Prejudice*. Cambridge: Harvard University Press, 1995.

———. *Seeing a Color-Blind Society: The Paradox of Race*. New York: Noonday Press, 1997.

Williams, Robert F. *Negroes with Guns*. 1962. Chicago: Third World Press, 1973.

Williamson, Joel. *The Crucible of Race: Black–White Relations in the American South since Emancipation*. New York: Oxford University Press, 1984.

———. *New People: Miscegenation and Mulattoes in the United States*. New York: Free Press, 1980.

———. *A Rage for Order*. New York: Oxford University Press, 1986.

Wilson, Amos N. *The Falsification of Afrikan Consciousness: Eurocentric History, Psychiatry, and the Politics of White Supremacy*. New York: Afrikan World InfoSystems, 1993.

Wise, Tim. *White Like Me: Reflections on Race from a Privileged Son*. Brooklyn: Soft Skull Press, 2005.

Wood, Forest G. *Black Scare: The Racist Response to Emancipation and Reconstruction*. Berkeley: University of California Press, 1993.

Woodward, C. Vann. *The Strange Career of Jim Crow*. 1955. Reprint: New York: Oxford University Press, 1966.

Wright, Bobby E. *The Psychopathic Racial Personality and Other Essays*. Chicago: Third World Press, 1984.

Wright, Richard. "Between the World and Me." *Partisan Review* 2 (July–August 1935): 18–19.

———. *Black Boy: A Record of Childhood and Youth*. 1945. Reprint: New York: Harper & Row, 1989.

———. *The Long Dream*. 1958. New York: Harper & Row, 1986.

———. *Twelve Million Black Voices*. 1941. Reprint: New York: Arno Press and the New York Times, 1969.

———. *Uncle Tom's Children*. 1938. Reprint: New York: Harper & Row, 1989.

Zack, Naomi. *Race and Mixed Race*. Philadelphia: Temple University Press, 1993.

Zangrando, Robert. *The NAACP Crusade Against Lynching 1909-1950*. Philadelphia: Temple University Press, 1980.

AFRICAN AMERICAN LITERATURE AND CULTURE

EXPANDING AND EXPLODING THE BOUNDARIES

General Editor
Carlyle V. Thompson

The purpose of this series is to present innovative, in-depth, and provocatively critical literary and cultural investigations of critical issues in African American literature and life. We welcome critiques of fiction, poetry, drama, film, sports, and popular culture. Of particular interest are literary and cultural analyses that involve contemporary psychoanalytical criticism, new historicism, deconstructionism, critical race theory, critical legal theory, and critical gender theory.

For additional information about this series or for the submission of manuscripts, please contact:

Peter Lang Publishing, Inc.
Acquisitions Department
275 Seventh Avenue, 28th floor
New York, New York 10001

To order other books in this series, please contact our Customer Service Department:

(800) 770-LANG (within the U.S.)
(212) 647-7706 (outside the U.S.)
(212) 647-7707 FAX

Or browse online by series:

www.peterlangusa.com